S0-BJI-870

A Rainbow
Travel Adventure
Book

In Search of
Lost Civilizations
Adventures in Archeology

Thom Tansey

RAINBOW BOOKS, INC.

Library of Congress Cataloging-In-Publication Data

Tansey, Thom, 1939-
    In Search of lost civilizations : adventures in archeology /Thom
Tansey.
        p.   cm.
    Includes bibliographical references and index.
    ISBN 1-56825-047-9 (alk. paper)
    1. Indians of North America — Antiquities. 2. Indians — Antiquities.
3. North America — Antiquities. 4. America — Antiquities. 5. Archaeology. I. Title.
E77.9.T36   1999
970.01—dc21   99-16249
                                                                  CIP

In Search of Lost Civilizations:
Adventures in Archeology
by Thom Tansey

ISBN 1-56825-047-9 / softcover / $14.95

On the cover: THE AUTHOR ENTERING KIVA AT PECOS PUEBLO, Joan
Cotton, photographer. All other photos are by the author.

Publishing industry inquiries (reviewers, retailers, libraries, wholesalers,
distributors/media) should be addressed to:

Rainbow Books, Inc.
P.O. Box 430, Highland City, FL 33846-0430
Editorial Offices—
Telephone: (888) 613-BOOK; Fax: (941) 648-4420
Email: RBIbooks@aol.com

Individuals' Orders: (800) 356-9315; Fax: (800) 242-0036;
Online: (http://www.) upperaccess.com, amazon.com, barnesandnoble.com

Printed in the United States of America.

CONTENTS

Other books by Thom Tansey

Adventures
Quests

To my mother, Elizabeth, for instilling in me the value of knowledge and inspiring me to seek it, thereby embarking me on a life-long journey of discovery and adventure.

INTRODUCTION

My interest in pre-Columbian archeology started innocently enough when I received a brochure in the mail from a local university, offering a varying handful of adult-education courses. I couldn't imagine how I got on their mailing list, but I'm ever thankful I did. One listing caught my eye. It was a beginner's course on the Maya. The course description intrigued me. Here was a subject, I thought, that I knew absolutely nothing about. It was an opportune time to correct that deficiency in my education. That course led me to sign up for a week-long course at the Smithsonian, conducted by Dr. George Stuart, one of the world's leading Mayan archeologists — and suddenly I was hooked in what has become a lifelong quest for adventure and knowledge.

I took other courses through various organizations. And I took to the field, first to Mesoamerican areas in Mexico and Guatemala. Next down to Peru. Then to the American Southwest. More recently to mound-builder sites along the Mississippi River. Every field trip has added a few more pieces to the puzzle, helping me to understand the life and times of these cultures as they existed and interacted before the arrival of the Europeans. Though all of these cultures had their own ways of doing things, they often shared many traits. For instance, the wheel, a basic device that arose at least 5000 years ago in the Old World, went remarkably undiscovered in the Americas before the arrival of the Europeans.

Not even the potter's wheel was in use in the New World.

The Iron Age never arose among the Indian societies. The Bronze Age made a feeble appearance in South America. Copper, while in use in North America, was only cold-hammered, never smelted and forged.

Writing was elusive in the New World. Some cultures, especially those north of Mesoamerica, never developed it. Others, like the Maya, had an elaborate system of writing that had progressed to the inclusion of phonetic elements. Yet an advanced group like the Inca of South America were entirely illiterate, though they did invent the *quipu*, a clever mnemonic device consisting of a system of knotted strings that recorded the likes of births and deaths, food stores, population numbers.

The New World cultures often built colossal monuments, rivaling those of their Old World counterparts. The Pyramid of the Sun near Mexico City is about as massive as the Great Pyramid at Giza, though it was constructed almost three millennia later. The Inca erected walls of stone so finely hewn and fitted that mortar wasn't needed. Of the walls not torn down by the Spaniards, the stone blocks are still so tightly in place that a knife blade cannot be inserted between adjacent blocks, a claim that I personally verified.

The Inca laced their empire together through a network of roads that ran for hundreds of miles, on par with those of the Romans. Thousands of miles to the north, the people of Chaco Canyon in the American Southwest linked their outlier settlements to their hub in the canyon via laser-straight roads.

The Inca engaged in trepanning, a form of brain surgery. With metal instruments, they chiseled out a section of the skull, apparently to relieve intracranial swelling caused by trauma, such as battle injuries. Though the Inca were probably unaware of the nature of infections, many patients survived. New bone growth is seen on excavated skulls. Some skulls dramatically reveal that there were patients who underwent multiple surgeries over time – and survived.

The Maya possessed a complex calendrical system that was highly accurate. Their astronomical observations and calculations allowed them to measure the period of Venus so precisely that by today's standards it was accurate to the second decimal point.

As with Old World societies, those in the Americas had their conflicts. The Maya, once thought to have been of peaceful disposition, were exposed for their warlike tendencies by the discovery of explicit panels such as those at Bonampak, which depict the torture and beheading of captive warriors. The Mayan cities battled one another from time to time as had the Greek city-states. The Aztecs established an empire from which they took captives to be slaughtered by the thousands in gory rituals. Recent evidence suggests that the egalitarian and docile Anasazi were not so docile and even engaged in cannibalism.

So who were these peoples? What tied them together? How did they differ? The reader is invited to join me in the journey through the book in search of answers and adventure. I've included a Resources section toward the back of the book for those readers who desire information on taking to the field on their own or with organized groups.

CITY OF THE GODS

The massive Pyramid of the Sun riveted my focus long before I reached the archeological site of Teotihuacán, thirty miles northeast of Mexico City, several years ago. As the tour bus rolled through the secluded countryside, still miles from the site, the pyramid's lofty spire poked above the tree line, blending with the distant hills, but its precise geometric configuration gave it away. This was no product of nature, no geological accident. The pyramid, with a base as extensive as that of the Great Pyramid of Giza, was a hallmark of a culture so long extinct that the awestruck Aztecs, who centuries later wandered onto the abandoned site, knew nothing of the former inhabitants or their culture.

Teotihuacán accreted in stages, starting in the Second Century B.C. Small farming villages along the Río San Juan and in the Teotihuacán Valley coalesced. Despite an elevation of greater than 7000 feet and an annual rainfall of fewer than twenty inches, the area supported a growing population. A plethora of natural springs moistened the valley's rich volcanic soil. The inhabitants had ready access to deposits of obsidian, a valued tool and trade item. The city was situated on a major trade route that linked the Gulf Coast to the Maya Lowlands. Teotihuacán was born.

By the middle of the Second Century A.D., the layout of the city had been established. Over the ensuing four centuries, the burgeoning metropolis continued to flourish. Teotihuacános extended their influence throughout parts of Mesoamerica — a vast blob of territory occupying parts of Mexico, Guatemala, Honduras, Belize and El Salvador. They were ardent merchants, trading in such diverse commodities as obsidian, seashells, feathers, incense, hides, textiles, cacao, rubber, jade, salt and medicines. In its heyday, the city was home to some 125,000 to 200,000 inhabitants, making it the largest human settlement in the Americas and the sixth largest in the world. It consumed nearly eight square miles of countryside, rivaling Rome, its contemporary, in size in the middle of the First Millennium A.D. More than 2000 walled apartment compounds were constructed during this time, only a few of which have been excavated.

I could hardly contain myself as our bus pulled into the site's extensive parking lot crammed with buses and cars. I set off on my own and headed straight for the pyramid, the third largest on the planet, which dominated the immediate landscape. The gray monolith burst forth from the flat terrain of the city like a miniature mountain. This truncated edifice loomed the equivalent of twenty-one stories into the air and spanned more than two football fields on a side. Some 300 million tons of rubble and adobe mud, all faced with stone, went into the construction of the pyramid. As there were no beasts of burden, all the materials were hauled on someone's back.

The stream of camera-toting climbers assailing its peak resembled a swarm of ants at a picnic. I crossed the wide Avenue of the Dead and joined the others scaling the monument. As I trekked up the long, steep stairway, I wondered how many countless thousands of others had ascended these very steps during bygone centuries. The majestic pyramid had borne not only the tread of Teotihuacános and their contemporaries, but of Aztecs and their ilk some 700 years later, and now of sightseers the world over. It would henceforth accommodate the passage of the curious for untold millennia, eventually rivaling its counterparts in Egypt. What secrets this omniscient eyewitness could divulge if the stones could talk.

The apex of the pyramid provided a commanding view of the entire site and surrounding countryside. In the distance jutted strips

PYRAMID OF THE SUN

of rugged mountains, including Cerro Gordo, the sacred peak from which emanated the springs that nourished the valley floor. The tropical sun had reached its daily zenith, washing the city in stark, abbreviated shadows. The buildings lining the two-mile-long Avenue of the Dead had been excavated. Most were remarkably well preserved, although extensive reconstruction was evident.

In 1971, a four-chambered cave, 330 feet in length, was discovered beneath this behemoth. The erection of the pyramid over the subterranean complex was no accident. Mesoamericans, including the Maya, and their contemporaries such as the Teotihuacános, viewed caves as gateways to the spiritual world. This cave contained offerings, perhaps attesting to its use for shamanistic rituals. It also contained skeletons, the hallmark of a burial practice; and large ceramic vessels, indicative of a storage facility. The chambers themselves resulted from the quarrying of volcanic stone used in the construction of parts of the city, probably in the residential sections. The largest chamber in the cave spans an area of more than half a football field.

I descended the stairs and turned left (south) onto the Avenue of the Dead, oriented slightly off from a north-south axis and aimed directly at Cerro Gordo to the north. I joined the parade of tourists strolling around within the Ciudadela (Citadel), a huge thirty-nine-acre enclosure near the geographic center of the city. The main plaza here, a civic and religious center, once had a capacity of 100,000 persons. I was drawn to the Pyramid of the Feathered Serpent within the enclosure. Although dwarfed by the structure I had just dismounted, this pyramid was noteworthy not for its sheer bulk but for its intricate stone carvings. Each successively higher level of this stepped pyramid was smaller in area than the level immediately below. The tablero faces on the western side were bedecked with bas-relief images of rattle-tailed serpents undulating across the pyramid. The edifice had once been brilliantly painted, almost entirely in hematite red. Time had scoured away almost all of the color. Bands of life-sized marine shells, also chiseled in low relief, shared the frieze with the serpents. Conch shells retained most of the original white pigment. Bivalve shells showed traces of red and white tint. Colossal stone heads, of fanged creatures resembling dragons, jutted out from the tableros and stairway balustrades. Each wore a collar of feathers bearing hints of the original red color. Another series of fanged monster heads was also affixed to this side of the pyramid. Obsidian eyes were set within "goggles," once painted blue-green, on a mosaic forehead. In all, there was once 365 such "masks" on the four sides of the pyramid. Time had eroded most of the features on the other three sides. It was only this western side that was beautifully preserved, having been ensconced beneath a platform for centuries, until excavated in modern times. I wondered about the significance of all this strange iconography, as I marveled at the exquisite craftsmanship. For all these icons had been carved by a stone-age people to whom metal tools were unknown.

The seashells apparently represented water and fertility. The "dragon" heads and serpent bodies seemed to be joined together into "feathered serpents," common images throughout Mesoamerica. There is a question as to whether this represented the similar-appearing deity the Aztecs later knew as Quetzelcoatl. To the Aztecs, Quetzelcoatl was a multifaceted entity, including a god of wind and a death-dispensing warrior aspect of the planet Venus. The Aztec's predecessors, the Toltecs, regarded the feathered serpent as a hero. Some archeologists believe the feathered serpent here was a manifestation of Venus, a god of warfare and blood sacrifice. The Teotihuacános engaged in sacred warfare and human sacrifice timed by the position of Venus, a practice of other Mesoamerican cultures such as the Maya.

Archeologists have uncovered burial chambers beneath at least two of the corners of this pyramid. The skeletons of eighteen young males were discovered in one corner, along with 169 obsidian points and 4000 pieces of worked shell. Most of these sacrificed victims had their hands bound behind their backs. Many wore collars, which contained human jaws and imitation maxillae, with artificial teeth carved from shells. Later, an excavation trench through another corner of the pyramid revealed eighteen additional male victims with similar funerary offerings. There was careful attention to orientation of the bodies when they were entombed. More recent finds have raised the number of human skeletons within the pyramid to 120.

Investigators concluded that the number of persons within each burial location, as well as their physical placement, correlated somehow with the pyramid's role in the religiosity of Teotihuacán. Numbers such as eighteen and twenty had calendrical import. Mesoamerican years contained eighteen full months of twenty days — five days were added to complete the 365-day cycle. A 260-day "sacred calendar," another Mesoamerican feature, was also used in Teotihuacán. It combined another magic number, thirteen, with twenty to achieve its cycle.

But archaeologists postulated divergent explanations for the derivation of the victims. One researcher argued the sacrificed were loyal citizens who were dispatched to eternally serve a departed leader, a practice not uncommon in Mesoamerica. Another asserted that the victims were enemy warriors captured in battle, specifically to be sacrificed in accordance with the doctrines of the Venus warfare cult.

Persons of status had also been interred beneath the pyramid. One of these tombs held the remains of an individual adorned with elegant earspools, a rectangular nose ornament, and twenty-one large beads, all of greenstone. A wooden baton, carved into the shape of a stylized serpent head, found with the body suggested that the deceased held a priestly office.

I departed the pyramid and strolled across the Avenue to the Great Compound, once the site of the main market now long gone. The market of this cosmopolitan society had been the focus of daily life, as it had been in Indian villages and towns throughout Mesoamerica, and indeed still is today. Hundreds of stalls here had once offered a great variety of food such as the Mesoamerican staples of maize, beans, squashes and chili peppers, as well as other vegetables, fish and game, including deer, turkeys, dogs, ducks and rabbits. Other stalls hawked avian goods such as feather headdresses and cloaks, and even live birds themselves. A wide variety of semi-precious stones and jewelry, and pottery, both decorative and utilitarian, as well as carved, stone masks and figurines, were offered. During ritual ceremonies, an alcoholic beverage, *pulque*, derived from the leaves of the agave plant, was eagerly consumed. Obsidian products such as scalpel-sharp blades, mined thirty-five miles north at Cerro de las Navajas (Mountain of the Knives), were in great demand. The market must have provided a stunning array of choices, and not just to the locals. Vendors and consumers traveled here from miles around. Distant foreigners, such as the Maya, were frequent visitors, as depicted by the wall murals in the excavated buildings.

I headed north, again joining the throng of pedestrians promenading along the Avenue of the Dead, making the long walk to the Pyramid of the Moon anchoring this road on the north. The excavated remains on both sides of me represented but a small fraction of the city in its zenith. I scaled the pyramid, not as massive as the one dedicated to the sun, but substantial enough to rank as the fourth largest in the prehistoric Americas. Now I had a commanding view of virtually the entire city, my vista bisected by the Avenue, wide as a modern ten-lane divided highway.

I wondered about the demise of this great city, the first true metropolis in the Americas. For centuries it had thrived before it fell into decline by the mid-Seventh Century. Several factors are implicated. The health of the population diminished. Infant mortality rates escalated. Environmental degradation depleted resources. Disease was endemic. Clean drinking water was getting harder to come by. But the city came to a *violent* end. Sometime in the first half of the Eighth Century, the ceremonial and administrative nerve-center of Teotihuacán, all up and down the Avenue, was systematically sacked and torched. Outlying sacred structures were also burned. Why?

One archeologist postulated that "warrior merchants" from neighboring towns "simply overran and destroyed the city." But time had already been running out for this grand metropolis for some reason or other. The warrior merchants simply administered the coup de grâce.

A great deal of mystery still surrounds the City of the Gods. We don't know the language of the inhabitants. No method of hieroglyphic writing, as was employed so vividly by the Maya, has come to light. Only traces of the Mayan numbering system, a combination of dots and bars with an occasional seashell, have been discovered. The origins of the Teotihuacános are unknown — as is their fate.

CLIFF DWELLERS OF THE SOUTHWEST

For years I had pursued an interest in Mesoamerican and South American archeology, attending lectures, taking courses, reading articles and books, even visiting ancient ruins in Mexico, Peru and Guatemala. All of my time and effort had been directed toward areas within the Western Hemisphere beyond the borders of my own country, for the legends of the Maya, Aztec, Olmec and Inca had totally enthralled me. These civilizations took my imagination captive and propelled it from vision to vision — of lofty stepped-pyramids, ball courts of varying dimensions, complex enigmatic hieroglyphs, impressive irrigation and road-building programs, precise astronomical calculations, even self-mutilation and human sacrifice. I eventually came to realize there were other remarkable pre-Columbian civilizations throughout what is now the United States. So I focused on those cultures that thrived in the Southwest, for no better reason than their proximity to their contemporaries in neighboring Mexico. There must have been an interchange of cultures, I surmised.

I started reading about those Southwest cultures, now vanished. One group appeared repeatedly in the literature: the Anasazi. This seemed a likely jumping-off point to embark on a journey of discovery, especially when I read about — and saw photos of — the remarkable, multistory cliff dwellings they left in their wake when they disappeared, structures unrivaled in the Americas. But reading about abandoned cities only took me so far; I had to physically absorb myself in the ruins to appreciate the builders. So I signed up for an archeological field trip to the Four Corners region (where Colorado, Utah, Arizona and New Mexico come together at one point), the former center of the Anasazi world.

Three months later I was in Colorado about to immerse myself in the Anasazi culture.

* * *

I was up early and out into the chilly, crisp mountain air. First destination would be Mesa Verde, site of renowned cliff dwellings — a spectacular tribute to a culture that has passed into history. There were some two dozen of us participants on this field trip. All came from the West Coast, the Northeast or Texas. My girlfriend, Joan, and I, being from Florida, were the aliens. Two "scholars" accompanied us, visiting archeologists invited along just for this tour. The sponsor, Crow Canyon Archaeological Center, conducted several field trips per year, mainly throughout the Southwest.

We were divided into four vans. The scholars doubled as drivers, a chore they seemed not to mind. We lucked out with Art Rohn in our van for the first day. A professor of anthropology, he has written extensively on the Southwest cultures, especially the Anasazi. Tall, heavy set, with a bulging midsection and a full head of uncombed hair, Art wore a turquoise choker necklace with an enigmatic gold pendant of a nude woman, which seemed totally out of character for him. There had to be a story that went with it, a mystery trailing an anecdote. A worn cowboy hat, the obvious loser of many battles with the elements, claimed the perch of honor atop Art's silver locks. His feet were shoved into ancient, scuffed cowboy boots that had yet to be blemished with polish. To the unknowing, Art could have just ridden in off the range, a genuine Marlboro Man, taking a breather before heading back out to repair more fences. He seemed as rugged and worn as the well-scoured landscape through which he had trod for decades in his search for understanding of the peoples who had once populated the area. Though he spent many hours each semester in the classroom, Art was more at home in the great outdoors of the Southwest, where he blended in with the canyons and bluffs and juniper trees. He was always quick on the draw with a joke. After everyone chuckled, including himself, he'd pause, then suddenly get serious and toss out some pearls about the Anasazi.

It's widely accepted that the Americas were populated by peoples who migrated from northeast Asia across the land bridge, about a thousand miles wide known as Beringia, that once connected that continent to what is now Alaska. The dates of these migrations are hotly disputed. Some estimates reach as far back as 30,000 to 40,000 years. More conservative guesses place the time closer to 14,000 years. Thus far the archeological evidence tends to support the latter date. But regardless of when the Asians reached the Americas, it's clear that over 10,000 years of human development preceded the Anasazi in the Southwest. These forerunners — hunters and gatherers — moved in small groups from place to place. The latter part of this stage in the Southwest is known as Basket Maker I, a cultural environment that endured for some 3000 years until a few centuries prior to the birth of Christ. Such neolithic peoples never discovered metal implements, relying instead upon weapons and tools of stone, bone, antler and other non-metallic materials.

These primitive cultures evolved over hundreds of years, passing through two other Basket Maker stages, then into the Pueblo phases, of which there were four, each progression generally leading to higher levels of complexity and development.

Art drove us higher into the mountains of the southwest corner of the state. We started a mile up and climbed. The warm air cooled. The foliage metamorphosed. Now waves of piñon pine and juniper bracketed the road. Art said this would in turn yield to other trees at higher elevations. At 8000 to 8500 feet, we'd encounter ponderosa pine. Farther up would be the spruce zone. Well below where we started lay the scrub and grassland zones and below that, the high desert. Each was a different ecological zone, each with its own flora and fauna.

The Anasazi generally chose to build in the piñon and juniper zones, said Art. But they would even inhabit the grassland and scrub sections. We climbed and twisted along the narrow road, the valley far below to our left. When the proto-Anasazi evolved from solely hunting and gathering to agriculture, their pace of development accelerated like a dragster, Art noted, as he wheeled us higher.

I asked Art whether the Anasazi had a social hierarchy. He thought not, in stark contrast to the cultures of Mesoamerica, which were highly stratified, especially during their classical periods. This surprised me, since I was aware, from my reading, of the spectacular architectural works of the Anasazi, the ruins of which were still visible around the Four Corners region. Surely such monumental undertakings were the product of the organization of the masses by religious or political leaders for public works projects which spanned years, even decades. But apparently this was not the case.

Our higher elevation allowed spectacular vistas still being chiseled by nature's deft hand. A vast plain spread before us, leading the eye to steep-sided monolithic plateaus and mesas that rose starkly for hundreds of feet into the crisp air far in the distance. Lined with countless horizontal layers of sandstone and shale, washed in pastel shades of rose, coral, lavender and tan, they had survived for 70 million years. They were still being shaped by nature, like an artist never satisfied, his painting always needing a dab here, another dab there.

We parked at an overlook and alighted from the vans, glad to stretch our legs. The view was unobstructed for miles across Montezuma Valley, set under a cloud-flecked sky of powder blue that went on forever. Three large birds, which I couldn't identify, leisurely glided across the valley in the distance, glancing about as though sightseeing. Some 30,000 Anasazi had lived in the towns and villages in the valley during the Pueblo III stage, from 1100 to 1300 A.D., considered the classical period for the Anasazi.

Art pointed out a shaggy-bark juniper, a cornucopia for the Anasazi. The branches snapped off easily and were used for firewood and roofing materials. The wood burned hot, making it most suitable for firing pottery. Juniper bark was also fashioned into menstrual pads for women and diapers for infants. The berries, though lacking in taste, were eaten. A different type of juniper berry has a more modern use: flavoring gin, as in gin and tonic.

Then on we went to our first site.

Southeast of the valley stood the Mesa Verde ruins. The cliffs and mesas were home to the Anasazi for 700 years (from 600 to 1300 A.D.), after which the area was abandoned. Along aptly named Ruins Road were several excavated sites that poignantly demonstrated the evolution of Anasazi architecture. Art led us through the progression.

One site contained a Basket Maker III "pithouse" dwelling dating to 595 A.D., which resembled a large, fancy hole in the ground, only slightly more technologically advanced than a bomb crater. Dug a couple of feet into the reddish earth, it was roughly twenty feet across. These unimpressive remnants had once been the proud home to at least one Anasazi family — its bedroom, living room, dining room and den all contained within this one earthen cavity. A circular, clay-lined fire pit — the family hearth — was centrally located. The room, now open to the sky, had been roofed over with timbers, sticks and mud when constructed. An air hole would have been left at the top. Attached to the room, like one bubble sprouting from another, were the remains of an antechamber, through which entry had been made into the main chamber. A stone slab, erected in the neck between the two rooms, served as a draft deflector during air circulation. When the fire was lit, smoke curled out through the roof opening, creating a negative pressure. This sucked air in through the antechamber and into the main room that housed the fire pit. To keep that draft from extinguishing the fire, the vertical slab was installed. It now lay flat and cracked. Four post holes were evident in the floor soil, though the posts themselves had long ago decayed away. When the pithouse was intact, these holes would have housed the timbers that supported the roof. The main chamber bore the remains of flat, rectangular, stone metates, each the size of an attaché case, used for grinding corn. It also contained the sipapu, a small, circular hole in the ground that had mythological significance for the Anasazi. This simple dwelling, modest as it was, served as the Anasazi equivalent to a fully equipped modern home in suburbia with an attached two-car garage.

Corn, which was often eaten fresh off the cob, hardly resembled what is found in today's produce departments. While selective breeding had then been going on for centuries, genetic engineering was hundreds of years in the future. Most ears of corn were small, the yields modest. A great advantage of corn was its shelf life, its ability to be dried and stored for months, even years. The main threat to its longevity came from insects and other pests. Often the kernels were laboriously stripped from the cob by the women. Bending over a metate, with its four short legs, the women ground the corn with a hand-held stone mano. They often worked in groups, catching up on the latest gossip, making a social event out of their arthritic-inducing labors. The corn meal was molded into flat breads or cakes, to be heated and eaten. This grinding method guaranteed a flour rife with stony grit. This abrasive diet, coupled with the lack of modern dentistry, took its toll on the Anasazi teeth, which gradually but inexorable wore down, often to nubs. These natives seldom were long-lived, which may have been a blessing to those who outlived their teeth.

As unsophisticated as the ubiquitous pithouse was then, the builders had made significant cultural advances over their predecessors from the two previous Basket Maker stages. Now, these peoples were cultivating beans, in addition to their mainstay crops of corn and squash, which they had grown for hundreds upon hundreds of years. In this, they had finally caught up to the dietary habits of their Mesoamerican neighbors, who were ahead of the Southwest cultures in many other ways as well.

For millennia, baskets had been woven in southwestern North America. High quality baskets, ranging in size from a few inches across to a more than a yard in diameter, often decorated with geometric designs in black. Some were so tightly woven they are *still* waterproof! Contrary to popular belief, making a basket was not child's play. Constructing even a small one involved hours of labor — and by an expert. First the materials (willow, squawbush or other supple twigs) were gathered. Then split, and split again, to get thin, pliable sewing splints a foot or so in length. These splints were then soaked to make them more pliable. Only then were they capable of being woven.

Though these natives hadn't yet learned of pottery, they were ingenious in their use of baskets. Seeds and corn were parched by dropping them into a large, flat basket with hot coals. The basket then had to be shaken briskly to keep it from burning. Not surprisingly, these baskets had a short longevity.

Other baskets were used for "stone boiling." Hot stones, heated on the hearth, were dropped into the liquid or mush in the basket to heat or cook the contents.

But baskets, even tightly woven ones, had their limitations. During the Basket Maker III stage, the art of making pottery finally found its way into the Southwest, another gift from Mesoamerica. Such innovative technology allowed a cooking vessel to be placed directly on hot coals, even into a fire. The clay pots also served as water jugs and storage bins. They were much more durable than baskets, unless dropped. An Old World invention, the potter's wheel, was one of those technological advances that forever escaped the Anasazi. Instead, the Anasazi coiled the tempered clay, then shaped and smoothed it before firing. Slips were applied. The ceramics were painted, generally with black designs. Other pottery, used for cooking, was left rough and unpainted. The vessel surface was corrugated by crimping the moist clay with the fingers. Perhaps this textured finish increased the surface area of the pot, allowing for better distribution of the fire's heat into the contents.

The bow and arrow, which today is considered primitive, was a substantial advancement in weaponry, replacing the even more primitive spear and atlatl. This now allowed the Anasazi to fell game at greater distances, bringing more meat to the table, feeding more hungry mouths, which in turn caused more hungry mouths to be born.

The Anasazi domesticated turkeys, essentially for their feathers. Arrows were fletched with split feathers. The feathers were also used in making blankets by winding the feathers around strings.

Robes were sometimes made from deerskin and occasionally from the hides of elk or bighorn sheep. The hides were sewn together with yucca twine — or with hair, human or dog. One site revealed six sashes made entirely of dog hair. The sashes, currently in a museum, are as soft now as they were when made 1500 years ago! The sashes used a total of more than a mile of finely spun dog-hair string.

These Basket Maker III peoples supplemented crops with the gathering of such goodies as piñon nuts, juniper berries, pigweed, rice grass, acorns and sunflower seeds. Populations expanded as populations tend to do when the food supply increases, right up to the Malthusian limits, just as they do today.

Though these later Anasazi still led a tough existence, there was now more time for leisure, even for fashion. Lapidaries kept busy. Beads of colored stones were ground, polished and bored for stringing. The natives also utilized beads of abalone shell, traded from the Pacific coast, and beads of local land-snail shells. Necklaces were manufactured from bright seeds or polished bird bone, cut into short tubes. Turquoise came into use, often being fashioned into pendants and beads. The stones were shaped and polished using only stone tools. Trading was ubiquitous amongst the pre-Columbian peoples, despite the wide diversity of cultures and vast geographic distances. Goods from the Gulf of Mexico and the Pacific Ocean reached far inland. Copper, from the Great Lakes region, was bartered from tribe to tribe, all the way down the continent.

But for all the rungs on the ladder of cultural evolution the Anasazi climbed, there were some rungs, hallmarks of civilization (at least as to the Eurocentric concept of the term), they never got a foot on. Such as the ubiquitous wheel, in use in the Old World for thousands of years, which amazingly eluded the Anasazi. And all other peoples of the New World as well! Also, the Anasazi, and the other cultures of the Southwest and even of Mesoamerica, remained essentially neolithic peoples until the coming of the Europeans. They did possess metal, such as copper, but it had mainly ornamental use and was never smelted or forged.

Nor did the Anasazi develop a written language, unlike some of their Mesoamerican counterparts, such as the Maya and the Aztecs. Their written record was essentially confined to rock art.

Art led us down Ruins Road to a later site surrounded by tall conifers. As we alighted from the vans, a chorus of songbirds opened up from the branches like Christmas carolers. Was this our unofficial welcoming committee? Were they out to serenade each other? Were they just overjoyed at the beautiful day it was turning into? The site, Deep Pithouse, at Twin Trees Village was built in the antechamber ruins of an earlier pithouse around 700 A.D. The Anasazi were noted for constructing one site upon another, a practice common among pre-Columbian peoples; the Maya did it regularly, in fifty-two-year cycles, which roughly equated to our century. Deep Pithouse had no antechamber itself. Access was gained through the roof opening, which doubled as a smoke hole. A stone slab was slid over the opening to keep out the rain. The floor was scooped out two feet below ground level. The room was circumferenced by a narrow earthen banquette upon which the wall poles would have rested. A major change from the previous site Art had shown us was the ventilation system. This latter pithouse brought fresh air in through a tunnel on the south side of the structure. This evolved into the ventilation system later found in most Anasazi sacred kivas.

As we moved on to the next site, Art pointed out several bluish-gray yucca plants growing close to the ground, their distinctive bayonet leaves projecting upward. To the unsuspecting, the needle points of the leaves can deeply pierce the skin — or an eye. But these cactus-like plants were a supermarket to the Anasazi. They wove the fibrous leaves into baskets, sandals, ropes and mats. The needle points were used for sewing. In the spring, milky flowers made a tasty addition to the diet. In the fall, the fruit, resembling a cucumber, had the flavor of a starchy melon. Even the roots yielded a soap that the Indians used to wash their hair.

Art escorted us to an even later site at Twin Trees Village, which consisted of two square pithouses, one of which had been backfilled (filled in) by modern archeologists to preserve it. Built circa 850 A.D., it contained the usual internal architecture of earlier sites. What had changed was the depth. Dug six or seven feet down, the pithouses were now substantially subterranean with their roofs at ground level.

The storage rooms had evolved into a combination of living quarters and storage facilities, Art said. Initially they were composed of jacal (wattle and daub), but later of masonry, usually sandstone. The Basket Maker III dwellings had reached the Pueblo stage.

In our progression through the ages of Anasazi culture, we were ferried to another site up the road. It was a square Pueblo II kiva dug deeply into the earth. This structure was a quantum leap in sophistication from those of the Basket Maker periods. Masonry lined the walls here. A stone banquette perimetered the structure a meter above the floor. The remains of eight stone pilasters, that would have supported the roof, were evident. I noticed a sipapu and a deflector slab. The square fire pit was no longer just a hole in the ground, but was masonry lined. Two oblong trenches — floor vaults — bracketed the firepit. They may have served as foot drums or storage space. Tree-ring samples pinpointed the date of the structure at 1074 A.D.

These kivas were sacred places. But they also served social and political functions. Meetings were generally secret and were certainly off-limits to the public at large. Kivas were sort of a combination of temple, caucus room and men's club. But some societies did use them for social or work activities.

As we departed the site, Art paused to forage along the ground beneath a piñon pine, picking up what appeared to be dark-stained pebbles. He placed one of the pebbles between his teeth and bit down on it. Crack! But it wasn't Art's tooth that shattered. The pebble split open, revealing a lighter-colored capsule inside. Art promptly gulped it down. Then cracked open the next pebble. And so on, through a handful of the pebbles. Art hadn't lost his mind. He was munching on the fruit of the piñon pine that dropped loose when the tree shed its cones. Art's snack turned out to be one of my favorite delicacies — pine nuts. I promptly bent over and scoured the ground. I leisurely strolled back to the van, munching on the succulent flesh of the tiny nuts.

The vans next stopped at Sun Point for one of the best views of Mesa Verde, which provided a breathtaking panorama of cliffs and canyons and ruins, all chiseled into a rugged, life-sized diorama. To the left, Fewkes Canyon ran away from us, cradling four major ruins within its embrace. Across the jagged, narrow canyon, Sun Temple, a small complex of sandstone buildings, perched boldly on the opposite sun-splashed bluff. Numerous sets of ruins of varying sizes popped into view to grab and hold the scanning eye. Here and there, trees and shrubs took up residence, singly or in small clusters, eking out an existence within the fissures of the cliff faces. Other irregular patches of trees sprouted haphazardly, like a bad haircut, from the summits of the cliffs.

Below and off to the right, I spotted the magnificent cluster of masonry buildings known as Cliff Palace tucked under an eroded-out overhang in the face of the sandstone cliff. That's the site I was particularly interested in visiting, for it was photos of these fabulous ruins that had helped divert my attention from Mesoamerica to the Southwest. Farther to the right and closer to the canyon floor sat Sunset House, another cluster of masonry dwellings. Most sites were surprisingly well preserved considering their antiquity, although there have been some restorations in modern times. Still, many of the buildings could have been made ready for occupancy by the original inhabitants, with a few repairs and some minor housekeeping.

Mummy House was visible in the cliff face beneath Sun Temple. A small complex, it consisted of twelve rooms and two kivas and, naturally enough, took its name from a well-preserved mummy found in a two-story building. It was the aridity of this place rather than some Egyptian-like embalming process that accounted for the desiccated corpse. Still, the mummy provided archeologists with a rare glimpse into the past through a window seldom open.

We were shuttled across the canyon to Cliff Palace, the largest, and perhaps most magnificent, cliff dwelling in North America. The Anasazi moved onto the overhead mesa around 500 A.D. During its heyday in the Thirteenth Century, Cliff Palace probably housed 2500 to 3000 persons, quite a metropolis for a cliff-dwelling community. We picked our way down the narrow stairway that folded back on itself, following the cliff line. A park ranger in a Smokey the Bear hat waited at the closest edge of the dwellings. Like a traffic cop, she pointed the way and told us to follow the directive placards and stay on the assigned walkways throughout the site. The midday sun blasted its fiery rays into the natural amphitheater to flash off the sandstone structures, highlighting parts and casting others in deep shadow, accentuating the architecture of the place and stirring up a sense of mystery.

The superstructures of the buildings had mostly eroded away, yet the buildings' multistory status was yet evident. But these weren't skyscrapers. Most of the sandstone edifices appeared to have reached only two or three stories. An exception was the relatively lofty four-story square tower. We were allowed to peek into this

CLIFF PALACE

building through the pint-sized door at the base of the ground floor. The rooms were confining, typical for the Anasazi.

The buildings of this cliff dwelling were skillfully crafted. The walls were flat, the squared-off corners straight, unlike many modern homes. The rooms were small, with a base averaging six by eight feet and a height that would cause a modern teenager to watch his head. The rooms were joined by small, rectangular or T-shaped doorways. Plaster on the walls was still evident, though most had eroded off. The colors of choice were earth tones such as off-white and reddish-brown.

No two in-ground kivas were alike, but similar blueprints were followed. They were circular, with a central fireplace and a ventilator tunnel on the south side with a raised deflector just to the north of the tunnel's exit. Masonry pilasters, usually six, rose from the encircling banquette. A sipapu was bored into the floor north of the fire pit. There was a recessed area, above the banquette, at the south end of the kiva. The kivas were generally dug beneath courtyard level so their roofs would form part of the courtyard.

The roofs of these kivas were no longer present. The interiors were completely visible from ground level by standing on top of the enclosing, subterranean wall. Some of the internal features indicative of a Mesa Verde kiva were lacking in the few kivas I peered into. On the floors of a couple of the kivas I discerned a loom loop, indicating the kivas here were in part used for weaving.

Beginning early in Pueblo III times, about 1150 A.D., the Anasazi began moving off the mesas and into the cliffs, perhaps because of hostilities from marauding bands of other Indians. By 1200, the Anasazi began constructing the great cliff dwellings. Over prior millennia, the caves had been carved out of the sandstone cliffs by percolating water. When the water froze, the ice crystals expanded. This action repeated itself indefinitely, causing sandstone to erode away and flake off, in grains, chunks, boulders and slabs. Holes, from baseball size to stadium size, have been thus scooped out along the bluff faces. They provided handy shelter beneath the overhangs for the Anasazi. Getting foodstuffs and building supplies up into the caves, however, must have been a backbreaking chore. Yet the caves' inaccessibility provided security from marauding tribes.

I noticed a group of rooms on an upper ledge tucked under the roof of the domed alcove. I thought them unreachable to the Anasazi. But a long-gone ladder allowed them ready access through a doorway on the upper level. Two vertical notches were yet visible in the sandstone where the ladder once rested. Such hard-to-reach storage rooms were handy. They were cool, dry and out of the way of mischievous children, curious dogs and hungry turkeys.

On the slope in front of Cliff Palace, the residents, in keeping with the times, dumped their trash, including shattered pottery, worn down tools of bone or stone, used up clothing and sandals, cold ashes from their fires, human wastes, uneaten or inedible foodstuffs. The effluvium, carried on an unfavorable wind, must have at times been overpowering.

We departed the ruins on the far side, climbing up through a narrow, steep stairway that barely cut through the rock, a stairway better suited to mountain goats. Off to the side of the passage were shallow niches cut into the sandstone by the Anasazi, which allowed access to the dwellings. Each notch would accommodate only the tips of the fingers or the ends of the toes. The Anasazi had to have been nimble — and with a firm grip. It's even more remarkable when considering that some of them would have scaled the sandstone mesa while carrying burdens on their backs or vessels on their heads.

Some of our group paused at the top of the stairway, heavily sucking in the clear mountain air in great gulps. As the rest of our group plodded up the stairway, I pondered the fate of these Anasazi. Why would they leave this magnificent place? They had taken such pains to construct their pueblo. The alcove in the sheer cliff face made their dwellings defensible from attack. The overhang at the mouth of the alcove would have shielded them somewhat from the summer sun. And the view was incomparable, so why then?

During the latter part of the Thirteenth Century they had started leaving in droves. By 1300 A.D., Mesa Verde had been completely abandoned. Perhaps the severe drought during the final quarter of the Thirteenth Century was a factor. But the Anasazi had survived earlier droughts, some of which were more severe. Maybe the lack of water came at a critical time. Perhaps other resources were also running short. Timber, for building and firewood, may have thinned out in the immediate area, necessitating longer and longer tree-seeking forays. Decades of farming may have depleted the soil. There's even speculation that pirate bands, such as the marauding Ute, had harassed the Anasazi into moving on.

Whatever, it is currently accepted that these Anasazi did not die out, but rather migrated generally south, where they commingled with other cultures in what is now northern Arizona and New Mexico. Today if one visits the Hopi mesas in Arizona, or the Zuni, Acuma or the Rio Grande pueblos near Santa Fe, New Mexico, he will come face to face with the descendants of the Anasazi of Mesa Verde.

We drove by Spruce Tree House. Our tour leaders thought this important enough to stop. The parking area also served the museum, restaurant and — finally, sighed the women — restrooms. After a whirlwind trip through the surprisingly complete museum, I hurried down the near canyon face, camera dangling from my hand, and scooted along the paved trail that cut back and forth. I weaved through the trees, crossed over to the other side of the canyon, which brought me to Spruce Tree House.

This site, harbored within a natural cave, was erected between

1200 and 1276 A.D. (Pueblo III). It had housed some 100 Anasazi. The convenient rock overhang provided maximum sunshine in winter and shade in summer. As I traversed the site, I noticed the kivas were lined up, more or less, from left to right, near the front. I wondered whether the alignment had any significance. No one could provide an answer. No matter how much we learn of the Anasazi, there will always be mysteries to solve, puzzles to piece together. Job security for generations of future archeologists is assured.

One three-story wall fronted what was once about twenty rooms. They were, of course, partially destroyed, but the diminutive size of the rooms was evident. The dimensions comported with those of the rooms at Cliff Palace, which apparently were typical for the Mesa Verde area. The living spaces brought to mind the close confines of the quarters in a Trappist monastery.

Many of the walls bore the distinctive and enigmatic T-shaped doorways. There was unbounded speculation for this peculiar shape, but nobody gave me a convincing explanation. This type of doorway was alternated with the rectangular type, for reasons unknown to archeologists. Beneath one of the ground-floor doorways was propped a sandstone slab. During cold weather such slabs, or animal hides, were fitted into the door frame, fending off the chilled air and sequestering the warmth within. But since the rooms were not well ventilated, I imagined the living quarters were sootier than a cigar-smokers' convention.

In addition to the blazes in the rooms, fires at the rear of the cave may have been kept lit around the clock during the coldest months. This was evidenced by the heavy patina of soot yet clinging to outer walls and cave ceiling.

Some original roofing timbers and balcony supports still survived. On favorable days, families lived and worked in the courtyards, on the rooftops, and on the balconies that extended from the fronts of the buildings. I could envision the women grinding corn, or weaving baskets, or preparing the food. The men may have been shaping stone tools, fashioning cotton or turkey-feather blankets, or preparing for the summer planting. The older folks might have sat around and soaked up the sun. Domesticated turkeys would have pecked across the ground, perhaps harassed by a pet dog. Children must have been at play in the courtyards.

I studied one deep kiva from the top of the circular wall. The roof was long gone, leaving the kiva exposed. The elements of a typical kiva were present: ventilator shaft, deflector slab, fire pit and sipapu in a line; a banquette ringing the interior; six masonry pilasters resting on the banquette. There was another element in this kiva that was not ubiquitous. Small openings, called niches, had been cut into the interior wall. These recesses usually contained ceremonial objects such as turquoise, shell beads and prayer sticks.

A ten-minute van ride brought us to Far View House on Chapin Mesa, one of the many finger mesas making up the sloping, flat-topped Mesa Verde. The site was a rectangular pueblo composed of forty ground rooms and five kivas. Constructed between 1100 and 1300 A.D. (Pueblo III), the entire site probably once contained more rooms. There had been a second story on some of the buildings, the upper walls having since collapsed.

The rooms here were more evenly spaced than the rooms in the cliff dwellings. At one location the trapezoidal doorways all lined up, giving a straight shot through three of the portals and into the fourth room beyond. These trapezoidal doorways bore a striking resemblance to analogous Inca portals thousands of miles to the south. I'd walked through many of them. I doubt there's a connection, just coincidence. Interesting, though.

I scampered over the walls like a curious child, peering down into the now unroofed kivas and rooms, wondering what life must have been like in those rooms centuries ago. The dwellings certainly were not comfortable by modern standards.

The villagers of Far View traded food, pottery and other goods with their Anasazi neighbors to the south. The influence of the Chaco culture, which we were to study firsthand, probably precipitated the building of kivas here, which resembled Chacoan style rather than that of the local Mesa Verde.

To supply the vast quantities of water to these sites in the Far View region, the Anasazi constructed a circular reservoir, almost as expansive as a baseball infield and twelve feet deep. It effectively trapped and held runoff from rain and snow. Uphill of the reservoir, a number of manmade channels collected the runoff. The main channel made a sharp right turn to deposit out any silt before continuing into the mouth of the reservoir. The Anasazi thus always had clean drinking water. For irrigation, the runoff was diverted before reaching the sharp turn and fed directly onto the crops, silt and all.

Then we went on to Bluff, Utah, for the night. We drove through a portion of the spacious Ute reservation en route to our motel. History has it that Bluff was settled by the Mormons in the 1860s. The current population hovered around 240. The village consisted of three service stations strung along the highway, three roadside cafes, a couple of grocery stores, two motels, a school, the office and boatyard of Wild Rivers Expedition, and a scattering of houses, some empty.

After dropping our luggage in our rooms and cleaning up, we all sauntered down the road to a white-man's hogan. Dinner time. The meal was put together by Wild Rivers Expedition, which would be the outfitters for tomorrow's rafting venture. The octagonal hogan was partially screened, allowing an unobstructed view of the russet sandstone bluffs jutting straight out of the ground only a few blocks distant. As the sun dropped, the long rays washed the sandstone faces in reds and oranges, providing a colorful backdrop to our communal repast.

✳   ✳   ✳

After breakfast we drove to our first display of rock art. On a sandstone cliff face, numerous figures and designs were etched into the rock. Erosion had faded some of the features and a few had been carved over by later Anasazi artists, but most were clearly discernible. Bighorn sheep (my guess) were depicted. I could make out an archer with a drawn bow. One of the scholars pointed out a stylized "flute" player, the legendary hunchback Kokopelli. This stick-like figure apparently held a musical instrument, which looked more like a clarinet than a flute, in his outstretched arms. The mouthpiece was between his lips, his hands grasping the tube of the flute. He was shown with a humped back. But maybe Kokopelli was merely bent over. I'd seen jazz players bent over as they wailed away on their horns. There was speculation that Kokopelli was a fertility symbol.

We assembled at the edge of the San Juan River, eagerly chattering like marmosets. Four large, gray rubber rafts were lined up along the water's edge. The guides passed out life jackets, plastic cups, and Army-salvage ammunition boxes for dry storage. We anxiously clambered aboard the rafts at random. A vinyl duffel bag on each raft provided additional storage for the forthcoming trip. A large jug of water, which we would drain during the trip, was fastened near each bow.

The early morning sun was softening the nip in the mountain air. No clouds were yet out. The river, only a hundred yards across at this point, was tame. This was not going to be a whitewater run.

Off we pushed into the slow, tawny current, one after the other. Our raft was second in line. The eight-horsepower motor casually propelled us downstream. The luck of the draw didn't seat one of the scholars in our raft. Our pilot and guide, Tom, an outdoors type in his thirties, was very knowledgeable of the archeology and geology of the region despite a lack of professional credentials.

The fields we leisurely passed gave way to sandstone cliffs on each bank. For untold millennia the river has been cutting its way down through the rock, baring layer upon layer of sandstone formations. There must have been thousands of layers, some no wider than a silver dollar. Even from the middle of the river, 300 yards away, the thicker layers were readily discernible, like a giant terracotta birthday cake. Tom indicated the layers were formed from sand dunes and blowing sand rather than from being deposited by running water. The rocks to our right dated to the Jurassic Period, during the age of dinosaurs.

The river meandered, changing course constantly, carving up the land into plateaus and canyons. The erosive power of wind and rain and temperature had further sculpted the rock edifices that the river exposed, creating an arty landscape of shapes and forms and colors. Our journey took us through the deepening, narrow canyons, propelling us backward into time, as the river twisted and turned. At every bend we were greeted by yet another scene, with different rock morphologies, varied shapes of cliffs and bluffs. The

BUTLER PANELS ROCK ART

only constants were some of the layers on the cliff faces. When we'd round a corner, often the bands of color would follow us like persistent shadows, sometimes dipping down, sometimes rising up, the result of ancient geological activity. We rounded endless river bends, awestruck, drifting serenely and unnoticed through a succession of our own private calendar-photo fantasy vistas, like Alice diving through looking-glass after looking-glass. We were floating through another world, another time, on an H. G. Wells adventure, blissfully ignorant of our own hidden world out there somewhere, happily out of sight, out of reach.

Our fantasy fleet veered toward shore and pulled up onto the bank, and we disembarked. On a cliff before us was an impressive sampling of rock art, more than a hundred figures and designs, etched into the stone — the Butler Panels. Most of these petroglyphs, spread before us left and right for some seventy feet, were the product of Basket Maker peoples. There were several rectilinear, anthropomorphic figures. Above many of them were "headdresses," a series of arcs, one atop the other, extending upward like some of the stacked, competition kites that are skillfully maneuvered above today's beaches. Neither Art nor the other scholar, Lex Lindsay, had any explanation.

Bighorn sheep were incised into the rock. Other figures were clearly human. One scene depicted a sheep being pierced by the spear from an atlatl. Perhaps a tribute to a successful past hunt. Perhaps a propitiation for a successful future hunt.

A horse head, clearly not Anasazi, adorned the cliff. Horses had long since died out in North America when the Anasazi ventured into the area. They weren't reintroduced until the arrival of the Spaniards. This figure was later chiseled by a Navajo artist in more recent times.

An even more modern etching, which I hardly classified as rock art, proclaimed "Fuck BLM." As I was shaking my head in disbelief and disgust, one of the river guides explained this was not graffiti but a political statement. It seems some of the land along the river was owned by the Navajo and some by the federal Bureau of Land Management. The Indians had a dispute with the bureau over land ownership, thus the "statement."

Back on the river. The sun was rapidly ascending to its midday perch directly overhead. No more jackets. My wide-brimmed Aussie hat kept my face safely in shadow. We passed close to an overhang where the cliffs rose directly from the river. Actually, the river has been cutting into the massive rock. Eventually, it will chew away the sandstone cliff, grain by grain, and completely hack through it. The overhang was being carved out by the flowing water. Affixed to the ceiling of the overhang were softball-sized, mud-colored protuberances. Each bore a hole at the apex. I immediately thought of mud-digger wasp nests.

"Swallow nests," Tom said.

As we floated by the sandstone cliffs, Tom pointed off to the right. "There's some Anasazi toeholds, going up the face of the cliff."

I didn't see them. "Where?"

"Over there," he said to me, gesturing. Apparently others in our raft spotted them.

"I still don't see them."

"Look right between the tops of those two adjacent cottonwood trees," he pointed in earnest.

What's a cottonwood tree? I wondered, never having seen one before. I kept my ignorance to myself. "Oh yeah," I nodded to Tom, still not having seen anything.

Farther ahead our guide pointed out the native trees along the banks. They were all strangers to me. I did figure out what a cottonwood tree looked like, however. The spade-leafed cottonwoods were putting on their autumn costumes. Most of the green leaves had metamorphosed to a vivid canary yellow.

"They suck up a lot of water," Tom noted, as he leisurely manned the tiller.

"That's a Russian olive," he stated, pointing toward a tree with dripping branches that overhung the bank.

Our convoy pulled off the river again. A half-mile trek through the brush brought us to the base of a bluff. Halfway up, ensconced within a cave, stood River House. These modest ruins consisted of but two kivas and two living units, which had been home to no more than twenty Anasazi. It was an easy hike to the site and a relief to be out of the cramped rafts for awhile.

Tiny, blackened corn cobs peppered the ground. The former inhabitants had grown larger ears as well, Art said, but those cobs had been used up. They burned well and provided a hot flame. Pottery shards were strewn about. Most contained black designs painted on white clay.

The rooms were diminutive, suggesting Mesa Verde influence, Art noted. The dwellings, beneath the overhang, faced the sun and were warmed by it. In summer months, the residents had sought the cooler, shady climate at the rear of the cave. It seemed an optimal place to live hundreds of years ago. A great view, not just for aesthetics but for defensive purposes as well. With abundant water for crops and direct human consumption from a nearby river that could have served as a highway, it was a place to bask in the sun or be sheltered from it, as the seasons dictated.

Farther along the river our rafts again banked — lunchtime. Amidst the cottonwood and tamarisk trees, some of the crew set up a picnic table and uncovered the food dishes. Another member of the crew, trained in geology, lectured us about the landscape.

Behind us rose an anticline, 300 million years old. This massive, rounded bulge in the earth was miles across, only one edge of which was visible from our vantage point. We'd have to drive for an hour to reach its opposite end. The upthrusting of the crust was obvious from the slanted layers of earth, each several yards thick, offset from one another and canted upwards. The dome of the anticline had long since been eroded off.

Our geologist guide noted that these anticline slopes were geologically distinct from the later 70-million-year-old sandstone formations we had passed through earlier. It was now getting warmer. I rolled up my shirt sleeves. Still no clouds. Occasionally a high-altitude jet would leave wispy vapor streaks across the expansive, empty sky.

After a surprisingly tasty picnic lunch, we saddled up and headed downriver. The canyon deepened, as the river cut through red sandstone, gray sandstone and siltstone. The walls rose to 500 feet, then to 700 feet, and higher, closing us in, but with a sense of privacy rather than claustrophobia. At the top of the walls, the elements had had more time to hack and grind away at the rocks. Some of the rocks were sculpted into boulders of all sizes and forms, with straight lines traversing the rocks, demarcating the sandstone layers. Beneath the boulders, the walls resembled the face of a stepped pyramid as the sections of sandstone got smaller toward the top. The cliff faces were crosshatched with cracks and fissures running vertically and horizontally, like aged elephant skin. Some walls resembled giant stacks of dominoes or poker chips. Others had been carved into towers and spires. A golden eagle majestically swooped low over the trees along the bottom of the canyon, hardly wiggling a feather, letting the currents carry it, totally unmindful of our insignificant presence.

Farther downstream a dozen bighorn sheep nonchalantly grazed between the river and the opposite canyon wall. Everyone in our raft swung around to look.

"They've been reintroduced," said our guide. "The native populous was hunted out."

Jane, a thirty-something physician isolated from wildlife within the concrete and glass canyons of one of the world's most populated cities (New York), was especially awed by these animals. Actually, by any wild animal. Even by some not so wild. On the initial ride from the airport at the start of the tour, she had expressed amazement at a cow grazing in a pasture along the road. A milk cow was just standing there in the open. Jane couldn't take her eyes off of it. Even as we had driven past it, Jane had craned her neck around, never having broken eye contact with the cow. I had ribbed her about it. And now she couldn't take her eyes off the sheep.

The solar globe had boldly commandeered the sky. Not a single cloud dared appear on the scene to challenge the brash sun. The deep, narrow canyon was silent save for the muted whirl of our propellers, the soft slapping of our rafts on the current, and the discontinuous spurts of our conversation. Tom, standing shirtless at the transom under a wide-brimmed, sweat-stained hat, would occasionally point off to the side and raise his voice above the din of the motor. He continued to amaze me with his knowledge of geology.

Another stop, this one for fossils. A hundred yards from shore we climbed over and between boulders strewn along the ground at the base of the cliff. Fragments of fossils were abundant, there for the taking. Debbie, one of the staff members, delicately picked up a tiny, mineralized cylinder, the size and shape of an aspirin, and carefully placed it on her palm for display. Three of us students gathered around and peered down. I immediately recognized the fragment. I'd encountered similar fossils during a dinosaur-digging excursion in Montana the previous year.

"It's a crinoid," Debbie informed us.

I groped over the rocks and found another piece of stem. Crinoid pieces littered the ground. Others in our group were also spotting them. Crinoids, also called sea lilies, still exist. They resemble long-stemmed plants, but are actually stalked animals. They belong to the echinoderm phylum, which they share with sea urchins, sand dollars, starfish and sea cucumbers. This area had obviously once been under the sea. Hundreds of millions of years ago, there were vast underwater forests of crinoids, ranging in height from several inches to several yards, swaying in the currents.

Then I noticed the indentation in a rock of a piece of shell the size of a fingernail. I readily recognized it as that of a brachiopod, from my experiences in Montana. This was more evidence of the submerged nature of this place long, long ago. When alive, this brachiopod would have superficially resembled a clam, though its two shells would have been of different sizes and shapes, in contrast to those of a clam with essentially identical shells. And brachiopods, which are assigned to their own phylum, are taxonomically distinct from clams, which occupy the bivalve class within the mollusc phylum, which also includes the likes of snails, slugs and the cephalopods. (Today they are represented by the squid, octopus, nautilus and cuttlefish, and in ancient times by the various ammonites.) Brachiopods, alive today in selected habitats, have an impressive lineage, dating back over half a billion years to the Cambrian Period. In fact, one Cambrian brachiopod genus, *Lingula*, still exists, though all of the Cambrian species within that genus have been replaced over the intervening hundreds of millions of years.

As we putt-putted and drifted down through the canyon, the sun plunged behind the steep walls, casting one side of the canyon and part of the river in deep, stark shadows. We passed cows strolling and grazing above the bank. I couldn't let the opportunity slip by. "Quick, Jane, get a picture. You can impress you friends back home."

She reached for a camera, raised it to eye level, thought better of it, lowered the camera, and chuckled to me. "I owe you one," she said, wagging a finger at me.

Late in the afternoon, a distinctive shape loomed above the tree line beyond the river bank. An outcropping had been chiseled away by the elements to form what resembled a sombrero precariously perched on a point of rock. We had reached the terminus of our trip — Mexican Hat Monument.

We offloaded from the rafts. Our river guides bid us a fond farewell, as they attended to the watercraft. We waited in the brush for the vans. In twenty minutes they made their way down the dusty, narrow road to the river's edge. We were off to Mexican Hat, Utah.

We rolled into town, which consisted essentially of a gas station and motel-restaurant-lounge complex, with all of thirty-eight inhabitants. Our gang almost doubled the population. The accommodations at the San Juan Motel, decorated with a Southwest motif, were clean and comfortable, more so than I expected in such a remote setting. But then, tourists were this tiny town's source of income, its life's blood. The motel was perched atop a short sandstone cliff, allowing a scenic view down onto the river.

* * *

It was up early and out into a cloudless, black, star-studded, western sky. The full moon's ghostly glow sparkled along the dark, lazy river, its beams poring down the cliff walls, highlighting their reddish tints. The crisp, chilly air nipped at my face. While the staff loaded the luggage onto the vans, our group straggled half-awake into the restaurant. Joan and I shared a table with Bob, an architect from New York. The service was slow by my city standards. For Bob, it was agonizing. But we were faced with a Hobson's choice — accept it or do without. Anyway, the coffee was strong and hot.

Then off through the vast expanse of flat, open terrain, punctuated by gigantic mounds of rock erupting boldly from the landscape. We were traversing a Navajo reservation. It would take another couple of hours, at least, to exit the other side of this largest of all Indian reservations in the United States.

Our driver this day was Lex, the other visiting scholar, on his premier trip for Crow Canyon. He was a research archeologist at the Arizona State Museum, and had been Curator of Anthropology at the Museum of Northern Arizona. He had twenty-five years experience with Southwest archeology. Lex, lanky and slow-talking, with glasses and thinning hair, was more serious than Art. He was not one to cut up. In the wrong crowd he might have come across as stuffy, but in the context of our trip I considered him astute. His studious, reserved mannerism served as a counterpoint to Art's more jovial, outgoing style.

We wondered what the nearly empty land was used for. Lex explained that the Navajo grazed sheep on it, "but it's becoming an outback.

"Uranium ore was mined and ground in a plant down the road

from Mexican Hat," he continued. "In the late Fifties, mining stopped, and the mines became dormant. Within six months, the Navajo miners came down with cancer. The government said there was no connection."

"Naturally," I said.

"It's like the Agent Orange thing from the Vietnam War," Lex added.

The day's first stop was on the outskirts of Monument Valley. Out across the expansive open prairie, which stretched in all directions as far as the eye could follow, massive plateaus and buttes jutted straight up into a cloudless, chalky-blue sky. White sandstone cliff faces were capped by layers of red rock. Water running off the tops of the outcroppings had carried the red stain down across the sandstone buttes, tinting them russet. The rising sun, barely peeking over the horizon, brushed its long, orange rays across the edifices.

Art explained that the entire area had at one time been flat, level ground, without plateaus. Running water had eroded most of the land into a vast prairie. The only remnants of the original ground level were the tops of scattered buttes and plateaus. It had taken millions of years, but the water inexorably did the job. The sandstone "monuments," which were 120 to 140 million years old and overlay a shale bed, were formed as sand dunes, rather than as sediment from a river. Rain runoff was still cutting away the land and monuments. Huge slabs of sandstone, separated from cliff faces by centuries of erosive forces, had crashed down, like calving glaciers, creating sheer, vertical walls with tons of rocky debris stacked at their bases, like the jumble of demolished skyscrapers.

With the help of the wind, the runoff also sculpted the mesas and other outcroppings. The rocky shapes bordered on the fantastic. Every manner of form could be imagined, like seeing shapes in clouds.

We continued through the reservation, all 20 million acres of it with its 200,000 Navajo inhabitants. Originally the reservation was much smaller, having grown by accretion. While most of the land was being held by the U.S. Government in trust for the Navajo, the Indians had purchased some neighboring lands outright. The modern Navajo, ever enterprising, augmented their income with royalties from oil and gas leases on their demesne. When these Indians were originally sent to a reservation by the U.S. government, no one considered the barren land's subterranean wealth, at least not gas and oil. Back then, these open spaces were deemed wasteland, of little use to whites.

We crossed into Arizona. Fanning out from both sides of the van, the flat, monotonous terrain was carpeted with low bushes sprinkled amidst tufts of mean-looking grass, from which an occasional sparse tree dared sprout. Buttes and mesas punctuated the dry, sandy background.

Off to the right, a phalanx of cars and pickups congregated around a couple of modest houses. Gray smoke curled skyward. Lex half-turned and pointed. "That's a Squaw Dance," he explained, over his shoulder.

We pivoted holus-bolus toward the scene. "It lasts three days. It's a curing ceremony," he added.

With a backward glance at us he said, "There's a medicine man who cures psychological problems. Family and friends are invited. A large fire is built. They dance and get drunk."

"Who feeds them?" someone asked.

"Oh, the family putting it on has to do that. And pay the medicine man."

"What's the cost?" someone else wondered.

"At least five thousand dollars." Not cheap.

Isolated Navajo residences dotted the land. Navajo didn't like to live close together, Lex noted. Most resided in modern trailers or traditional hogans. Many of the Indians clustered together recently to avail themselves of modern conveniences such as electricity and plumbing.

Our journey took us through the community of Kayenta. Prefab houses were the dominant dwelling, with trailers running a close second. There was no consistency or pattern to types and locations of residential dwellings or commercial buildings. Lex confirmed the obvious, that there were no building or zoning codes anywhere on the reservation.

The local Burger King marquis heralded "Happy Columbus

Day." I pointed it out, asserting that the restaurant couldn't be owned by Indians.

"How insensitive!" burst Jane from the rear of the van.

We rode into Tsegi Canyon to view ruins of the Kayenta, a sub-culture of the Anasazi. We had climbed over a thousand feet in elevation. As we ascended, we encountered more and more piñon pines. The junipers became smaller, their populations sparser. Sage was appearing, although in petite versions. Lex indicated that atop Navajo sandstone, with cooler temperatures, the piñons could achieve "full growth potential."

We parked and wandered through a museum perched on a lofty mesa. One noteworthy exhibit was a mockup of a Kayenta house of jacal construction, with puny rooms reminiscent of what we had seen in Mesa Verde. One room was devoted to grinding corn. Three stone metates, replete with manos, were lined up side by side. Art mentioned that corn was passed down the line from one metate to the other, being more finely ground with each transfer, sort of a prelude to Henry Ford's assembly line centuries later.

The room clusters of the Tsegi Phase of Kayenta architecture were similar to Mesa Verde cliff dwellings of the Pueblo III stage, with the exception of the ratio of rooms to kivas. The Tsegi Canyon people built a living room and several storage rooms that opened onto a courtyard, but they did not regularly construct kin-group kivas. Also, there were no great kivas in the Kayenta region. The few kivas that were built served as kinship kivas and ceremonial centers.

Entry into Tsegi living rooms was via a door or roof hatchway. Some of the doors were T-shaped. Living quarters were heated by a slab-lined fire pit located beneath the hatchway, which doubled as a smoke hole. A deflector modulated the draft.

These Anasazi were farmers who subsisted on the traditional diet of corn, squash, beans, domesticated turkeys and wild game. They also cultivated cotton and produced unadorned, utility pottery for cooking and general storage. Decorated pottery was used for eating, drinking, carrying water, and for storing charms and jewelry.

We trekked down the side of the mesa along a steep, paved

trail. Halfway to the canyon floor, we reached the lookout point. Far across the canyon, embedded in a cave at the base of the opposite sandstone cliff face, sat the remains of Betatakin. The cave, a giant amphitheater, was voluminous enough to house a battleship. The ruins along the floor of the cave were extensive, yet the enormity of the high-domed space made the dwellings appear as doll houses from across the canyon, perhaps a mile distant. Oak, aspen, Douglas fir and box-elder trees clustered at the mouth of the cave. I doubted that all those trees would have been left standing had the place still been inhabited. For the Anasazi, despite their primitive technology, made a tremendous demand on the neighboring woodlands, usually depleting the nearby trees and shrubs, then expanding their harvest farther and farther from home until it became too burdensome to continue, in which case they generally moved to a new site.

Betatakin was erected over a short period during the middle of the Thirteenth Century (late Pueblo III). The population, peaking at 125, started to depart after 1286, and was gone by 1300 A.D. The reasons were still debated. The water table may have lowered. To keep up with demands for wood, for building timbers and fire logs, the men had to venture farther afield. The weather may have been arid, drying out the soil, which eroded away. There might have been a change in the political structure. No one was sure.

Most of the buildings appeared single story, some two stories, though upper floors may have vanished with the passage of time. The courtyards were on the roofs of adjoining structures. Nothing in the architecture suggested a hierarchy, according to one of Art's books, **Anasazi Ruins of the Southwest in Color.** In fact, Art was so emphatic on this point that he stated in black and white that no evidence at any prehistoric Anasazi sites indicated the existence of an elite class. He reiterated this to me at least twice during the field trip. But in his book he did concede that, at least at Betatakin, there was "some sort of community decision-making."

We were back on the road, heading south, still on Navajo land. A herd of sheep, intermingled with a few goats, strolled across the road. Glancing at the herd, Lex explained the curious mixture of animals.

"The goats lead the sheep to the corral. Sheep are too dumb to find their way there by themselves."

A pause. "Only turkeys are stupider," he added.

As the sparse countryside rolled by, Lex filled us in on the Navajo. He prefaced it by alluding to the Anasazi, to whom the sun and rain were important. Their world view was one of harmony with nature, as was that of the Navajo. The Anasazi had no written language, he said. It fact, there was no written language in all of North America above Mesoamerica.

"The Navajo are divided into chapters," he went on. "Eighty-seven representatives meet at Window Rock. This tribal council makes the laws for the reservation. It has its own courts, own political system, all similar to ours."

Lex mentioned that hogans were constructed today of logs, plywood or railroad ties. They were frequently octagonal.

"The hogan is a sacred place," he stated. "But it can be residential."

Lex pointed out that Navajo society was matrilineal and matriarchal. The daughter inherited from her mother. A man moved into the wife's house, bringing his rifle, horse and sheep.

"If the woman wants a divorce," Lex said, "she puts his saddle outside. Adios."

The ladies in our van liked that one.

The paved roads turned into dirt sideroads. The terrain became even more desolate, consisting mostly of tufts of rugged, brownish grass with a scattering of stubby trees. Clouds still hadn't found their way here. An occasional car passed us in the opposite direction. The dusty rooster-tail we kicked up swallowed the trailing vans, momentarily eclipsing them from view. One would not have lasted long on foot here without an abundance of shade and water, both of which were in short supply in this parched environment.

With one's seating location within the van came certain responsibilities, we had decided. Bob, sitting shotgun in the front seat, was in charge of the drink cooler. The rest of us in the van would make requests, and he'd pop open the cooler and hand out a soda, juice or bottled water. We kept him busy.

We crossed into the Hopi reservation, completely surrounded

by the Navajo reservation, which dwarfed it and was a source of friction for the Hopi. It was also a source of litigation. A court battle had been raging for years between the two tribes. Interest in 7 million acres had been in dispute. A 1934 act of Congress made that land part of the Navajo reservation. The Hopi, who were on much of the land before the Navajo wandered in, felt as though their interests were not protected by Congress. They sued.

One federal district-court judge ruled against the Hopi, awarding them only 60,000 acres. They were appealing.

Lex cautioned us that the Hopi didn't allow cameras to be used on their reservation. No recorders, either. Not even note taking!

Lunch was at Novaki, a modest Hopi roadside restaurant. We filed in, past the seated diners — men, women, families, most of whom were clearly Indian — and into the back room that was reserved for our gang. We filled the tables and the room, with its stark-white, bare walls. The Hopi families glanced at us as though we were an oddity. Some of the Indian kids held their stare, as though we were the first whites they had ever seen in the flesh. I felt I was in a foreign land. I was, therefore, somewhat taken aback when our waiter, a handsome Hopi lad with jet-black, shiny hair and pearly, straight teeth, took our orders in perfect English. He was quite friendly and seemed anxious to please. I gambled on the taco platter, with rice and beans — a poor choice as it turned out, but then there weren't any good choices. The portions were small, about what I imagined condemned men received on Devil's Island when Papillon was a guest of honor there. This stuff would never sell off the reservation, but it did temporarily abate the hunger pangs. Some of them, anyway.

Pueblo Indians have resided in the American Southwest for two millennia. Modern-day Hopi, who count the Anasazi among their ancestors, numbered about 9000, of which 7000 lived on the reservation in twelve villages.

The Hopi Indians currently occupied three mesas, which were actually fingers of a larger land mass known as Black Mesa. In historic times, a fourth mesa, Antelope Mesa, was also occupied. West of Antelope Mesa, the other three mesas were lined up to the west, appropriately dubbed First Mesa, Second Mesa and Third Mesa.

We zigzagged from the canyon, across the face of the steep cliff, to the top of lofty First Mesa. Upon this narrow precipice three hamlets were queued. We wheeled into the nearest village, Hano, and stepped out onto a hot, dusty plaza.

Art led us to the visitors' center, where a petite Hopi woman about fifty, with long, lampblack hair and lined, leather skin cheerlessly greeted us. Art reminded us about the cameras and tape recorders. The woman, who identified herself as Loretta, ushered us inside. As Loretta gathered all of us together and briefed us, I noticed a sign on the wall prohibiting photographs — in three languages no less. Did today's Hopi really believe that a camera capturing their image would rob them of their persona or their spirit? Or were they merely camera shy, like the Amish?

Our group was divided into two segments. Loretta would escort our flock. We weren't allowed to stroll freely through the villages. The rules mandated that we be accompanied by an Indian guide. Loretta, fluent in English, led us through the packed-dirt streets. We passed drab, dust-colored, single-story dwellings of stone, some with wooden timbers. There was a scattering of cars, some drivable, others in various stages of decomposition. Mangy but friendly dogs trailed mutely behind us. Or trotted silently ahead to lead the way. I wondered how they knew where we were headed. But then, there was only one short road into town, and one out. Other hounds were dispassionately flopped into the dust, their tongues hanging. They hardly looked up as we passed. There were no clouds to be seen, even from our lofty vantage point, which provided a sweeping, unobstructed panorama to all horizons. At the edge of the road, six women sat on the ground or in chairs, effortlessly shucking corn while making small talk. The completed ears were tossed onto an expanding pile in the dusty road.

After only two quick blocks, we were out of town. The next village, Sichomovi, immediately followed and was contiguous with the first. More short, drab dwellings. More dusty, curious dogs. This hamlet, like its neighbor, was devoid of color, as though a dust storm had powdered the buildings and roads. There weren't many people about, outside of our split group. A hush seemed to pervade the place. But that would change when the kids got home from school down in the valley.

Another two abbreviated blocks and we were already on the outskirts. The utility poles and plumbing ended. But there were houses still ahead. Across a skinny, dirt causeway stood legendary Walpi. There was no one to be seen from where we stood. Loretta informed us that only old people now lived there. The younger ones had moved into the valley below.

We crossed the causeway. Locked outhouses sprouted alongside the road and partway down the side of the steep mesa like trees. The one- and two-story buildings were even older and more drab than in the first two villages. Loretta pointed to one edifice that supposedly was 300 years old. But other constructions were much newer, even into recent decades.

An old, tanned, wrinkled woman suddenly emerged from one of the doorways. She held a doll aloft. It was a kachina doll. As we passed, the old woman waved the doll to us, offering it for sale. Some member of her family had carved it, she said in halting English through a tooth-poor mouth. We all paused, smiled, nodded, complimented her on the workmanship, and filed past. One of the guys in our gang had second thoughts. He doubled back, forked over some greenbacks, and hurried back to the group proudly clutching his trophy.

I scanned the edifices of recent vintage. They were built of concrete block. But others were constructed of stone, replete with mortar and stone chinking.

We quickly reached the end of the town, which coincided with the end of the mesa. A few more steps straight ahead and we would have taken the abrupt shortcut to the valley a thousand feet below.

We circled around the last house and headed back on the other side of the dwellings, down a parallel, narrow, dirt road. Loretta pointed out two kivas, both covered and off limits. To our right, the mesa dropped off precipitously. That edge of the mesa was protected by a short wire fence that would not have withstood the challenge of an assertive toddler.

Beyond a shady overhang that spanned the narrow road, another elderly, wrinkled lady with bad teeth squatted at her doorstep, offering two small ceramic plates. They were crudely done. Again we all looked, smiled, waved and moved on. This time there were no takers.

I didn't see anyone else in the village, nor any cars. Except for the two old women hawking their wares, the place seemed completely deserted. Surely the village, though only a couple of blocks long, housed more Hopi than this, I thought. But where were they? Why was no one walking on the road? Or standing outside tending to their houses? Where were the young adults? The pre-school kids?

Walpi has deep roots. It's been continuously inhabited since 1680. Before then, Walpi stood on a lower terrace of the mesa, closer to the farmlands on the bottom of the valley. Prehistoric Anasazi had moved into the Hopi mesas after 1300 A.D.

To walk through Walpi is to travel though time as well as space. It was like nothing I'd ever experienced. It was a scene straight out of a National Geographic documentary. This couldn't really be the United States, or the Twentieth Century. It was another time and place, one that no longer existed, like Tibet from centuries past. I was a time traveler, magically whisked backward through four centuries for a glimpse at a prehistoric village, like mockups I'd seen in museums with painted dioramas and plastic mannequins. But these mannequins moved and talked, and the diorama was three dimensional with sounds and smells and dust and sun — truly a mystical encounter.

Loretta felt Walpi would soon become a ghost city, since the younger people no longer lived there. Once the old folks died off, they'll be no one to replace them, she said. But this hamlet had been around for centuries. Surely *someone* would move in and carry on, I mused aloud to Loretta. She just shrugged her shoulders and kept walking. I wondered dolefully about the fate of this unique aerial sanctuary. It would be a shame to have it just fall into disuse and disappear. Should Walpi fade into history, it will carry away with it some of the Hopi tradition and culture — indeed the very soul of the people — to be forever lost, irreplaceable even by all the trappings of modern civilization. In fact, it will be the Twentieth Century itself that will doom Walpi, rendering it obsolete by the seductive appeal of television, automobiles, indoor plumbing, Monday-night football and canned beer. And once gone, there will be as little chance for a resurrection of Walpi as there is for a patch of tropical forest, cut down and paved over, to sprout anew. Destruction of a culture is a one-way trip, like passing through a revolving door, like the time-direction arrow of the Second Law of Thermodynamics.

After we had retraced our steps across the causeway, Loretta released us. We were free to roam the first two villages (but not Walpi) unescorted. We only had twenty minutes, but I set off to make the most of it.

I returned to the corn shuckers. They were friendly and amenable to chatting with me while they worked. Most of the ears were white, a minority blue. They all went into the same pile. One of the women told me they had different uses, and would be separated later. It would take three days to shuck the entire batch. By the time I had gotten these few tidbits, all six women had turned away from me and toward their work, their fingers nimbly stripping the ears.

I had noticed that several of the homes in Hano and Sichomovi had signs in the windows or on the doors, advertising pottery or kachina dolls. Loretta had informed us that the signs automatically gave us permission to knock on those doors and enter the houses.

I peeked through one door that was partially ajar, then entered. A small room was partitioned into even smaller rooms: a bedroom, a living room and a kitchen. A young Hopi couple sat on the bed watching our group parade in and out. They were quiet, unsmiling, and seemingly anxious to have their privacy restored. In the kitchen a middle-aged woman, presumably the mother to one member of the couple on the bed, was vending kachina dolls. She assured me they had been made by a member of her family. I handled the dolls, admired the work, thanked her and left for the next open house. I was more anxious to see how these people lived than I was in buying the dolls.

Across the road, a sign proclaimed dolls for sale. I ventured in. Three young Hopi men in jeans stood around a table in the living room, looking at me hopefully, like puppies at a pet store waiting to be bought. A block of wood was in the process of being transformed into a kachina. For the first time I actually believed the dolls were being carved locally. For all I knew before then, they could have been imported from somewhere in Asia. Other finished kachinas were lined along a ledge near the table. I pored over them, turning them over to be sure I didn't see a "Made in China" label. Hanging from another wall were colored-pencil drawings, sketched by one of the young men, depicting Hopi men in native attire and kachinas in decorative costumes.

It was time to return to the vans, but I wanted to see more. I quickly popped into another house. The kitchen and living room were combined into one. A hallway, draped with a curtain, apparently led to the bedroom. An infant, strapped into a high chair, sat against one wall near the kitchen, complaining about something. A woman in her thirties, probably the baby's mother, pointed me to another wall with rows of shelves. The ceramics along the top shelf were done by her, she proudly claimed. The kachinas on the shelves below were fashioned by her husband and son. On the wall above the shelves were family photos. One was years old and of a young man in Army dress greens. I guessed it to be of her husband.

One of the ladies from our group caught a glimpse of me and mentioned that Joan was looking for me. It wasn't hard for me to find Joan. It wasn't hard to find anyone on First Mesa. Joan hurried me to one of the open houses. She wanted me to see a particular kachina doll that had caught her eye. She assured me it was magnificent, the best she'd seen in the villages.

We walked right in and rapidly scanned the living room. Other dolls were about but not *the* doll. Joan asked about it. Art, standing against a side wall and holding a wrapped package, smiled and piped up that he'd just bought it for 125 dollars. Joan was crestfallen. It was a kachina dedicated to some watermelon spirit, intricately carved and painted, apparently. I never got to see it. In fact, I didn't want to see it. I didn't want to know what I had missed.

The carver offered me another kachina for the same price. I held it, rotating it quickly and assessed it. Joan told me it wasn't as beautiful as Art's. Nonetheless, it was finely crafted and splendidly painted, and I wanted it — for the right price. Unfortunately, I didn't know what that price was. I hadn't shopped for — or even seen — kachinas previously. Time was running out. Most of our group was already back in the vans. I was keeping them waiting. I didn't have time for protracted negotiations.

I handed the doll back to the carver. "I'll give you seventy-five dollars," I stated emphatically.

He paused momentarily as if weighing the offer. I figured he'd lower his price. After all, Art bought the other doll for 125 bucks and his doll was better than the one this guy was now holding.

"One hundred twenty-five dollars," he smiled evenly.

I asked him to go lower, as I glanced toward the door. He knew I was leaving and that I was the last of our group to whom he could sell. He'd come down. My I-am-leaving ploy had always worked when purchasing a car. When a salesman had realized I was about to walk out, he had inevitably dropped his "rock-bottom" price. And it had proven effective when haggling in South and Central America. It would work here, too. I'd get that doll, and at my price.

"One hundred twenty-five dollars," he repeated, undaunted.

He was hanging tough, but I knew he'd fold. He had to. I was the only game left in town. "Will you take seventy-five dollars?" I said, my tone revealing a hint of urgency.

He smiled and casually shook his head.

"What will you take for it?" I was prepared to increase my offer, but only slightly. I started toward the door, waiting for his lowered price that I knew had to come.

"One hundred twenty-five dollars," he reiterated calmly but firmly. He was as likely to budge as the Rock of Gibraltar.

He was as stubborn as I. Maybe more so. The haggling session had become a battle of wills. Neither of us was willing to concede to the other's price, or to even approach that price. So while I didn't lose the battle of wills, I did lose the war of negotiations. I left empty-handed. I just couldn't see paying what Art paid and not getting what Art got — a big mistake as I was to later learn.

Driving back down First Mesa, we reflected on what we had just witnessed. Jane thought it was too much commercialism with the selling of pottery and kachinas.

"It's a degradation of their culture," she felt.

"But it does keep them producing some of their traditional wares," I countered. "So in an ironic way, it actually fosters their culture."

Lex digressed. "The Hopi are very religious. They believe in spirits that dwell in the neighboring San Francisco Mountains."

These spirits were part-time residents of the peaks. Starting in late December and continuing into February, the spirits migrate to the Hopi villages, staying around until late July. They may be the ancestors of the Cloud People. They could bring on rain, fertility or general good fortune. Or they could withhold their blessings. During ceremonies, they are portrayed as intermediaries between the Hopi and their gods. The kachina dolls are carved representatives of these beings.

We made a shopping stop at a trading post in the valley. Kachina dolls lined the shelves. Display cases showed off silver and turquoise jewelry, but it was a doll I was after. From the large selection, I figured I'd have no problem picking one out. My searching eyes summarily rejected most of them as not being of the same quality as the one I had haggled over on First Mesa. Few were. I picked three or four off the shelves for closer examination. They were in the same class as the one I had passed up. But the prices weren't. When I flipped these dolls upside down to check the price tags, I gaped. They were three times as expensive as the one I had walked away from. I really blew it, I gulped. Now there was no way I would pay these retail prices. I left empty-handed again.

Art, seeing my frustration, assured me I would have no problem buying a top-quality kachina when we reached the Crow Canyon gift shop at the conclusion of the trip. "They have a great selection, and at good prices," he guaranteed, as he smiled broadly and patted me on the shoulder. I sighed in relief, for now I simply had to have one of the dolls, one on par with Art's.

Dinner was back at the Novaki. The service was friendly but oh so slow. The cup of watery gruel the waiter placed in front of me was charitably referred to as chicken soup. It would have passed muster at a vegetarians' luncheon, being totally devoid of meat. The "steamed vegetables" amounted to a half cup of overdone, soggy carrots and cauliflower, cooked long enough to ensure that all the nutrients were depleted before arriving at my table. The portion of rice barely filled a tablespoon. More Devil's Island rations. Oh well, I wasn't very hungry.

We spent the night at the Hopi Cultural Center, which was in part a motel. The museum portion was closed when we pulled in. Our rooms were new, clean and neatly decorated in Southwest motif.

The Navajo had figured out how to capture the tourist dollar, at least at the motel.

* * *

The next day we got another early start. Our luggage had to be at the vans by 6:30. The sparkling stars were sprinkled across the wide-open black sky like diamonds strewn on black velvet. There was no light pollution to dim their brilliance. There's Orion, I noted to myself.

We headed east, beyond First Mesa and into Keams Canyon, still within the Hopi reservation. A gas station/restaurant combination offered breakfast. The service was friendly though agonizingly slow like that in the Out Islands of the Bahamas, where time just casually shuffled along. But the Hopi blue-corn pancakes here were filling and the coffee hot, for which I was thankful.

We exited the canyon, continuing east. The Hopi land ended, and we were once again driving through Navajo territory. The Hopi, who were Pueblo people, had their roots deep into the Southwest soil. The Navajo, on the contrary, were not Pueblo dwellers and did not descend from the Anasazi. The Navajo had only been in the area for a few centuries, but their population vastly dwarfed that of the Hopi, and they'd grabbed up most of the land.

Near Ganado, still in Arizona and within the Navajo reservation, we pulled into the parking lot at Hubbell's Trading Post. The one-story structure spread out to take up one entire side of the lot.

Inside we were treated (subjected?) to a showing of Navajo rugs. The proprietor, a white man, peeled one rug after another from a bottomless stack, holding them up and rattling on about the native craftsmanship. The rugs may have been native, but the prices weren't. The price tags were in four, and sometimes five, figures.

There were hand-woven baskets fastened to the walls and rafters. They were also for sale, and also for lofty prices. Many were offered for hundreds of dollars, some for thousands.

A park ranger guided us through a tour of the adjacent Hubbell house. The bedrooms were roped off but otherwise open to view. The place was covered from floor to ceiling with baskets, pictures and drawings, dating to the late 1800s or the early 1900s. The baskets had been hand-crafted by the Navajo. The pictures and drawings were of them. It was a mini-museum and the highlight of the stop for me.

Back inside the trading store I bought a copy of the **Navajo Times,** the official newspaper of the tribe. While the rest of our group roamed through the store looking for bargains (their quest would go unrewarded), I sat out front and leafed through the modest paper. It seemed these Indians still liked their liquor. But the reservation was dry. Farmington, New Mexico, was the nearest off-reservation border town. Some Navajo made the trek for a drink or two (or more), sometimes getting assaulted by town bullies. Others were arrested for drunken driving by the local gendarmes. Dipsomaniacal drivers even ran the gauntlet back on the reservation. The paper published a (lengthy) list of Indians picked up for DUI by the Navajo police. We later noticed numerous crosses planted at various spots along mile after mile of the highway, memorials to those inebriated Indians who never made it back to the reservation.

Then on to Chinle to the north. As soon as we rolled into the Navajo-owned Thunderbird Motel at midday, we were rushed onto two open trucks, like the two and one-half ton, four-wheel-drive trucks used by the Army for troop transport. But these had the canvas canopy removed from over the troop compartment. And the seats were in several rows that faced ahead, rather than in two rows that faced inward toward each other. Each truck carried a Navajo driver who also acted as guide. We were on our way to Canyon de Chelly (pronounced "shay").

A short drive took us into the canyon, which was actually a two-canyon complex of Canyon de Chelly and Canyon del Muerto. The two canyons were shaped and joined like a wishbone. We took the fork to the left, the one into Canyon del Muerto. As soon as we entered, the reason for the rugged-terrain vehicles became obvious. The ground, from one sheer canyon wall to the other, was a sea of tire-grabbing sand. I couldn't imagine a car trying to drive through the stuff. Yet cars do — or did. Now they've been banned because too many got bogged down and had to be towed. I'm surprised the towing companies didn't lobby against the ban.

We slowly plowed our way through the thick sand. There were, of course, no trails, just wheel ruts going in varied directions down the canyon. The reddish sandstone bluffs, with their sheer faces, erupted perpendicular to the ground. The ancient sandstone, almost as old as time itself, was chiefly from the De Chelly Formation and predated even the dinosaurs, dating back into the Permian Period, more than 248 million years ago. Running water has cut through the land, forming a channel that was the canyon floor. But despite what appeared to be parched desert sand, running water still coursed through the canyon at times. There were flash runoffs that sent torrents of water surging along the canyon, covering the arenaceous floor from wall to wall. Where the canyon narrowed, the water would rise to several feet. You didn't want to get caught here in a flash flood.

The canyon widened slightly as we slowly churned our way along. The cliff faces reached skyward for 300 feet. Cottonwood trees were clumped along the ground where water pooled or ran. A thin rivulet of water meekly coursed between the trees. I spotted an occasional Russian olive or tamarisk tree. A strange, burnt gassy odor wafted over me, emanating from the truck's chassis. I couldn't place it, although it faintly reminded me of propane when it was fired to provide lift to a hot-air balloon. The sun was above the canyon walls and taking a straight bead on us. My Aussie hat deflected part of it. But there was nothing to fend off the swirling dust cloud our trucks were generating. I should have brought a bandanna.

We stopped. Bennie, the Navajo driver of the other truck, stood on the sideboard and pointed to the wall on the left — rock art, including Anasazi pictographs. Bennie, in his mid-forties and heavy set, with a wispy mustache and bad teeth, enlightened us. In singsong monotone, he explained what we were seeing — or were supposed to see. I could make out a recumbent Kokopelli, the enigmatic hunchback flute player who pervaded Anasazi rock art. There was an anthropomorphic "frog" figure similar to one I had seen while rafting down the San Juan River and which no one had been able to explain.

Bennie sang on, pausing only to suck in a breath. I understood virtually nothing of what sounded like an incantation. I wasn't sure whether he was speaking English, Navajo — or in tongues. He would take getting used to. I did discern a zigzag on the wall. Someone translated Bennie for me and said it represented a snake, but she didn't catch what Bennie said about it.

Besides the Anasazi art, there were depictions from more modern times. Some unknown Navajo had painted two men on horseback chasing a deer. An amorphous blob was supposedly a deer kidney. The Navajo used to let a rattlesnake strike the deer kidney, lacing it with venom. Then they dipped their arrowheads into it.

There was also Hopi art. A stylized bear claw represented the bear-claw clan. A four-leaf clover stood for the wolf clan.

We moved on. Another group was filing along on horseback. It seemed the perfect way to explore the canyon. The terra-cotta-hued cliffs were further tinted by clumps of algae and sheets of dark "desert varnish" — manganese and iron oxides. Trees sprouted from cracks in some of the cliff faces.

The canyon complex now held the remains of several hundred prehistoric Indian villages, most constructed between 350 to 1300 A.D. The inhabitants grew the traditional crops of corn and squash, and wove baskets, sandals and other items. They originally lived in pithouses, eventually building masonry dwellings, mostly during the latter 200 years of their occupancy here. By then the pervasive drought that lingered over the Four Corners region for the last quarter of the Thirteenth Century finally drove the Anasazi out of the canyon, scattering them to other parts of the Southwest.

Another stop. Our guides pointed out a complex of cliff dwellings partway up the cliff face, under an overhang a block wide that spanned two adjacent alcoves — Mummy Cave, named for two well-preserved mummies found there and for which Canyon del Muerto was named. I broke out the binoculars. I could make out what appeared to be two groups of buildings of sandstone masonry. The set to the left sat on a ledge between the alcoves. It contained stone walls that were partly crumpled but revealed the buildings' multi-story origins.

The series of buildings to the right was tucked into the right alcove. I couldn't discern any evidence of lofty structures. The remains were now low-lying, hugging the ground.

The most spectacular parts of these ruins were erected in late

Pueblo III times. Tree-ring dating put a three-story tower at 1284 A.D. When abandoned, circa 1300, there were seventy to eighty rooms and at least three kivas in use in Mummy Cave.

The Anasazi of this canyon complex, like their cousins in the Kayenta region, built few kin kivas and no great kivas (at least none had been found).

The site had housed Anasazi for centuries. Portions of the cliff dwellings were built over much earlier Basket Maker II habitations. Rooms and storage pits dated from 300 to 400 A.D.

Back through the sand we went.

After twenty minutes of more cliffs and canyons, we parked at the edge of an infield-sized clearing amidst a thicket of trees. I noticed the trucks were not propelled by gasoline, or even diesel fuel, but by liquid propane, just like hot-air balloons.

Beneath a sweeping Russian olive, the staff spread out the noonday meal — brown-bag lunches and drinks from the jugs. Over sandwiches, potato chips and lemonade, Joan and I joined another couple on a picnic table shaded by the Russian olive. The rest of our group spread out along the tables lined up end to end in the clearing, but protected by a roofed pavilion with open sides. It wasn't haute cuisine, but the food filled a pit in my stomach and the lemonade washed down the road dust.

Surrounding the clearing on three sides were the sandstone bluffs, boldly rising to 400 feet or more and partially veneered with huge draperies of desert varnish, sometimes running down almost the entire height of the bluff. The walls throughout the canyon were peppered with pockmarks. The holes, placed at random on the cliff faces, ranged in size from a basketball to a Volkswagen. I asked Art about them.

"The bigger ones are from water flowing from the top and eroding out the holes."

"And the smaller ones?"

"Those are ant holes."

Did I hear him right? "Ant holes?"

"Yup," he affirmed, as though it was obvious to everyone in the world, as he turned and walked to the lemonade jug, cup in hand.

I'm still wondering about that one.

Our driver and guide, Lewis, also a Navajo, was chatting with some members of our group. I ambled over. In his late thirties, with an ample belly, long, ebony hair, and a hooked nose, he stood under a sweat-soaked, off-white cowboy hat relating the story of his family. I didn't catch it all, partly because of his monotone chant that broke in mid-sentence. He was more intelligible than Bennie, though.

Lewis was one of eleven children; he had seven sisters and three brothers. Not one for breaking tradition, he had ten kids — and counting. The Navajo currently had about the highest birth rate of any ethnic group in the entire country. I later read that there were more Navajo living now than when the white men started their incursions into the Southwest.

Back on the trucks. We swung close to a prominent overhang that fanned out low over the sandy canyon floor. Then paused. A solitary anthropomorphic stick figure bedecked the wall. Swallow nests were stuck to the sandstone beside it. But they weren't the reason Lewis pulled over.

"It's called Martini Rock," he smirked.

We all sat there still as dummies. No one got it.

"Big hangover," smiled Lewis, quite pleased with himself.

We chuckled, more out of courtesy than humor.

We retraced our route to the mouth of Canyon del Muerto, disembarking at a major site, Antelope House. The sandstone masonry structures spread out along the base of a towering cliff, against a slight indentation in the sheer wall. There was yet evidence of at least four multistory buildings, although the walls had partly tumbled down or been eroded out of existence. Seasonal floodwaters, which could rage through the canyon as though a dam had given way, had also taken a toll. The ruins were moderate in size, containing almost a hundred rooms, with two or three larger kivas and several smaller ones. Originally the building walls were dressed inside and out with plaster, most of which has since worn away.

The cliff face boldly displayed pictographs, in an excellent state of preservation given their constant exposure to the elements for over a century and a half. Life-sized deer, antelope and a horse stood in profile, the work of a single Navajo artist, Little Lamb, done in 1830, centuries after the Anasazi had departed the canyon. The pronghorn antelope were vividly depicted in their natural coloration of orange and white with black trim.

A white swastika also emblazoned the cliff, easily visible from the opposite canyon wall. This was not a Nazi logo. In fact, the arms of the hooked cross pointed backwards from that used by the Nazis. The American Indians were using the symbol long before Hitler was even conceived. To the Navajo it may have represented the four seasons someone said, although I heard other explanations as well.

An anthropomorphic frog-like figure decorated the cliff behind the highest building yet standing, its meaning uncertain. Despite decades of field work and academic study into the Indians of the Southwest, many aspects of their lifestyles are still shrouded in mystery. Perhaps always so. And maybe it should be that way, never having all the answers, for often the adventure, and even the satisfaction, lies more in the journey than in the destination. Some things are better left unsolved, lest our curiosity, then our interest, wane.

The ruins that were visible dated to late Pueblo III, being occupied during the 1200s. This pueblo had been abandoned by the Anasazi around 1270, earlier than other canyon habitations. Despite the ramshackle appearance of Antelope House, the presence of its last inhabitants still pervaded the place as though they might return any day to reclaim their homestead.

Beneath these constructions lay the remains of a pithouse from late Basket Maker III times, dated to 693 A.D., indicative of prolonged Anasazi tenure in the canyon.

Our scholars suggested that some of the building walls looked Kayenta — there were no T-shaped doorways; the rooms were "large," unlike in Mesa Verde; there were no pilasters on the banquettes in the kivas. But there was a tower that suggested Mesa Verde. Lex was still undecided about the origins of these buildings.

"I've long agonized over it," he lamented.

Cotton pieces and cotton textiles have been found at the site. Art postulated that Antelope House may have been a factory.

"It's one of the best examples of craft," he added. "Nowhere else farther north are cotton parts and textiles found."

The sun started on the descent portion of its daily arc across the heavens. Parts of the canyon were draped in shadows. When we passed through shade on the canyon floor, the temperature dipped noticeably. But the naked sand on the floor reflected much of the sun's energy back at us. Some of the vertical walls were heavily riddled with huge scoops, reminding me of gigantic slabs of Swiss cheese.

We stopped to observe huge Navajo pictographs on a clear cliff face. They displayed men on horseback — Spaniards. The scene, painted by a Navajo named Gray Moustache, had historic significance for the Navajo — tragic significance. The Navajo started occupying the canyon circa 1700, some four centuries after the departure of the Anasazi. Unlike the Anasazi and their Pueblo descendants such as the Hopi, the Navajo were culturally and linguistically related to the Apache, both being linked to the Athapascan peoples of the Northwest. The Navajo also differed from the Pueblo peoples in being more aggressive. For a century and a half the Navajo raided Spanish settlements and Pueblo Indian villages along the Rio Grande Valley, where many of the cliff dwellers had settled when they abandoned their Anasazi homesteads. Successive governments in the region — Spanish, Mexican, American — sought reprisals. The Navajo ensconced themselves within Canyon de Chelly. For awhile they were safe in this stronghold. But in 1804, fate caught up with them.

A troop of 300 Spanish soldiers, on a punitive mission under the command of Lt. Antonio Narbona, patrolled down the canyon one cold morning, looking for trouble. About 150 Navajo, including women and children, were hidden in a cave high above the canyon floor, their presence undetected. The Indians shied themselves away from the lip of the cave, safe for the moment, keeping silent as the unsuspecting soldiers passed by down on the canyon floor — except for a single, but fatal, slip-up.

One of the Navajo, an aged grandmother, had once been a prisoner of the Spanish. When the soldiers were filing by beneath the cave, the old woman couldn't contain herself and let loose a startled cry. It carried to the hellkites below. In an instant they had their rifles to their shoulders, the denouement tragically obvious.

The Indians crept farther back into the cave, preventing the soldiers far below from drawing a bead. And the sheer cliff wall was unscalable. But the cave's role as a sanctuary was illusory, for its domed geometry sealed the fate of the Indians.

The soldiers unleashed volley after murderous volley, not directly at their quarry for they were unseen, but into the roof and sides of the cave. The ricocheting bullets created a field of fire within the cave from which there was no escape. Most of the Navajo were killed or wounded. Their refuge became their tomb, now known as Massacre Cave.

I tried to bring the scene to mind. Though almost two centuries had elapsed, the landscape was substantially unchanged: the same sheer, naked cliff with its domed cave several stories above the sandy, barren bottom of an isolated section of the canyon. I could almost see the soldiers abruptly rein in their horses at the cry from above, dismount hurriedly, draw their weapons, point up toward the sound, while the frightened Indians scurried back deeper into the cave, calling on their gods to save them, gods who were not listening. I could just about hear the shots ring out, on and on without relenting as though ushering in the end of the world, which for many of the Navajo it was. Their chorus of wails and cries, from anguish and fright and grief, still faintly echo along the sandstone walls, a haunting accompaniment to the spirits of those departed Navajo that yet linger in the canyon.

The wind picked up, funneling through the canyon, throwing even more dust in the face. I tugged the brim of my hat lower. As we would plow through the viscous sand, the driver would shift up through the gears, then down again. We weren't setting any speed records. Although the canyon floor was carpeted with a heavy layer of sand, the ground was not smooth. The truck bumped and bucked along, jerking and tossing us around in the rear like so many rag dolls.

We rounded the head of the wishbone and turned into Canyon de Chelly. The canyon took its name from the Spanish corruption of the Navajo word *"Tsegi,"* meaning roughly "rock canyon." We

passed more ruins on a ledge on the north side of the canyon —
First Ruin, a diminutive Pueblo III dwelling composed of but ten
rooms and two kivas, hardly more than on outpost. The canyons
were peppered with ruins from small to moderate. We would not
encounter a large set of ruins here. For that, we'd have to wait for
Chaco Canyon. Art had tantalized us with his promises of massive,
sprawling ruins there, causing our curiosity juices to flow freely.

Ahead loomed more ruins. We stopped and broke out the binoculars. The site was unusual in that there were two sets of dwellings, one above the other. The lower site was stacked on the sandy
floor at the base of the cliff, the other a hundred feet up the cliff
face. This was White House, a Pueblo III site so named by the U.S.
Army in the 1840s because of the white plaster adorning some of
the building walls. More accurately, the soldiers had dubbed the
site "Casa Blanca."

Originally, the two levels of buildings had been connected by
four-story buildings on the lower level. Many of the canyon-level
rooms have been destroyed by high water. At its peak, White House
included some eighty rooms and kivas and probably housed 100 or
more persons, according to Art's book. The inhabitants must have
ranged far and wide for sustenance, for the canyon seemed sterile
throughout most of its length, hewn from rock and sand with only
a spattering of fauna and flora. There were certainly animals beyond the canyon, and even within its confines, though, except for
an occasional lizard, they were keeping out of sight of our entourage. The search for game must have been a constant challenge.
And for edible plant products, though when the rains came enough
water flowed to nourish crops of corn, squash, beans, cotton. Yet
there were patches of vegetation that somehow managed to survive
from year to year, as evidenced now by the cottonwood and tamarisk trees, so dependent on a steady source of water. The vegetation
and the rivulets of water that periodically snaked through the canyon would have drawn the birds and animals, further adding to the
meat supply. But for this fragile ecosystem to work, for it to sustain
the Anasazi, there had to have been water — constantly. With a
sustained drought, one enduring for many years, the chain would
have been broken, the canyon's Achilles' heal severed. After 250

years of continuous occupation, the site was abandoned, perhaps for this very reason.

Through the binoculars I could make out that the eroded walls were thick near the base, unlike what I had seen in the Mesa Verde area. Rather than consisting of walls one or two stones in depth, these were five stones across. Our scholars indicated this was evidence of Chaco Canyon influence. Also, the large size of the rooms, the banded masonry, and the accuracy of setting the masonry were Chacoan in nature. More fodder for our curiosity.

As we slowly bore through the sand, bucking and jerking, with Lewis grinding mercilessly through the gears, we passed a hapless would-be sightseer. He had defied the ban on autos in the canyon. And paid for his hubris or ignorance. His car was buried to the chassis in the middle of the canyon floor. The driver helplessly stood beside the car, waiting for the tow truck, frowning as we passed, all of us staring at him and his plight.

Back at the Thunderbird, I sighed under a well-needed shower, then off to the gift shop. Perhaps I'd find a kachina doll. They had dolls all right, but the selection was lacking. And most of the dolls were carved by Navajo artists. I had been warned by Art to only buy "genuine" kachinas, which meant Hopi-made. After all, he had pointed out, the Hopi were the originators of the dolls, the Navajo just imitators. The prices, whether of Navajo or Hopi dolls, were even higher than those back at the trading post on the Hopi reservation. Except for postcards and a T-shirt, I walked out empty-handed — again. But I knew I'd be able to get a doll at the gift shop at Crow Canyon. Art had figured there would be plenty of them.

✳ ✳ ✳

Another early start; our driver was Mel, one of the staff members and not an archeologist. His training was in environmental health, of all things. About thirtyish, with dark hair and glasses, he'd been with Crow Canyon about a year. Despite his lack of credentials, Mel was very amiable and most helpful, definitely an asset on the trip. We headed north, eager for the day's encounters.

We crossed Washington Pass at close to 9000 feet. At that lofty elevation we were amidst aspen wrapped in white bark, spruce cast in muted blue, ponderosa pine draped with long needles.

We turned off the asphalt road onto one of dirt, driving past a scattering of Navajo dwellings, some with corralled horses. A sheep herder tended his flock in the distance. I wondered what the animals could possibly graze on as the brownish grass appeared most unappetizing.

From the dirt road, we ventured onto a path that curved up onto a mound. I saw nothing of interest at first. But we had arrived at Skunk Springs Ruins, an *unexcavated* site. I didn't know the origin of the site name, but I didn't care to try any of the local water.

We poured out of the vans and over the rock-strewn, windy, barren landscape. Despite the land's emptiness, the site was alive with telltale fragments. I found potsherds, black on white or corrugated gray, distinctly Anasazi, then more shards. Everyone was finding pottery chips, which were as plentiful as confetti at a wedding. I stumbled upon a fist-sized chunk of petrified wood, which had nothing to do with the archeology of the site. Others found similar pieces. One of the group picked up an arrowhead. Whatever we came upon, we were allowed to pick up and examine. Then the artifact had to be put back where it was discovered. The unimpeded, whipping wind threatened to carry my hat away.

Art and Lex guided us over the site, which was composed of mounds and depressions, covered with rocks, pebbles, clumps of grass and brush, and a sea of savage stickers and burrs that ambushed a trodding ankle or probing finger. To the untrained eye, the site was a natural mound with bumps and dips, nothing special. But to the scholars, it represented dwellings yet uncovered. The ground upon which we trod was probably at least at the level of the second floor, said Art. This had been an "outlier" for Chaco Canyon, sort of a suburb.

Art pointed out that many of the stones strewn on the ground weren't there naturally. They came from the building walls. The mud mortar had weathered away, allowing the stones to tumble down. Most of the structures were probably underground by now. The ground had become covered by wind-blown sand and dirt over the centuries.

Although unexcavated, Skunk Springs had been studied. Ceramic materials suggested a Pueblo I habitation, circa 850 to 950 A.D., and a Pueblo II to Pueblo III component, around 1005 to 1250. Preliminary investigation revealed a great kiva complex backed by a multistory masonry house. Overall, the pueblo consisted of three great kivas and about forty ground-floor rooms and sixteen second-floor rooms. I couldn't see any other mounds in the distance that might have also contained delitescent buildings, and certainly there were no other ruins visible for miles. I could only surmise that this outlier must have been an isolated, and perhaps lonely, place in a vast wind-scoured badland. Living conditions must have been harsh. The site name implied a source of water, though of dubious quality, which might account for the presence of these buildings.

The staff circled the wagons against the wicked wind and spread out the tables. Lunch time.

Then it was on to the next site, many miles distant. It was north, then a sharp right turn to east, through Farmington and on to Aztec, New Mexico, where we encountered Aztec Ruins, another Anasazi site. Conventional wisdom being what it was when the site was named in the latter part of the 1800s (and it wasn't much), it was assumed that indigenous peoples couldn't have constructed such an advanced site. No, these buildings had to have been erected by the Mesoamericans, in particular by the Aztecs or Toltecs.

Wrong.

The large set of ruins sat on the north bank of the fertile Animas River, within a large rectangular site, with twenty-eight kivas and multistory buildings containing 405 rooms. Our scholars detected evidence of Chacoan influence, such as the large rooms and high ceilings. Many of the rooms had later been subdivided into smaller Mesa Verde-style rooms. Art said the site may once have been a Chacoan outlier, later occupied by a Mesa Verde group.

"The Chacoans weren't the earliest on the site," said Art. "The pottery here from Pueblo I, black on white, was common in the San Juan area. Then the Chacoans moved in. They were absorbed by the inhabitants then in place, or they later moved out. Then the Mesa Verdeans moved in and took over the site."

I later read in an article by Steve Lekson, Crow Canyon's president, that this site was populated by the Anasazi from 1100 to 1275 A.D.

In the northwest section of the site, there was a series of contiguous rooms connected by doorways oriented north to south. Early this century, intruders had cut east-west doorways into the walls for better access. One by one, we filed through the rooms, pausing to stoop through the tight portals. By Anasazi standards, the rooms were indeed spacious, with ten-foot ceilings. Fifteen of us could stand in a room together without discomfort.

Ceiling beams, a millennium old, were still visible and in a remarkable state of preservation. The dry Southwest air probably played a role in that. Three large timbers, each sixteen inches in diameter, once spanned the ceiling of each room. Above this layer of timbers would have been a layer of smaller poles, four inches in diameter, and arranged at right angles to the larger timbers just below. The third layer up would have been of split wood, possibly juniper. Above that, clay was spread. The roof of the ground story served as the floor of the second story.

There were two porthole-sized ventilator shafts at the top of the north wall of each of the rooms. The air was heavy, the lighting poor. The rooms, despite their volume, summoned in me the close feeling of a dungeon.

In adjacent rooms directly south, metates were recumbent in the soil, lined up as though waiting faithfully to undertake their corn-grinding role, a wait that had endured for centuries.

Then to the great kiva, the dominant feature and star attraction of the site. It squatted in a courtyard southeast of the rooms we had just explored. Although reconstructed in modern times, it was well worth seeing. From the outside, it was shaped like a giant cheese box with a tab protruding from the north side. The circular walls rose ten feet or so above ground level. From an aerial view I imagined it to have a keyhole shape.

We ambled down the staircase into the belly of the kiva. Its behemoth dimensions caused me to suck in my breath. I paused at the bottom of the short stairway, eight feet below ground, to pan the scene. The inner diameter reached over forty feet. The structure was completely roofed but allowed subdued sunlight to filter in. I took a seat on the raised masonry lip of one of the two rectangular floor vaults, recessed four feet into the earth.

Near the north end of the kiva a square fire pit, four feet long on a side, was dug into the earth, its boundaries marked by a raised masonry lip. The inner enclosing wall of the kiva was ringed with a low, stone banquette. The roof was supported by four massive columns, composed of alternating layers of masonry and wood. These sturdy square pillars were attached to the transverse roofing beams and rose eighteen feet from the floor. Each pillar was supported by three thick, circular, sandstone disks, stacked one atop the other. This kiva dwarfed anything I had thus far seen, making it a virtual auditorium to the Anasazi. During its tenure centuries ago, this vast kiva must have witnessed all manner of events in its service as a government center, religious facility, social club.

Art took center stage on the dusty floor. "These great kivas are not found in Kayenta. They are found throughout Chaco and down to the Zuni area."

Lex stood up. "In Kayenta there may be a Basket Maker III great kiva. There's a circle in the ground with a bench, but it's poorly dug, without vaults or a circle for a fire hearth, no roof posts, and the walls are not there. It may have been only a gathering area. It was excavated in the early part of this century, and not excavated carefully."

"The Mogollon to the south have the earliest great kivas," Art continued. "After the Anasazi left the area and went south, kivas stayed in style until at least 1400."

Bob, the architect, abruptly rose, facing Art and Lex. "These columns are a significant leap out of the Twelfth Century," he said skeptically. He didn't think it possible for the Anasazi to suddenly develop the technology to erect such a structure. From an architectural point of view, he didn't believe the columns, as reconstructed, could be accurate. He felt they had to be shorter, mumbling something about the weight-to-distance ratio, which went right over my head.

"Most archeologists would agree that the height has been exaggerated," Lex offered pensively.

Art asked us to reserve judgment on this kiva until we'd been to Chaco Canyon. "A lot of your questions will be answered there," he smiled assuredly.

Then back to Farmington for the night.

* * *

This morning Lex was at the wheel. We were finally going to see the great kivas of Chaco Canyon we had heard so much about, as though everything we'd thus far seen was merely a prelude to Chaco. But, of course, Chaco was but one piece in the giant, fragmented puzzle, albeit a big piece. Steve Lekson, a renowned archeologist himself, would be along. We trekked south. Paved road yielded to packed dirt. We crossed the Escavada Wash. There wasn't much to see, basically barren scrubland, but I for one was filled with anticipation. Art had assured us that some of the answers we sought about the Anasazi would be awaiting us at Chaco.

We suddenly parked along the dirt road and alighted. Steve hurriedly stepped ahead, eyes to the ground, frantically searching through the sparse grass and brush like a bloodhound after a scent. Whatever he was seeking, he found. We all scurried over. I didn't see a thing. Supposedly we were at the Great North Road that stretched from Chaco Canyon, miles away, to an unexcavated site nearby, and beyond. The road once ran laser-straight over all terrain. If a mesa had the audacity to get in the way, the Anasazi cut steps into it.

Steve, tall, light haired, lean and an energetic, boyish forty, pointed along the ground, his eyes following something. I saw the unexcavated mounds several yards away, covered with earth and grass, but no road. We were all poring over the ground, eyes down, straining to see whatever Steve was onto. After a couple of minutes, Steve realized we weren't seeing any North Road, just uninterrupted prairie.

"You really can't see it from the ground," he said defensively — a colossal understatement.

Supposedly the concave road was visible from 300 feet up. That didn't help me. Satellite-generated infrared photographs have revealed an elaborate network of roads, centered around Chaco Canyon and spreading through more than 100,000 square miles. The invisible road before us, unseen by all except Steve, was part of the 400 miles of ancient roadways radiating out from Chaco Canyon to its outliers. Outposts, discovered atop high mesas around Chaco Canyon, served as signal stations, conveying line-of-sight messages, presumably by fire, smoke or reflected light. But this system of roads, tying the Chaco culture together, paled beside its counterpart constructed by the Inca thousands of miles to the south. That road system spanned 12,000 miles through present-day Ecuador, Peru and Chile. Still, what the Chacoans produced was unparalleled in the American Southwest before the arrival of the Europeans.

In half an hour we were in the canyon, occupying some thirty square miles of the San Juan Basin in what was now northwest New Mexico. To the west, the Chuska Mountains ran generally northward, straddling the state's border with Arizona. Within the confines of the canyon were the remains of more than 2400 archeological sites, including ten bona fide towns (Great Houses), each containing hundreds of rooms.

First stop was Casa Rinconada, built by the Chacoans during the last half of the Eleventh Century. The ruins actually consisted of three Anasazi house sites and the great kiva of Casa Rinconada. Still buried were some of the first homes in the canyon. The ancestors of these Anasazi settled into agriculture around 400 A.D. Initially they resided in pithouses, occupying these rudimentary dwellings for 400 years before they were superseded by the sturdier masonry buildings.

I was particularly interested in the great kiva. I stood at the top of the kiva's circular wall, three feet above ground level. The roof had long since eroded completely away. The kiva was now wide open to the elements.

Steve, standing nearby, mentioned that "there was no wood, little water, not a lot of game, a short growing season. But there's plenty of sandstone. There were 5000 souls living here at one time. They had to haul wood from over sixty miles away."

I peered down into Casa Rinconada, which was over sixty feet in diameter. I readily recognized the important features: square fire pit, perimetered with raised masonry blocks and bracketed on either side by a rectangular, masonry vault; circular, masonry-lined post holes cut into the floor, devoid of any remnants of the posts themselves; banquette, two-feet wide and a yard above the floor.

The kiva was oriented along a north-south axis with an antechamber attached to its north side. The architecture of this kiva was
remarkably similar to the reconstructed version back at Aztec Ruins. It couldn't be coincidental.

There had originally been an unusual feature here, a subfloor
passage, since filled in. A yard wide and a yard deep, it had been
roofed over and connected a room in the north antechamber with
the kiva. The apparent purpose had been to allow a costumed religious figure to appear suddenly in the center of the kiva, adding
drama and excitement to a religious ceremony.

I entered via a short set of steps and parked myself on the banquette. I noticed thirty-four niches ringing the inside of the wall.
No one knew for sure what they represented. However, another
great kiva at a different site in the canyon had similar niches that
were sealed until uncovered in modern times, yielding shell and
turquoise necklaces, precious commodities to the Chacoans. Turquoise was so valued that it became a medium of exchange and
even engendered a cult, beginning by the early Eleventh Century,
that filtered out across the vast regional network. The raw ore was
processed into intricate jewelry, often with mosaic patterns.

We wondered why the Anasazi chose to live under such spartan
conditions. Steve conjectured that Chaco might have been a distribution center for the outlying, productive areas.

"Lots of wood, corn and pots were brought in. Two-thirds of
the pots were from the Chuska Mountains about sixty miles to the
west," said Steve.

The great kivas in the canyon attested to Chaco's status as a
ceremonial mecca, but the variety and number of consumer goods
that passed through told of its role as a commercial center, the hub
of an expansive trade network.

I asked whether there was some sort of hierarchical structure.
Art thought not. "It's just barn raising."

I looked at him and shook my head, smiling. "I have a hard
time accepting that," I responded. "It seems there had to have been
someone in charge, some organizational levels."

Art retorted didactically. "Think of how *they* might have
thought, not like we tend to do things." He explained that the
Anasazi were more egalitarian than we are. They did things with-

out a leader. There were no chiefs.

I couldn't argue with him, but I wasn't convinced.

We were ferried down the canyon to the compact museum. The crew set up the serving tables and put out the dishes. We enjoyed our tasty buffet lunch on the picnic tables in front of the museum with the stark sun as a canopy and the sandstone bluffs as a backdrop.

There was time to explore what little there was of the austere museum. Joan and I spotted an antique photo of Walpi, taken in 1897 and remarkably well preserved. Walpi was instantly recognizable. It looked virtually the same a century ago as it did now! There were no cars in the photo, no power lines either — just as when we visited. We had indeed been time travelers on First Mesa.

We sat through a twenty-minute film about the Anasazi. One couldn't do justice to the Anasazi in such a short time, but the movie did bring out some interesting points. The Anasazi believed they were in the fourth period of history. The previous three periods had each come to a crashing end by either wind, fire or flood. Interestingly, that greatly coincided with beliefs in Mesoamerica, where an additional previous historical period was terminated by wild animals. The Mesoamericans believed they were in the fifth period of history.

A short ride brought us along the canyon to Chetro Ketl, a vast, D-shaped, masonry pueblo set against the towering sandstone cliffs. It was massive compared to what I had thus far seen on this excursion, containing over 300 rooms and more than a dozen kivas, including several tower-kivas. Probably the rear wall reached four, maybe five, stories, a skyscraper to the Anasazi and surely one of the tallest buildings of its time in the entire Southwest. Most of the upper walls were now long gone. Tree-ring dating revealed that this site was erected in fifteen stages from about 1010 to 1105 A.D.

As we strolled over the site, I noticed a horizontal line of saucer-shaped holes poked into the cliff above the pueblo. From the distance, it resembled the results of a burst of machine-gun fire raked across a wall.

"Post holes," said Art.

Steve eagerly pointed out a rare feature on the front of one of the buildings. Atop a low masonry wall a row of square columns had been erected, apparently to support the horizontal timbers forming the roof of a gallery. The spaces between the columns had later been filled in during ancient times to make rooms.

"This could be evidence of Mexican influence," hypothesized Steve, himself not convinced.

"I don't think so," Art quickly responded with certainty. His index finger drew a bead on the edifice. "These columns are on a wall. The columns in Mexico go to the ground."

That comported with the colonnades of the Toltec building, the Temple of the Warriors, I had seen at Chichén Itzá in the Mexican Yucatán. That temple supposedly was the twin to one at Tula in central Mexico, which Art had apparently visited.

We traipsed to the top of the great kiva, its roof also gone. It was sixty feet in diameter and fourteen feet deep. Another behemoth. It contained essentially the same features as its counterpart at Casa Rinconada.

"This was a planned community," said Steve confidently. "When the Anasazi built here, they knew they were going up to five stories. The top rooms weren't merely an afterthought."

How did he know that? I wondered.

Steve pointed to the bases of the ground-floor walls. They were fully five blocks across. Steve gestured higher on the walls. The walls of the second floor were slightly narrower, only four blocks across. And so it went as far as can be seen from what walls remained. The walls become narrower with each ascending floor. Steve assured us that the lower floors were indeed designed to support the weight of the floors above.

I took a closer look at the lower floors, particularly the bottom floor. Yes, it had a width of five stones. But more importantly, it was only at the edges of the outside stones that the wall was smooth. The interior three blocks of the ground floor had never been chiseled smooth to form the edge of a wall. Had there been a row of interior blocks that lined up neatly to form a clean edge, I would have known the bottom wall was originally narrower and had been widened only later. Steve was right, the Anasazi started off with a massive architectural project in mind. Which made me wonder about

Art's pronouncement that there were no chiefs. How could such a prodigal undertaking be planned and built and administered without levels of hierarchy? I had to doubt Art on this one, though he was eminently qualified to render an opinion while I wasn't remotely so.

We walked the quarter mile up the canyon in the stark sun to Pueblo Bonito, another extensive, D-shaped, masonry pueblo spread below sandstone bluffs. During four construction eras, from 850 to 1125 A.D., some 800 rooms and thirty-seven kivas were built — a metropolis, even larger than Chetro Ketl. In the last half of the Eleventh Century, the then-existing 600 rooms were home to a thousand persons (other rooms were added later). Along the wall, the pueblo once rose to five stories. Most of the upper floors were now gone. But in its halcyon days, Pueblo Bonito was so huge that its size remained unsurpassed in America until the Industrial Revolution in the Nineteenth Century!

As we strolled between the two pueblos, Steve said he would prove the Chacoans built these pueblos themselves, without direction from Mexican architects. Once within the ruins, Steve became animated. He had some definite ideas about Chaco. This was the place to demonstrate them. As we sat along walls and steps, Steve stood before us. His eyes sparkled in the bright sun. His arms and hands came animated like those of a marionette.

"Here you can see the Anasazi taught themselves," he said. He pointed to various portions of the ruins, indicating where the Anasazi initially erected their buildings. They didn't get it right first, he continued. They made mistakes. The upper parts of buildings didn't remain standing. The Anasazi made the appropriate changes. He showed where the construction styles evolved.

On one wall Steve demonstrated that the wall couldn't have borne the load. The walls were of veneer blocks on the outside and core blocks inside. The veneer blocks bore the load, he said. When the upper floors were falling down, the builders added chinking, thin strips of stone between the blocks, which provided support and increased the load-bearing capacity of the walls. "You can see it right here," he gestured.

He pointed to another wall. It was crumbled and buckled. Not only was it without chinking, but it was narrow at the base — too narrow. It was another mistake the Anasazi corrected in later construction.

"Without the chinking, the mud mortar washed out. The wall was already too narrow. It therefore gave way and buckled."

There was another important evolvement. "The Anasazi eventually made the rooms *smaller*, so there could be crosswalls for added support of the high walls," he noted.

I was taking it all in. I could readily see for myself what he was talking about. There did appear to be corrective developments in the construction here.

"The Mexicans did not build Chaco, the Anasazi did," he stated positively. "There *is* Mexican influence in the canyon, but it came at the *end* of Chaco, not the beginning."

He let that sink in.

"The copper bells and macaws came late. The Mexican influence doesn't explain the buildings," he reiterated.

I knew the Anasazi had prized the macaws for their feathers. The birds weren't indigenous and had to be imported from the south. The copper for the bells couldn't have been mined locally and also had to be brought in. So, that was the extent of the Mesoamerican influence in the canyon — trade — Steve was saying.

Steve shifted gears. He alluded to the two burials found in the rooms, unusual for the Anasazi. They had been discovered in log-lined crypts with several other skeletons heaped above them.

"I wouldn't be surprised if the dead persons scattered around were sacrificed for the other two burials," Steve mentioned. "Those two were middle-aged men who were killed by being hit on the back of the head."

He shifted his stance. "There were some funerary goods."

I was digesting that, waiting for the punch line.

"This could be a sign of leadership," he said offhandedly.

You bet it could! There's no way all of this could have come about without leaders and a social hierarchy. Steve hadn't gone quite that far, but he had opened the door, at least for me.

Art and Steve led us through a series of connected rooms within the pueblo. Most of the rooms had walls remaining that reached the second or third floor, although many were without roofs now.

The rooms were tall by Anasazi standards, but the doorways small. We had to stoop going through, walk a few steps to the next doorway, stoop again, and so on through a maze of sandstone-block walls. If I had to live here and walk through all these doorways repeatedly, I'd be in dire need of a chiropractor.

Steve gathered a bunch of us in one room. He explained that the lower rooms had been used for storage, with the upper rooms reserved for dwellings. He pointed out an unusual feature. In an upper corner of the room was a portal, a strange place for a doorway. The roof of the room we were in was gone, so that doorway would have been at floor level on the second story. But what made it odd was its position. It was not cut through any individual wall, but into a corner, thereby carving a piece out of two intersecting walls.

So what?

As if to answer my unasked question, Steve pointed to the doorway, noting that it didn't help support the structure. In fact, it weakened the building.

The lady standing directly beneath the doorway quickly and silently moved to another part of the room, accompanied by a chorus of snickers.

Once outside in the courtyard, Art observed that when a population reaches about 2500, it becomes hierarchical and buds off. This would be true worldwide and for all cultures. Art believed this threshold stopped the Anasazi from blossoming into a fully hierarchical society like their Mesoamerican counterparts. "At 2500 population, humans tend to develop crafts and architecture," he said.

I later read there had been as many as 6000 Anasazi (which roughly comported with Steve's figure of 5000) in 400 sites within the canyon area by 1100 A.D. Their population had doubled over the previous fifty years. That population would easily have surpassed Art's critical mass of 2500. Why, then, no social hierarchy at Chaco?

The Chacoans had a florescence: the fabled Chaco Phenomenon. It began, flourished and crashed in exactly 200 years, from 920 to 1120 A.D. Their culture then had been far more spectacular than that of their neighbors at Kayenta, Mesa Verde or Canyon de Chelly.

The Chacoans had reached the Pueblo III stage fifty years ahead

of other Anasazi. In turn, the Chacoan Pueblo III phase had dis-
solved nearly a century earlier than its counterparts in Mesa Verde
and Kayenta.

By 1020 A.D., the Chacoans had been well en route to creating
a Mesoamerican-style culture. Their architecture, ceramics, roads,
jewelry, agriculture, commerce and administration had made them
the forerunners of Pueblo III culture in the Southwest. They had
been on their way. But they never quite made it — a renaissance
manqué.

The sun was dropping below the canyon walls. Time to go. Too
bad, as I was enthralled by Chaco Canyon. We headed north to spend
the night in Mancos, Colorado.

✳ ✳ ✳

As the rising sun ushered in the new day, we drove through the
Colorado countryside to the Crow Canyon campus in Cortez. On
the grounds of the small campus a mockup of a pithouse had been
erected. We had seen actual pithouse remains, which were often
little more than shallow depressions scooped into the ground, superstructures worn away. But now we would actually get to enter
an intact pithouse. A Twentieth Century reconstruction of a
pithouse, that is.

We ducked in through the low portal, took a few steps down
the antechamber, emerging in the main chamber. The room, squarish with rounded corners, reached twelve to fourteen feet across.
The walls, slanted inward from bottom to top, were supported by
four upright posts in the main chamber. Vertical logs interwoven
with horizontal twigs formed the walls, which were finished with
coats of mud. An eight-foot ceiling joined the walls. We were
two feet below ground. Logs at the base of the ceiling rested on
the four wooden pillars. Twigs had been placed above the logs
and at right angles to them. Mud and dirt had been packed on
the exterior walls and atop the outside roof, into which a smoke
hole had been cut.

On the floor were two corn-grinding metates and accompanying manos. The fire pit was slab-lined. Between it and the doorway
a deflector slab rose from the packed earth. I couldn't imagine call-

ing this home, but a thousand years ago I'd have been thankful to spend the night in a place like this.

The students at Crow Canyon who had labored to create this model a few years ago did a credible job. They provided a glimpse into pithouse accommodations from 600 A.D. As with the Anasazi, the students had to make constant repairs as the rain washed away the mud mortar. Through trial and error, the students found they could fortify the mud with the addition of fine sand, fire ash and vegetable matter. Interestingly, they later analyzed samples of Anasazi mud mortar. The Anasazi had come up with the very same formula centuries ago!

Outside the pithouse, the staff had set up an atlatl "firing range." A life-sized turkey mannequin had been positioned in an open spot in the brush. A makeshift atlatl and spears were passed to those of us who were not timid about making fools of themselves. I promptly volunteered. One of our group got first try. He flubbed terribly, missing the mark by several yards.

My turn — but would I fare any better? After all, I hadn't thrown an atlatl either. None of us had. I'd thrown a spear before, but not without actually grasping the projectile. Now I would be flinging the five-foot spear without gripping it. I slipped my right index and ring fingers through the two finger holes in the leather strap attached to one end of the atlatl. The spear rested horizontally in a groove on the topside of the atlatl. I cocked my arm with the atlatl lined up parallel to the ground, the spear pointing forward. The spear was loosely held onto the atlatl by the longitudinal groove. A notch at the leather-strap end of the atlatl lightly secured the feathered end of the spear. It was this back end of the atlatl that would transfer the force of my arm into the feathered end of the spear, sending it (hopefully) toward the target.

I was all set up, ready to go. The atlatl and spear were in position. My arm was cocked. I grasped the wooden stalk of the atlatl with whatever portion of my right hand that wasn't occupied with the finger strap. It was awkward. I looked downrange. The turkey was only forty feet away, only two-thirds the distance from the pitcher's mound to home plate. It should be an easy throw. But this wasn't a baseball. And I couldn't do anything fancy with my arm or wrist. No curve balls, or sliders, just straight over the plate in the strike zone.

I envisioned how I would heave a baseball if I absolutely had to get the ball in for a called strike. I had to come straight over the shoulder. And keep the wrist from rotating. And follow through.

Here I go. I snapped my arm forward at three-quarter speed to keep control. I kept my index and ring fingers straight up, so as they released the spear they followed through right down the body of the turkey. The spear soared toward the target in a slight wobble. It was right on course. But too high. The spear flew over the turkey and landed in the brush fifteen feet beyond. The atlatl had extended my lever arm and provided more power than expected. With a baseball I'd have beaned the turkey. With the atlatl I needed to underthrow.

Several of the others took a turn at bat. No one hit the mark. Most missed wildly. One guy came oh so close. He was right on line, but the spear dug into the dirt at the feet of the turkey — just six inches higher.

Back in the vans for the short ride to Sand Canyon, one of two sites Crow Canyon was excavating. Bruce, the project manager, greeted us. In his late-thirties, bespectacled, with a moustache, goatee, dirty hands and soiled jeans, he was fresh from the dig site. He stood before us, eager to explain his project. His eyes danced, head bobbed, hands darted. His crew was interested in exploring late Pueblo III ruins, circa 1250 to 1300 A.D. They had scoured the surrounding hills and canyons and settled upon this site.

"There are no antecedent sites here. It's a clean site, only one time span to worry about," he said. "We'll only excavate twelve percent. That's enough for now." He added that this would provide most of the information they could have gotten if they excavated the entire site. The small increment of additional information would not warrant the excess outlay of time and money. They had to move on to other sites. Future archeologists, with access to better tools and methods, would have the option of re-digging the site.

Bruce was initially interested in ascertaining certain particulars. "We want to know when the Anasazi built this site. Whether it was erected according to a plan. How it grew. What the individual configurations were. If the population lived in kivas. What the units functioned as."

Bruce led us single-file along a sparse trail that wound through the trees and underbrush. The pleasant, spicy scent of juniper wafted over the trail. I didn't see any site. Bruce paused by a long stonestrewn mound. It was the remains of a wall, he observed. Good thing he told us. Below the wall sat a depression carpeted with rocks and foliage — a kiva.

Bruce pointed in various directions through the trees. More unexcavated mounds and depressions that were disguised as merely bumps and dips in the terrain. They were all rooms, walls or kivas. The site, encompassing three city blocks, contained about 420 rooms and ninety kivas. I thought that to be an extraordinarily high number of kivas. Bruce must have read my mind.

"The room-kiva ratio here is highly unusual," he said. "The ratio is three or four to one. In Mesa Verde, for example, the ratio is around eleven rooms per kiva. Actually, the ratio varies dramatically within this site. Some areas are two to one, some twelve to one, one is over thirty to one."

We followed Bruce to another part of the site. Almost all of the site was unexcavated. How could they know so much? From a double pit ten feet down, two student volunteers were scraping and scooping along the dirt walls and earth floor. After they sorted through what they uncovered, they toted the buckets of discarded dirt up ladders to the top of the pits, where the buckets were handed off for disposal. An adjacent pair of wire screens sifted the dirt for any artifacts the volunteers missed.

The volunteers, women in their fifties and sixties, were caked with soil. Cloth gloves provided some protection as they wielded their brushes and tools. The musty odor of newly exposed dirt filled my nostrils. The sun, not yet having reached its daily zenith in the cloudless sky, would pore straight down into the pits in a couple of hours. It would get sticky in those holes with the sweat and heat and dirt. You had to love what you were doing to be in there. These women apparently did. Despite their labored movements and baggy eyes, they were cheerful. The older woman had spent several weeklong sessions on these very digs.

Bruce estimated the population of the site at 250. He believed the residents had migrated away by 1300 A.D. He wasn't sure why. "Unlike at other sites, these Anasazi could have gotten all the wood they needed locally. A study showed they could have obtained the wood for construction within 1.2 kilometers from the site," said Bruce.

"What about firewood?" asked Steve, not trying to be funny.

Bruce didn't directly address the query. "I don't think they ran out of wood," he responded, with a tone that didn't invite debate on the point.

There are five cultural signatures that enable archeologists to define the Anasazi. First is the kiva, which belongs to the Anasazi and is not found anywhere else.

Second is the unit pueblo. This formed the modular unit of standardized design that was multiplied to form larger settlements.

There is also the orientation of kivas and unit pueblos toward the south or southwest.

Fourth is the pottery. The Anasazi fired their pottery in a non-oxidizing atmosphere. Many pots were decorated with black paint, producing the distinctive black-on-white pottery.

Last is the pattern of burials. The bodies were lain to rest with legs flexed against the chest, on their sides with the heads oriented directionally — often toward the east — or parallel to the slope if the grave was on steep terrain.

After a picnic lunch on the site, we were ferried back to the campus. Cruising along the back roads I spotted an oddity in a corral. The horses belonged there, of course, but that large-eared, four-legged animal with its back to me did not. Somehow a deer, probably a mule deer from the size of its ears, had hopped the fence and was casually nibbling grass near the horses.

"Look at the deer," I pointed, for everyone in our van to see.

Debbie, our driver for the day, shot me a weird look as though I told her I had just seen a spaceship land. "That's not a deer. That's a mule!"

"A mule?" I stammered, turning red. "Are you sure?"

"Positive. I've seen it there before."

Jane heard it all. She wasn't about to let me get away with that one. Her laughter ricocheted throughout the van. "Oh, Thom, you don't even know a deer from a mule!"

Touché.

Back on campus, we were ushered downstairs to the lab, the nerve center of any archeological project. This was where all the raw artifacts wound up, at least those that could be transported. We filled the seats as Melita, the lab director and herself an archeologist, stood before us. In her early-thirties, with dark hair, she seemed too young to be in charge of such an important laboratory. But she was sharp and seemed to know her business.

She explained the dichotomy between archeological artifacts and features. Artifacts include: seeds, potsherds, food matter, tools, clothing, pollen samples, animal bones and human remains. "Flotation samples" were also brought to the lab. Samples from the hearth or floor were put in water, with the organic matter being skimmed off. Features stayed at the site. The walls, pits and kivas obviously didn't make it to the lab. A field report of the site did get to the lab, where Melita and her associates used it to catalog and analyze the artifacts from the site.

Work in the lab was by no means perfunctory. "For every hour in the field, it's four to five hours in the lab, preparing and analyzing," said Melita, allowing that to sink in.

"The artifacts are unwrapped and washed first. Then catalogued. They're sorted into such groups as: pottery, bones, carbon, tools, chips. The pottery shards are assigned a style, to get a relative date for the site."

Melita explained that the materials were analyzed, the results published, the artifacts curated (stored). Melita led us to the storeroom. Rows of shelves lined the walls and filled the room's interior. Temperature and humidity were closely regulated. Pottery vessels crowded the shelves, totally covering them. Some vessels were intact. Most had been shattered and were now glued together like a three-dimensional jigsaw puzzle, some of the pieces yet missing.

In another room of the lab we spread out along two workbenches. Bags of artifacts had been dumped on the benches. We were challenged to figure out what we had before us. The artifacts were genuine, but they had been sorted through and compiled just for our training.

We easily recognized bits of pottery. Our bag also held chunks of carbon, remnants of a cooking fire. I retrieved a sliver of obsidian, volcanic glass, invaluable for its razor-sharp cutting blade. There were pieces of bone, probably from food items. Some of the chunks of stone could have been axe heads. There were chips of stone that may have flaked off when a larger stone was worked. Some of the chips themselves were useful as cutting tools, though none bore as fine an edge as obsidian.

Last stop was the gift shop, my last chance to go home with a kachina doll. I had my credit card in hand as I enthusiastically walked through the door. But my anticipation soon dampened. One of the staff members warned me that most of the dolls and other items were out of stock. Some group had gone through the store during the week and cleaned the place out.

Sure enough, the selection was bare-bones. There was nothing worth having. I left the store empty-handed — once again. No doll this trip.

I never did hear the story that went with Art's pendant. I had to know. Curiosity was eating my insides out. So a year later, I called Art at work, at the anthropology department at Wichita State University. He was more than willing to chat. When I mentioned the pendant, he chuckled. It has given him "faith far and wide." He said that women more often noticed the pendant than did men.

"Ninety-five percent of the women remark that they like it," he told me.

He didn't wear the nude lady as a symbol of male chauvinism, but rather to "honor women." Art "appreciated women." He relished female company, so much so that he had "more female friends than male friends." But he didn't "hit on them."

I asked the source of the pendant. It seems that in 1989 Art was visiting the town of Lijiang, in extreme southwestern China, home of the Nahki, a minority people. The culture was unusual, Art told me, in that "descent was through the females " and "the females dominated."

"The females owned the houses and controlled the bedrooms. The matriarch had the master bedroom. The women routinely got to select their bed partners."

Which usually translated into multiple sex partners for the females, especially the unwed ones. But even the married ladies got to pick and choose their companion for the night, a custom apparently acceptable to the husbands. Art said that in town the women were always on the prowl. Some married couples did, however, maintain a monogamous relationship throughout their lives, Art was quick to add, as if to preempt any moral objections I might voice. (I didn't have any.) But I had the impression that this monogamy was the exception not the rule among the Nahki.

One day Art was shopping at the market in Lijiang. The pendant, cast from lead and dangling from a string, caught his eye. He had to have it. Art successfully "bargained for it" with the lady who ran the stall. As Art reached for his purchase, a female bystander, whom neither Art nor the proprietor knew, suddenly snatched the pendant and draped it around Art's neck.

"I had to wear it then," Art said. "What else could I do?"

"Was there anything symbolic in the woman's actions?"

"Not that I know of . . . I never saw her again."

Art took the pendant back to the U. S. and wore it faithfully, a token of his appreciation of women. A couple of years later a friend mentioned to Art that the lead in the figurine was poisoning him. What to do? Anyone else might simply have stashed the nude lady in his jewelry box. After all, the pendant wasn't a gift from someone special. And even if it was, it wasn't worth being poisoned over. But stashing was not an option for Art. The pendant had to be worn. So Art had the lady copied and cast in gold. He has since worn it proudly.

TEMPLE OF THE GIANT JAGUAR

From my window seat in the aging, twin-engine DC-3, I could see the eroded peaks of man-made structures poking through the dense canopy of forest cover and into the pristine sky like freshly germinated shoots racing for their very existence toward the precious light of day. First one, then two, then yet a third stony summit popped into my limited view. This early-morning, hour-long flight was shuttling a hodgepodge group of us from Guatemala's capital northward into the country's panhandle, to spend a couple of days at the ruins of Tikal. This had once been a thriving city in the Classic Mayan world, a hub within a vast trading network that spanned Mesoamerica and stretched from the Pacific Ocean on the west to the Gulf of Mexico and the Caribbean Sea on the east. Tikal's influence also spread in ways less peaceful than commerce. This relatively advanced (for Mesoamerica) community was often at war with one or another of its neighboring city-states, standard fare for the times and region.

In turning onto the final approach path to line up with the skinny gravel runway, the plane banked steeply, dipping the inboard wing so that its tip seemed about to carve a deep arc in the blanket of trees. Sitting on the inboard side, I was able to admire the unobstructed view now presented by the wing being dipped sharply and out of my range of vision. The rudimentary landing strip was scraped out of pervasive jungle as though by a giant fingernail. I could make out several thatched-roofed huts with solid walls set inside the edge of the jungle at the far end of the runway. A cluster of individuals stood at the side of the runway, shielding their eyes to watch our progress — our welcoming committee, no doubt. But several of my fellow passengers were less concerned with the sights than with their safety. Gasps and other guttural sounds of distress, as well as a few carefully chosen invectives, uttered in Spanish, reverberated through the cabin.

Once lined up with the runway, the plane dropped quickly the moment it cleared the trees. There was enough runway to allow for a shallower glide path, but this pilot wanted on the ground now. The jungle was close in on all sides as though awaiting an unguarded moment to spring forth and reclaim the airstrip.

With a bump and a bounce and another bump, we were on the ground, brakes applied, gravel spraying, then a long roll to a dead stop. The stewardess sprang to life and unbolted the door. The two-man ground crew mechanically secured the exit stairs. A land rover roared along the edge of the runway toward us, then stopped abruptly to let out the lead member of the welcoming committee. As we deplaned, the trailing dust cloud overtook us, triggering a spasm of coughing among us passengers. Welcome to Tikal, one of the wonders of the ancient Mayan world.

We were escorted along a tree-shrouded path to an oversized, thatched-roof hut. It served as an administrative center and doubled as a mess hall. Some twenty of us were here, separately as singles, couples or small groups. I was alone. Our accommodations would be at the Jungle Lodge, whose scattered buildings I had seen from the air. The ruins themselves were nowhere in sight, just jungle in all directions as far as the eye could wander, which wasn't far given all the foliage here.

After the requisite orientation by the Lodge's staff, we were assigned our quarters. My two-person hut, which I had to myself, tried to blend into the dense thicket, as did the rest of the huts, with some success. Agoutis, resembling long-legged guinea pigs with pointed snouts, darted in and out of cover to forage for some morsel or other. When I settled in at my concrete, thatched-roof hut, I went straight for the shower stall. And quickly learned there was no hot water in this place. Nor would there be, at least not in the huts such as mine. The water was not merely unheated but darn-right cold, as though from a spring. Which ruled out shaving for the next two days. Hot water wasn't the only luxury in short supply. Electricity, being generated here in the camp from gasoline flown in, was supplied for only an hour or two per day, in the evening.

A guide, Julio, a skinny campesino in worn clothing and with a shaky grip on the English language, gathered us up for a tour of the ruins, a fifteen-minute hike distant. It was mid-winter and mercifully cool once hidden from the fierce tropical sun by the interlocking leafy umbrellas. An alert guard in a clean uniform collected the admission price from Julio and waved us into the park, of which the ruins occupied but a small fraction. The park gobbled up some 222 square miles of jungle and was rigidly protected, a tribute to the planning and foresight of the Guatemalan government.

Julio led us along a dirt trail that wound deeper into the jungle. Booming bass calls from far off on one side of the trail alerted the entire world to our passage. Howler monkeys, said Julio in fragmented English. Other howlers in different directions answered the trumpeting. A primate verbal tug-of-war, apparently. There were strange bird calls, too. When I asked Julio for a translation, his response was as incomprehensible as the bird calls. Julio warned us to stay on the trail and not wander into the brush for fear of snakes. Some lady nervously asked him what kind of snakes. I was able to make out "coral" and "fer de lance" from Julio's fractured response. Were they dangerous, the lady wanted to know. "Deadly," said Julio in surprisingly good English.

Off to the sides of the trail mounds of earth, overgrown with trees and shrubs, hid unexcavated Mayan structures buried for over a millennium. Stelae, resembling large tombstones, were strewn face down in the ground, amidst the rocks and trees, where they had fallen centuries ago. On their undersides would be incised in bas-relief the story of the Maya of Tikal, or at least of their leaders. Birth, death and ascension to the throne of the rulers, as well as their capture of enemy chiefs, was recounted in pictures and hieroglyphs. There were so many hidden buildings and toppled stelae here that the archeologists would be busy for generations.

One branch of a fork in the trail suddenly erupted into a clear-

ing large as a soccer field. This was the Great Plaza, completely
excavated and remarkably preserved and restored. We were standing in what had once been the city's downtown. On the eastern
flank of the rectangle, the Temple of the Giant Jaguar (Temple I)
majestically reached more than seventeen stories into the air, its
top as lofty as the tallest of the jungle's trees. The temple, composed superficially of limestone blocks, had been erected around
700 A.D. by order of a chief, Ah Cacao, whose remains were entombed within. This leader's name, and the names of other Classic
Maya, was merely a guess by modern archeologists based upon their
interpretation of the name-glyphs carved into the stelae. This temple
dominated the clearing. I headed straight for it.

Temple I, facing the plaza, resembled a truncated pyramid on
the order of a Babylonian ziggurat. There were nine (a sacred number) sloping terraces, stacked up like a layer cake but with each
higher level being smaller in area than the one immediately below,
causing the structure to incrementally taper toward its flattened
summit. A set of steps ran along the face to the top level. The steps
were unusually high and narrow, making ascent awkward; but I
bolted up the edifice like a mountain goat. A metal chain, anchored
into the steps, ran up the face of the temple to assist the more cau-
tious climbers.

At the top level the structure supported a three-room stone
temple that occupied virtually the entire summit of the pyramid.
There had once been a carved wooden lintel over the entrance to
this temple, bearing the likeness of a jaguar, hence the alternative
name for Temple I. The lintel now resided in a Swiss museum, having been pilfered by an archeologist in the Nineteenth Century. The
remains of a towering roof comb, partly eroded, extended up from
the temple building like a giant Carnival headdress. In life it had
been richly painted, but time had worn the colors away. From the
platform summit I had an unobstructed view of the entire plaza,
bordered on every side by stone buildings and framed by the ever-
encroaching jungle.

I strolled into the temple building. The rooms, set one behind
the other, were narrow and tall, necessitated by the Mayan corbel
arch. The Maya never discovered the true arch as used by the Romans (who themselves borrowed it, probably from the Etruscans).

The Mayan arch used height to span space, thus the odd dimensions to their chambers. The rooms here were cool and dimly illuminated by the sun's rays sneaking through the entrance. There were about two dozen of us wandering between the rooms, crowded enough to elicit pangs of claustrophobia in these close quarters. I noticed a series of red imprints of human hands on one of the walls. I turned to Julio, who was standing nearby, for an explanation. He shrugged his shoulders. Then as an afterthought he started mumbling something about "workers," but by then I was already on my way into another room and didn't bother to stop. I spotted a pair of carved beams still in place across the middle doorway. I was pleasantly surprised that some archeologist hadn't hauled them off to a museum somewhere. I could barely make out what looked like a seated figure, possibly a priest, and an enormous serpent of some sort, highly stylized. I made my way through the crowd and out of the building.

To the west, at the far end of the Great Plaza, sat Temple II, another limestone pyramid. I descended Temple I and crossed the grassy field to that other pyramid, which was shorter and less grand than the one I had just left. It also differed in consisting of only three terraces. But like Temple I, it was erected by Ah Cacao about 700 A.D. I easily scaled the steps up 125 feet to its summit platform, which also supported a three-room temple. A pair of oversized masks of a grotesque design, which time had almost erased, bordered the stairway in front of the platform. But the masks gave this temple its nickname, the Temple of the Masks. The temple building also had the remnants of a roof comb, which would have, when in good repair, added another fifteen feet to its height. A face, mostly destroyed, now occupied much of the front of the roof comb. The figure was decorated with elaborate earplugs, still visible.

I wandered through the vaulted rooms, which were otherwise unoccupied. These rooms were unusual in that there were numerous incised drawings, arranged in haphazard fashion, scattered across many of the walls. I detected images of temples. There was one scene of a hapless victim, securely bound, being pierced with a spear hurled by a masked executioner. I suspected graffiti, perhaps by Classic (and post-Classic) Maya. Graffiti was probably too harsh a term to use today, several centuries removed from the rendering of the drawings. By now the drawings themselves had archeological significance. And they added a bit of prehistoric human presence to the rooms. But there were other graffiti of more modern vintage that added nothing of value. Many visitors over the past century had scratched their names and initials into the walls. Such senseless mutilation.

As I descended the pyramid, I passed Julio and the crowd on the way up. I considered temporarily joining Julio's posse to get the benefit of his lecturing, but then thought better of it. I opted instead to rely upon a guidebook authored by a leading archeologist, Michael Coe. He and his teams had spent several years excavating in Tikal, and his English read much better than Julio's sounded. I cut diagonally across the grassy plaza, aiming for the complex of buildings comprising the North Acropolis. By now other groups were being led on tours. I could hear fragments of Spanish from a couple of the groups and bits of German from another.

Along the northern edge of the plaza stretched two rows of upright stelae, like unconnected fenceposts. Many were accompanied at their base by a stone "altar," the size and shape of a hassock. Some of the stelae were plain, just blank slabs of limestone (or, in some cases, dolomite). If a stela bore carvings, its altar did also. Unlike the other stelae we had passed on the trail, these monuments were open to view. I noticed that many of the monuments were damaged, and not merely from the normal erosion processes. Chunks were missing, and some of the human figures depicted appeared to have been defaced. Per the guidebook, the mutilations were deliberate. When a ruler died, his stela was often "killed." Unlike the Egyptian pyramids, these monuments were not meant to endure throughout the ages — at least not so far as the survivors were concerned once the honored ruler or priest was dead. The carved stelae originally contained the date of construction, depicted as a series of glyphs together with the Mayan numerical system of bars and dots. Some of these dates were now either missing or worn away. The latest detectable date on a stela here was 869 A.D. When new, these stelae were brightly decorated. Archeologists have found traces of red paint. What was amazing about all of these Mayan structures was not just their complexity and intensity but the fact that they had all been cut and shaped with stone (and sometimes bone) tools! Metal tools were unknown in the Mayan world. We in the so-called modern world often tend to underestimate the capacities of the so-called primitive peoples.

I clambered over the extensive North Acropolis, set on a platform encompassing two and a half acres that was elevated above the Great Plaza. In the forested background, three spider monkeys picked their way through the network of branches, keenly aware of nearby human presence. These buildings over which I roamed were merely the outer layer of a series of earlier constructions superimposed one upon the other like Russian dolls. The Maya routinely erected buildings directly over existing structures. At times the consumed buildings were partially destroyed, by design. Archeologists have discovered at least a dozen earlier versions of the Acropolis. Remnants of some 100 buildings were still ensconced within the complex, some dating as far back as 200 B.C. Coe's crews had found evidence of even older habitation: charcoal from fires that glowed in 600 B.C. Parts of the Acropolis have been restored; parts were still badly eroded or damaged. The original polychromed stuccoed façades have been worn off. Much of the original grandeur of the Acropolis has passed into history, leaving ample fodder for the imagination.

The visible superstructures of the Acropolis also hid previous development. Modern excavations have revealed two earlier platforms, one atop the other, and tombs. One, apparently of a priest, also held nine of his retainers who accompanied him into the afterlife, as did some turtles and a crocodile. The tomb contained pigmented ceramics in the style of Teotihuacán, Tikal's neighbor from the Valley of Mexico to the north. This could be evidence of a cultural link between the two powerful cities, though Teotihuacán was in decline during the latter part of Tikal's Classic Period.

Another temple had been excavated sufficiently to reveal two prior Russian-doll temples, each now partly visible. The outer shell of temple, still suffering the ravages of time despite extensive restoration, was mounted on a pyramid. In better days, the entire structure had been brightly decorated and reached skyward the equivalent of eleven stories. Built around 600 A.D., it predated Temples I and II by a century. Two tour groups had caught up with me and were pouring over the complex, so I moved on, pausing at the Great

Plaza to take a last look back at the Acropolis. From my wide-angled perspective, I could take in and appreciate the widespread sculpturing that adorned the pyramid. The temple itself was embellished by large, fantastic masks. The stairs, providing access to the underlying platform, were flanked by monstrous stone heads bedecked with ear spools, intertwined with stone serpents. Symbolism played a large role in Mayan society.

I made my way past Temple I, dodging the stream of sightseers climbing and descending the structure, to a small ball court just south of the temple. The ballgame is one of the criteria that define not only the Maya but Mesoamerican cultures generally. It even spread up into the prehistoric American Southwest. Today various forms of the game are still played in parts of Mexico. In the ball court before me, two walls, each with a sloping bench that faced the opposite wall, formed the lateral boundaries of the rectangular court, which was open at the ends.

The Maya inherited the game from their Olmec forebears, who developed it as long ago as 1500 B.C. The game played a far greater role in Mayan life than does, say, professional football in ours. At stake in an NFL game is a chance to be at the next Super Bowl game without having to buy a ticket. And bragging rights for the fans. But for the Maya, elite and hoi polloi alike, the ballgame had immense cosmic and religious significance. The movement of the ball across the court was a metaphor for the sun's movements across the heavens. The dynamics of ball movement and player interaction, as well as the game's outcome itself, all had a vital effect upon such concepts such as creation and death, fertility and warfare.

I sat on one of the sloping, stone benches, gazing onto the playing field, trying to conjure up images of long-gone players struggling against each other as hundreds of spectators cheered them on. The players of the Mayan game wore protective padding, generally on their hips and knees, to knock a solid-rubber ball back and forth. Like today's sport of soccer, hands were not allowed to contact the ball. The game, involving two teams each usually consisting of from one to six players, could endure for days and was a highly ceremonial affair. Woe be it to the losing team, for those players didn't have the luxury of retreating to a locker room for a hot shower and a rubdown while licking their wounds and contemplating next week's game. More likely, the losers were subjected to a career-ending penalty — decapitation!

Beyond the ball court to the south, lay another complex of restored ruins. The Central Acropolis engulfed some four acres on the southern perimeter of the Great Plaza. The conglomerate was a blend of low-lying masonry buildings, one to three stories tall, often with multiple rooms, grouped around half a dozen courtyards. Stairways and passages tied everything together. The buildings in this Acropolis were referred to as "palaces," though their function was as yet undetermined. Speculation held that priests and other elites resided here periodically, or that the structures served administrative functions. Michael Coe, in a dated book, took the middle ground: "It is felt that the best explanation is one of duality of residence and administration."

In going through the palaces, I again encountered the tall, narrow rooms spanned by the corbel arch. Some exterior walls were generously cut with windows, allowing sunlight to reflect into the white-plastered rooms. Long, knee-high, stone benches grew out of the walls in some of the rooms. I plopped down on a couple of them. They were comfortable enough to sit on, for a while anyway. They might also have doubled as beds, though I couldn't imagine spending a night on one — at least not without a mattress, a thick one.

From one of the windows I caught sight of Julio rounding up his charges. He was yelling something in English and then in Spanish, neither of which I could make out. But his hand gestures were clear: it was lunchtime. We all trooped back to the dining hall at the Lodge for a midday repast. Some of our group opted for a siesta. Julio seemed anxious to join them. But there was a handful of us who wanted back into the site, so Julio's nap would have to wait. I didn't actually need Julio to lead me around since I had an informative guidebook replete with a detailed site map, but I did need him to get me back through the entrance.

Once in, I was on my own again. I made my way back to the Great Plaza to orient myself, then headed west for another huge pyramid, Temple III, 180 feet tall. Also known as the Temple of the Jaguar Priest, it was erected early in the Ninth Century. There's something about tall buildings that beckons me to climb them. As a sixth grader on our graduation bus tour of historic Boston, I led the charge up the Bunker Hill Monument. Many years later, as an adult, I scaled the inside of the Washington Monument while visiting the city on an archeology seminar.

Steps now led me to the temple on top of the pyramid. No one else was around at the moment, which suited me just fine. There were only two rooms, corbelled like the others I had visited here. A wooden lintel, with faded but discernible carvings, spanned one doorway. A standing figure, splendidly attired in jaguar-skin garments and a massive, ornate headdress that engulfed his head and flowed down his back, took center stage. He held a staff in one hand, perhaps a badge of office, and a three-pronged knife in the other, perhaps a sacrificial device. Two other figures, smaller and plainly dressed, flanked the main dignitary like janizaries. They were relegated to the edge of the scene, obviously signifying their relative lack of importance. This lintel gave the pyramid its more colorful appellation.

Human sacrifice was an integral part of Mayan life, a relatively recent revelation. For more than a century, it had been thought that the Maya were a peaceful lot, keeping to themselves within their city-states. The graphic murals discovered, a few decades ago, at the ancient Mayan city of Bonampak forever dispelled that delusion. In vivid color, dejected captives from a neighboring city were depicted staring at their bloody fingertips, their fingernails apparently having been ripped out. Others captives had already been decapitated.

I made my way back down the Temple III and followed a causeway that led westward toward an even higher pyramid a ten-minute walk away. At 212 feet in height, Temple IV was the highest standing structure in the prehistoric New World (although there is evidence that the Pyramid of the Sun at Teotihuacán may have been slightly higher, but its summit temple was now long gone). The spire of Temple IV was surely one of those I saw poking through the canopy on the flight in. So massive was this structure that 250,000 cubic yards went into its construction. Even today the surrounding grounds were pockmarked with quarries from where the construction materials were taken.

From the pyramid's summit I had a commanding view in all directions despite the pervasive mat of dense foliage. Searching eastward, I readily spotted the eroded roof comb of Temple III rising from a gap in the interlocking branches. Farther east I could make out the tops of Temples I and II. A jumble of a skyline to the southeast represented the South Acropolis. Beyond it loomed the summit of Temple V, another giant whose tip I had seen from the plane. I wouldn't have time for it today, perhaps tomorrow before the flight out.

Two doorways to the temple were once spanned by intricately carved lintels. Sad to say, they were now in a Swiss museum. Hieroglyphic inscriptions on the lintels dated to 741 A.D. All Guatemala wound up with was an epoxy cast of one of the lintels for its national museum. I made my way back to the Great Plaza just in time to join Julio's group for the hike back to the Lodge.

After washing up and changing clothes, I rendezvoused with the group at the mess hut. Over a hot meal of familiar vegetables and strange meat (I didn't ask), some of us got acquainted. Rebecca, a vivacious twenty-something stewardess from California, and I shared our peregrinations of the day. It was her first trip to any type of archeological site. She was overwhelmed by the magnitude of the experience. This would not be her last such site, she assured me. Randy, a laid-back, longhaired "naturalist" in his mid-thirties from Colorado, joined the conversation. He was more interested in the wildlife and ecology of the park than in the Mayan features, though he had an "interest" in archeology.

Randy's trained eyes and ears had detected a myriad of bird types, which he rattled off by common name as well as by genus and species, all of which went right by me. He had also seen monkeys, several groups of them, he claimed, and a coati-mundi — a long-nosed relative of the raccoon. He was hoping to spot, or at least hear, a jaguar before we flew out the next day. Best chance of that, he said, was at night. Rebecca piped in that she'd rather not have a jaguar skulking around our camp. That wouldn't happen, Randy said. Jaguars would avoid a noisy human settlement.

The discussion switched to the Great Plaza. Randy suggested offhandedly that it would be exciting to stroll around the plaza and climb its pyramids at night, without guides and sightseers. Rebecca and I casually nodded in agreement. Our positive responses, mild though they were, fueled Randy's crescendoing enthusiasm. His idea suddenly became a plan, to sneak into the park under the cover of darkness that very evening. The scheme was starting to appeal to me, and to Rebecca. Randy seemed as though he'd go for almost anything that had an air of illegality to it, purely for the sake of an adventure. He had graduated college and drifted through a smorgasbord of jobs, none of which held his interest. Problem was he couldn't land a worthwhile job within his field of study with only a bachelor's degree. There was an open offer to work as a park ranger, but that wouldn't do. It wasn't "scientific enough." Randy sought something "more challenging." For that, he'd have to return to academia and earn a doctorate, something he'd "eventually get around to." Looking around to be sure we weren't overheard, we three co-conspirators hatched our plan. We'd meet later and sneak off into the bush.

At the appointed hour, we met back at the dining hall and set off for a supposedly leisurely stroll in the woods. The park was officially closed, and a guard was hanging around the entrance. We simply made our way along the perimeter of the park until we were out of sight of the guard, then stole our way in. It was easy. We cut through the brush hoping to come across a trail. There were lots of noises in the dark. Rebecca kept tapping Randy. Could that be a jaguar? Nope. I was more concerned with snakes, since I could barely see the ground over which I was carefully stepping. But for the moon, now almost full, it would have been pitch dark. There were small open spots in the canopy that formed oases of moonlight. Our journey took us from one dimly lit patch to another, like connecting the dots. After half an hour of groping through a dark, alien world, we stumbled upon the very trail that had taken us in and out of the park earlier.

There was not another soul around, though animal life abounded along our route. There were many calls, mostly monkeys according to Randy. Even I could pick out the booming basso profundo of the howlers. There were cat-like calls and bird-like shrieks and an occasional squeal, but nothing that sounded like a jaguar. Which suited Rebecca just fine. There were branches twitching and leaves rustling off to the sides of the trail, so we knew we had company. But we didn't spot a single creature amidst all that foliage. The darkness hid them well, at least from our eyes. No doubt the night-adapted predators (and prey) saw, and otherwise sensed, an entire world almost invisible to us. In our evolutionary climb culminating in a highly convoluted brain capable of abstract thought, we have abandoned much contact with the outside world through our senses. We do possess, it is true, a remarkable eye, better than most organisms that are capable of capturing light impulses. We are a visual species. But even here, at our best sense, we are deficient compared to many of our vertebrate cousins. Besides lacking keen night vision, our visual acuity lags behind, say, the eagle. I have read that if an eagle only had 20-20 vision, it would be extinct.

Light was being reflected up into the branches ahead. We were approaching a large clearing. The Great Plaza, its milky temples and palaces and pyramids bathed in pearly moonlight and accented with stark shadows, loomed before us like an apparition. I almost expected it to dissolve at any moment. We stood spellbound at the edge of the clearing, still hidden by trees and darkness, taking it all in silently. The plaza was vacant, not another soul around. We scanned the tree line of the plaza's perimeter, what we could see of it. We indeed had this all to ourselves.

The plaza, and its surrounding structures, at once beckoned us and repelled us. Its mystery, its magnificence, its power drew us to it. But those same attractive forces stayed our approach. It was as though we were about to violate hallowed ground, like sneaking into a Buddhist temple. Our plan only took us this far. From here we would be improvising. In hushed tones we debated our options. We quickly reached a consensus: we would make straight for the Temple of the Giant Jaguar, our primary goal, then decide upon our next step.

Taking one last scan of the area, we broke out of our cover and strode purposefully into the Great Plaza, past Temple II on our right, past the North Acropolis fronted by the double row of stelae and altars on our left, across the grassy field to the foot of the Temple of the Giant Jaguar.

"Ladies before gentlemen," Randy said to Rebecca, as he gestured toward the stairway.

Rebecca hesitated, then guided herself along the low chain that ran up the steps to the top. Randy and I eagerly followed in turn. At

TEMPLE OF THE GIANT JAGUAR

the summit we took another quick look around, then ducked into the temple. A shaft of moonlight managed to make it into the outer room, providing enough illumination to keep us from bumping into one another. It also created creepy shadows on the wall as we moved.

"This is spooky," Rebecca said. "I'm going back outside."

Randy and I continued inward, as far as the light allowed, then turned back to join Rebecca. She was seated on the top step just out the front doorway, wistfully gazing off into the distance. Randy and I plopped down, one on each side of her. Rebecca said she had never experienced anything like this before. As a stewardess, she had done lots of travelling, albeit only domestically. Being city born and bred, Rebecca had always been attracted to the big cities with their fancy restaurants, fashionable boutiques, and upscale nightclubs. Not that she personally spent a great deal of money on such pursuits, since she was quite attractive and did date frequently. For her, there was no need to stray from city life, which offered all she could possibly want.

Randy was just the opposite. He couldn't wait to get away from a metropolis. He did acknowledge that a big city provided at least one useful feature: an airport, so he could quickly get out of a city and far away from it. He took pride in announcing that he didn't own a single suit or a necktie. He was truly in his element here in the jungle.

We sat there at the top of the stairs, amidst the moonlight and shadows and temples and pyramids, serenaded from every direction by the conflicting sounds of the jungle at night, trying to absorb it all. I strained to visualize what I would have encountered had I sat here 1200 years earlier. The buildings totally intact and brightly painted with magnificent, undamaged roof combs stretching above the jungle canopy. The beehive of activity throughout the plaza, a city going about its daily business of staying alive. A population striving to feed itself, tending to its religious needs, carrying on warfare, all within a rigid, highly stratified society commanded by chiefs and priests. How different that life and society would have been from what we are so accustomed to in the hustle and bustle of the technologically advanced, but socially deprived, Twentieth Century.

Fleets of clouds sailed across the moon, playing with the light. Despite the obvious decay of the buildings, unused for centuries, the plaza retained the presence of its former occupants, like a stage set with its props all in place, waiting only for the actors to come on stage from the wings and play out the next scene. Randy sensed it, too.

"This is a very mystical experience," he said.

A strange cry suddenly pierced our reverie — a loud, snarling growl from just beyond Temple II, on the far side of the plaza.

"That's your jaguar," Randy smiled to Rebecca.

She gasped and looked at him incredulously. "You're kidding," she said, knowing he was not.

"Nope."

"What do we do now?" Her voice was tinged with terror.

"Nothing. He'll move on. He's not interested in us."

"Are you sure?"

"Yup. Jaguars don't eat people."

I had doubts about that one, but I suspected Randy was simply trying to allay Rebecca's fears.

"But what if this one doesn't know that?" Rebecca asked seriously.

"Don't worry," I chimed in. "We'll just wait him out." I didn't want to admit that I, too, was nervous. After all, that bloody cry emanated from just about where we would pick up the trail to lead us out of the park.

The call came again, softer, more of a throat rumble, and farther away. Perhaps the cat was moving on. A minute later we heard voices, seemingly coming down the trail toward the plaza.

"It's the guards," said Randy excitedly. "They're making their rounds. We gotta get out of here."

We all rose and quickly started down the stairs. Rebecca hesitated. "What about the jaguar?"

"To hell with him!" said Randy, his voice starting to raise. "It's the guards I'm worried about."

"Maybe we should just wait awhile to be sure it's gone."

Randy and I were nearing the bottom of the stairs. Rebecca was hanging back. The voices were getting closer, probably not far from Temple II by now.

"C'mon," Randy said urgently to Rebecca, extending his hand to her.

"I'm scared," she said anxiously, still paused halfway up the stairway.

It occurred to me that if we could hear the guards, they might very well be able to hear us. "Keep it d-o-w-n!" I urged softly.

"Let's get out of here," Randy said to Rebecca, straining to keep his voice low.

"But I'm scared."

"Do you want to get arrested?"

"No, but I don't want to get attacked by a jaguar either."

"Come on, Rebecca," I finally blurted out, trying to keep my voice low as I motioned her downward. "Let's get out of here! The jaguar's gone. The guards scared it off."

That worked. Rebecca hurried down the steps. We scurried across the plaza to the edge of the bushes on the opposite side of Temple II from where we could hear the voices. We were safely under cover when two uniformed guards, still oblivious to our presence, casually strolled into the plaza, their flashlights scanning the buildings of the North Acropolis, illuminating the shadows. They headed for the complex, still blabbing away. When they ducked out of sight on the far side of the Acropolis, that was our cue.

We scooted around the backside of Temple II, found the trail, and walked rapidly down it. Rebecca kept scanning the trees on both sides, keeping a lookout for the jaguar, no doubt. We didn't hear from it again, though that was no guarantee it wasn't still around, watching us.

We made it back to the Lodge without further incident. That night I lay awake thinking of the plaza and its people. I imagined Rebecca lay awake thinking about the jaguar.

* * *

In the morning, at breakfast, Rebecca plopped down beside me, a tray of food from the buffet line in her hands. As I stuffed a forkful of eggs into my mouth, she asked if I was scared last night.

"Where?"

"At the plaza?"

"Oh, you mean where the guards were coming through. Yeah, I was nervous. I didn't care to get caught."

"Come on. You know what I mean," she said, as she loaded up her fork.

I continued to play dumb. "No. What?"

"You know I'm talking about the jaguar," she said, chewing away.

"Oh that. Kind of neat, wasn't it?"

Rebecca stopped chewing, while her fork hung in midair. "Neat? You gotta be kidding. I was scared to death."

"Really," I offered weakly, as I nonchalantly continued eating.

"Don't give me that. You were scared, too."

"Yeah, of the guards."

She watched me for a couple of seconds, her fork still suspended above her tray, hoping, I guess, to see me crack a smile. But I remained poker-faced. "It was no big deal," I said. "We were in no real danger."

Rebecca shook her head in disbelief and resumed eating. I finished first and left her there as I had to pick up some things at my hut before we set off for the ruins again.

I hooked up with Julio's group to get into the park. Randy was off by himself somewhere, wandering through the woods, checking out the wildlife. Rebecca was part of the group. On the hike to the park she asked me again if I had been scared of the jaguar.

"Naw. In fact, I hope we run across one this morning," I lied.

"I sure don't!"

Once at the Great Plaza, I broke off on my own. I invited Rebecca to join me, but she opted to stay with the group. Safety in numbers, I guess. I worked my way to the East Plaza, lying east of the North Acropolis and northeast of Temple I. It encompassed some five acres or so and was plastered throughout. Two causeways linked the plaza to the rest of city. The center of the plaza was consumed by the "Market Place," a quadrangle of long, low buildings with a network of passages and stairs that led into an inner rectangular courtyard framed on each side by a low building. The appellation was just a guess, though its location would have made it readily accessible.

That Tikal once had ties with the Valley of Mexico to the north, particularly with the city Teotihuacán, was made strikingly clear by one building I happened upon. It was a small and low structure, made even lower by the ravages of time. Most of its superstructure had been reduced to rubble. Normally, it would not have merited much attention given the limited time I had to explore the city. But this building's foundation walls were what gave away its pedigree. Along the building's front, on either side of the entrance stairway, was the unmistakable pattern of talud-tablero architecture I had witnessed in Teotihuacán. Set within that pattern was the goggle-eyed stare that I had seen at the Temple of the Feathered Serpent in Teotihuacán, here repeated lineally along the front wall. There was nothing in the guidebook as to its date and use. I could only wonder.

My watch warned me that my time here was nearing a close. Already the plane which would ferry me back to Guatemala City was winging its way over the jungle, bring in a fresh group. I hoofed it back to the Jungle Lodge to pack up before lunch, after which I would be boarding the plane. I caught up with Rebecca and bid her farewell. She was staying another night, as was Randy and a couple of others. I managed to catch him after lunch and shake his hand goodbye, as I was rushing to catch the plane. We chuckled about Rebecca and the jaguar.

STELA

On the plane ride back to Guatemala City, I pondered the demise of Tikal, as perhaps amateur archeologists a thousand years
from now might ponder the demise of, say, Los Angeles. How did
this magnificent metropolis ever come to be abandoned? It seemed
to have had everything going for it. A lush jungle environment teem-
ing with plant and animal life for the taking. Ample water, made
more available by the construction of reservoirs. A captivating and
reassuring system of cosmic and religious beliefs, replete with deities and heroes and myths. The security of strong leaders preserving a highly stratified and organized society. The building and maintaining of magnificent pyramids and temples to occupy and coa-
lesce the workforce and give it a sense of accomplishment. An occasional war with a neighboring city to rally the troops. So what
happened?

Though Tikal was no Garden of Eden, it did hang together, more
or less, for several centuries, like other lowland cities of the Mayan
Classic Period. There were intercity raids, and even wars, to be sure.
Armies captured the warriors and leaders of their neighbors, hauling them back home as so much booty, to be humiliated and eventually sacrificed. Enemy chiefs were prized sacrificial captives. Yet
these cities endured, and even thrived, at times. It all started to
unravel around 800 A.D. Over the course of the next century, in
city after city, the erection of stelae ceased, the construction of public
buildings ground to a halt, populations declined, all sure signs that
the leadership had weakened, that times had inexorably changed.
The social and political fabric of the culture was in tatters.

The decline of the Classic Period for the lowland Maya did not
sweep over the cities in a single stroke. Some population centers
became abandoned while others survived with varying degrees of
success. For a time anyway. But eventually the society-destroying
epidemic, whatever its cause, claimed them all. One city after
another was abandoned to the jungle, their populaces drifting
off in smaller groups to lead simpler lives. Complex society had
run its course for them. Perhaps the cities had been too successful, taking more from the environment than it could continue
to offer century after century. What had allowed populations to
expand when managed properly, may have caused them to con-
tract when abused. Which might have led to civil strife which the

leaders and institutions could not contain.

There was a later renaissance of Mayan culture, in the Yucatan Peninsula of Mexico that endured for several hundred years before finally succumbing to the Spanish invaders. The conquistadors not only decimated the Mayan populations, but their culture as well. Though the Mayan populations have recovered, their system of hieroglyphic writing was lost for centuries, thanks in large part to the burning by the Spaniards of the Mayan codices (books), only a handful of which survive. It's only been in the past few decades that Mayan scholars from North America, Europe and Russia have deciphered most of the hieroglyphic symbols, which are now unreadable by the native Mayan descendants who still populate the region. The Maya were forced by their conquerors to adopt Christian religious practices, while their own religious beliefs and ceremonies were suppressed. Yet many Mayan traditions, religious included, have survived, often blended perforce with Western customs and practices. But the glory of Mayan civilization has passed into history.

CANAL BUILDERS OF THE SONORAN DESERT

For 1700 years, a culture subsisted, even thrived, in the surprisingly fertile Sonoran Desert, tapping the bounty offered by the generous environment and supplementing its diet with cultivated crops. The Hohokam, whose epicenter was the Phoenix Basin covering 4000 square miles in south-central Arizona, siphoned off immense quantities of water from the nearby Gila and Salt Rivers through a network of canals and ditches. They were able to divert the flowing waters to their irrigated fields up to ten miles from the rivers. The main canals, up to fifty feet wide, were painstakingly dug with hand-held sticks. An army of laborers monotonously chipped at the ground, scooping away the dirt by the basketful. It took years to tunnel even a single main canal. And there were miles upon miles of these channels. Once excavated, the canals required constant maintenance. Truly a Herculean task.

But the rivers' life-giving water allowed the Hohokam to raise such staples as corn, squash, beans, cotton and tobacco to augment the seeds, fruits, vegetables and game their habitat otherwise provided.

During their tenure, from 300 B.C. to 1450 A.D., their technology expanded and their numbers swelled. They emerged from their crude wood-and-brush pithouses to dwell in solid adobe structures. Customs evolved. Ball courts, reminiscent of those in Mesoamerica, came into vogue. Cremation of the dead, unknown in the Southwest, became popular.

So who were these interesting people? From whence had they originated? What caused their florescence? Why did their culture decline? What became of them? Joan and I headed for the Southwest to find out. We signed up with another Crow Canyon Archaeological Center field seminar.

Once we students were settled into our hotel in Scottsdale, Arizona, we rendezvoused in a meeting room. Over drinks, the twenty-six of us got acquainted. Then, one of the scholars who would be accompanying us throughout the trip, Dr. Bernard "Bunny" Fontana, presented an overview of the Hohokam. Ever jovial and friendly, Bunny, in his fifties I would guess, would have made a perfect shopping mall Santa Claus, though he would have needed a pillow stuffed under his belt. He made it obvious that there were not the volumes of data on the Hohokam that were available for the Anasazi. Hohokam archeology lagged behind at least four decades.

Millennia before the birth of Christ, bands of hunters and gatherers roamed Arizona, part of a continent-wide Archaic culture. Their houses (huts, actually) were quickly erected once the building materials had been marshaled. Vertical wooden beams provided the initial framework. Smaller beams and brush were packed between the beams. The roof was thatched. Mud mortar was dabbed on for waterproofing. These Archaic peoples directed rainwater onto their small plots to raise corn and squash. They carried spears for hunting, knives for cutting. Their dead were buried in a curled position. These Indians, in the southern desert, were termed Cochise. Some archeologists considered them the direct ancestors of the Hohokam, a position subject to lively debate. But for sure, the Hohokam evolved through a succession of periods: Pioneer, Colonial, Sedentary and Classic.

* * *

My search for answers continued the next morning when our group rode into adjacent Phoenix, which has unfortunately been constructed over many Hohokam villages. One site that didn't get totally bulldozed was Pueblo Grande, presently owned by the City of Phoenix. Remnants of a large platform mound remained, but the ball courts and most of the habitation areas were invisible, either paved over, unexcavated or backfilled. The mound, in a sorry state of disrepair, provided only a hint of the culture that once inhabited the area. The mound once occupied an area about the size of a football field. Ruins were built upon ruins, generation after generation. The original inhabitants controlled the nearby Salt River, plugging into its water as though it were an intravenous line. Some forty platform mounds were erected, spaced every three miles along the prehistoric irrigation canals of the Salt and Gila Rivers.

This platform mound at Pueblo Grande was the hub of a sprawling village that once encompassed an area of over a mile in diameter, occupied by some 1500 persons.

A paved trail meandered up to the top of the truncated mound, wound between the ruins there, and passed down the other side to ground level again. I paused at the crumbling walls in the southeast corner of the platform. In one room wall I noticed a hodgepodge of building materials — chunks of hardened caliche, river cobble, granite and other blocks, all set into a mud mortar. Breaking with the normal architecture, a corner doorway, facing northeast, had been cut into the room. There was another door on the south wall. At sunrise during the summer solstice and at sunset during winter solstice, a curious alignment occurred. A shaft of light reached from one doorway to the other, signaling the midpoint of the solar annual cycle. At least a basic familiarity with astronomy was a must for the Hohokam, as with virtually all agrarian cultures, to accurately gauge the planting seasons.

Bunny pointed out that even a few feet of elevation provided a commanding view of the flat countryside. To the northeast I could make out the oval impression of a ball court, one of three known on the site. The court was built and used between 1050 to 1200 A.D. Once the ballgames fell out of favor, the people started tossing their junk into the court's depression, a convenient dump site.

I continued along the paved path. No clouds were to be seen. Only the wispy trails of overhead jets marred an otherwise clear, pastel-blue sky. An adobe wall, three feet thick and eight feet high, once completely surrounded the mound. Little evidence of the wall remained. Another set of rooms, built around courtyards, contained interesting features and articles: kitchens with large cooking pots, wind screens, caches of obsidian nodules, shell and stone beads, piles of stone axes, quartz crystals and pottery from Indians to the north. This might have been an area where feasts were prepared, or tools made, or jewelry fashioned.

Bunny pointed out the obvious: "Pueblo Grande was clearly a preeminent place for the Hohokam. The time and labor they invested indicates it was not an ordinary village. The location and size of the site and the presence of the platform mound and the ball courts point to this importance."

Although Pueblo Grande exposed me to only a fragment of Hohokam life, it was a start, fueling my curiosity.

My thoughts ran back to Bunny's orientation discussion that traced the development of the Hohokam. During the initial phase, the Pioneer Period (300 B.C. to 500 A.D.), the pithouses grew larger, villages formed. Pottery became a mainstay sometime before 200 A.D., probably the result of Mesoamerican influence to the south. The local potters gathered clay from selected sources on the desert floors or in the adjacent mountains. They mixed sand and micaceous schist with the clay to prevent shrinking or cracking during the drying and firing processes.

Like their Anasazi neighbors to the north and east, the Hohokam never invented the potter's wheel. Instead, they fashioned their vessels essentially from coils. Thin ropes of rolled clay were spiraled, one atop another, to form the vessel. The walls were thinned and smoothed by scraping with a pottery fragment, gourd or stone.

Other pots were shaped from thicker coils, to be smoothed by the paddle-and-anvil technique. The potter would place one hand, clutching a stone "anvil," inside the forming pot. The other hand, grasping the wooden paddle, would slap at the clay as the potter worked her way around the circumference of the pot. The anvil acted as a backing to the smacks from the paddle. Thus was the clay thinned, smoothed and strengthened.

The vessels were fired in pits using mesquite wood, which yielded a high temperature. The pits permitted air to have free access to the pots, allowing for complete oxidation of the iron in the clay. The pots generally ran the gamut of various shades of brown. Some bore incised sets of lines on their exteriors.

* * *

The following day found us on our way to Casa Grande, a set of impressive Classic Period ruins located near Coolidge, Arizona. We rode in a van driven by Larry, an affable sixtyish volunteer for the trip. As soon as the seminar ended, Larry would have to hop on a plane and hurry back to his office in New York, where he practiced psychiatry. Bunny rode shotgun.

"Was their society hierarchical?" I asked Bunny.

"I think someone had to be in charge because of all the irrigation projects."

Bunny explained that "Early Pima" referred to the residents of the Gila River area from 1450 to 1700 A.D., when the Spaniards found the present-day Pima. The Pima Indians have replaced the Hohokam as residents along the Gila River. The Papago Indians now occupied territory the Hohokam inhabited in the desert south of the Gila River. But Bunny wasn't ready to state that the Pima and Papago followed the Hohokam in an unbroken lineage. There was an interrupted history and absence of data during this period. In fact, Bunny said, we didn't even know what the Hohokam called themselves. "Hohokam" is a Pima Indian word for "those who have gone" or "all used up."

After riding southeastward through the Sonoran Desert, we wheeled into the parking lot of the site. An archeologist, Jerry Howard, ushered us to a covered set of benches for his briefing.

Casa Grande was the largest Hohokam site on the Gila River, he explained. Over Jerry's shoulder the massive shape of the adobe Big House loomed in the background. Its eroding four-story walls were now protected by a modern, four-legged, metallic monster of a canopy, which bore a striking resemblance to the above-water portion of an oil-drilling platform. Jerry mentioned that there were three main features at the site. One, of course, was the centerpiece, Big House, after which the site was named. Then there were the plat-

BIG HOUSE AT CASA GRANDE

form mounds. And a ball court. The structures at Casa Grande were generally oriented along a north-south axis, he noted.

With that brief introduction, Jerry led us into the compound. First stop was the Big House, the main attraction. This structure, completed in the early Fourteenth Century, was now the tallest and most massive known in the Hohokam world, with dimensions of eighty by sixty feet. Its mud walls, four feet thick at the base of the lower floor, have been partially reclaimed by the elements over the ensuing centuries.

I moved in for a closer look. The tan, sun-baked, mud walls had been intentionally infiltrated with pebbles. I didn't see any sign that individual adobe bricks were used. Jerry explained that the mud was packed with caliche, which comprised much of the sub-surface dirt in the area.

Jerry noticed puzzled looks when he mentioned "caliche." "Does everybody know what caliche is?" he asked, scanning the audience.

Most of us shook our heads vacantly.

"It is a calcium carbonate material. It is formed by rain transporting minerals down through the soil, which brings particular carbonates down, and they start forming a hardpan under the soil. If you dig anywhere around the Phoenix area, as many gardeners find to their dismay, you find this hard, white layer buried under the soil."

In what is called coursed-adobe architecture, this caliche mud was piled two feet high and shaped to form the bottom of a wall. When it dried, another two-foot horizontal segment was added to the top. And so it went until the wall reached the planned height. More than one wall could be erected simultaneously. Thus was the entire monolith constructed — no bricks or blocks. Erosion has exposed the seams between the two-foot bands. I was surprised that the building wasn't worn completely down over the centuries by rainfall. Perhaps the infrequency of the rains in this part of the country explained it. No doubt, though, the structure required constant maintenance when occupied.

Some of the original timbers used in Big House's construction were still in place. The larger beams, from juniper, fir and pine trees, had to be hauled in from fifty miles away — a prodigal undertaking considering the Hohokam never had the wheel or beasts of burden! The bottom floor of the building had originally been filled in, such that the first floor actually occupied the second story. The wooden ceiling of the one story doubled as the floor of the next higher story. These wooden beams spanned the width of each room. Wood-like, dried-out "ribs" from saguaro cacti were placed atop of and perpendicular to these. Then reeds were set on this framework. The floor was capped off with a layer of caliche.

A horizontal groove was obvious partway up one exposed interior wall. I asked Jerry about it.

"It's where the floor once joined the wall."

The Hohokam smoothed and plastered the insides of the walls, which handiwork was evident now despite nature's hand of erosion.

I turned the corner of the rectangular building. Set high in the west wall were two small "windows," at opposite ends of the wall. It was discovered that the circular window in the upper left portion of the wall aligned with the setting sun on the summer solstice (June 21st), the year's longest day. The square window on the upper right lined up every eighteen and one-half years with the setting moon at an extreme point in its cycle. Other doorways and windows aligned with the sun or moon during significant times of the year. Based upon these revelations, it appeared the building served in part as an observatory. The Hohokam may even have devised a calendar system based on the motions of the sun and moon.

The Big House formed the focal point of what was now labeled "Compound A," which had once been perimetered by caliche-mud walls. The remains of other smaller buildings were in place around the compound, which I guessed encompassed ten acres. In the open areas between the buildings, I could imagine the Hohokam going about their daily business over six centuries ago. People would be crossing from one building to another, stopping in the compound "square" to chat. Kids would be frolicking with one another, getting filthy in the dusty courtyards, dogs yapping at the excitement or just lying around. Men would be in the fields during crop season, or repairing adobe walls, or discussing social issues in the courtyard. Women would be forming baskets, weaving clothes, shaping pottery vessels, grinding corn, socializing, minding the smaller kids.

The Casa Grande community was far more extensive than just Compound A. It was spread across a square mile of the desert. There were other compounds, free-standing and separately walled, within the community.

Jerry led us out of Compound A, across the parking lot to the ball court, located on the perimeter of the community plaza, in the approximate center of the community. From the top of a short staircase, Joan and I scanned the fenced-off ball court, a pebble's toss away. The site hadn't been excavated, and no one was allowed any closer. To the untrained eye, the overgrown site was simply an oval depression, perhaps seventy-five-feet long. It certainly paled in comparison to some of the more impressive ball courts, which have been excavated throughout the Hohokam domain. In Snaketown, a site lying to the northwest, halfway to Phoenix, there was now excavated a large ball court on one side of a central plaza and a small court on another edge of the plaza. The larger court, an oval depression surrounded by earthen embankments, was 200-feet long and half as wide, encompassing about two-thirds the acreage as a modern football field.

The ball courts were a later development for the Hohokam. No courts were now known from the Pioneer Period. It was only during the following phase, the Colonial Period, that the courts appeared. The Hohokam modified the design of the courts from the flat rectangular form of Mesoamerica to an oval shape with slightly sloping floors. A rubber ball, almost three inches across, was uncovered at a Hohokam site in Arizona. The Hohokam game may have involved two opposing teams, as did the Mesoamerican games. Whatever their significance and rules, the ballgames were an integral part of Hohokam life. More than 200 Hohokam courts had thus far been discovered in Arizona. For reasons not clearly understood, the courts ceased to be built and maintained sometime during the Classic Period.

From the Casa Grande ball court, Jerry took us through a gate that normally blocked the public's access to the remainder of the extensive site. We followed single-file northward through the open brush to Compound B. This segment of the community at one time also had its separate retaining wall. But if Jerry hadn't pointed out its low-lying remnants, I never would have known one existed.

Jerry directed our attention to the compound's two platform mounds, overgrown for centuries with brush. These unexcavated, flat-topped structures contained several thousand cubic yards of fill. Early mounds throughout the Hohokam world were constructed from sterile desert soil capped with a layer of caliche plaster. These mounds were initially used for ceremonial purposes. Dances were held on them. In later centuries, buildings were generally set atop the mounds. Single-story adobe houses once sat on the platform mounds of Compound B. The conventional wisdom held that such structures were homes for elite, but Jerry wasn't convinced.

"There are a lot of changing ideas as to what these platform mounds were."

The ground surrounding the mounds was virtually paved with fragments of brownish-black pottery. The archeologists and tourists hadn't had the opportunity to make off with the potsherds. The sun-drenched terrain around the compound was dotted with the black skeletons of mesquite trees, which seemed misplaced in an otherwise verdurous landscape. Their grotesque, branching remains resembled giant pieces of driftwood stuck vertically into the ground, creating a fantastic, almost surreal, landscape. The park guide accompanying us explained that the water table had dropped precipitously in modern times, so the roots of the mesquite trees no longer reached the moisture.

Jerry said that such sites often contained compounds within compounds, which were divided into one or two "major areas." Each major area had a plaza with rooms bordering it that faced onto the plaza courtyard. People carried out many of their daily activities in these courtyards. Jerry mentioned something about "interactive residential groups of houses" as representing extended families.

Another characteristic of a compound with a platform mound was the location of the entrance, said Jerry. It was always situated in the center of the eastern wall.

"That entrance led into a major plaza, the largest open space inside the compound containing the mound."

Jerry continued. "These rooms are enormous. They could be used for people perhaps getting ready for rituals. These rooms are often connected to the public plaza by corridors. It's almost like this was a staging area, where people got ready to come out the corridor, and you can just imagine they come out dancing into the major plaza."

As we exited Compound B and followed a path into the brush, Bunny Fontana pointed out that trash mounds, accumulating debris over hundreds of years, yielded important artifacts. The people of Casa Grande dug pits to excavate caliche. The pits performed a dual role, later being filled with trash.

I strolled off into the bush to nose around on my own. The circle of canary-yellow fruit sitting atop a squat cactus caught my eye. The aptly named fishhook barrel-cactus, shaped like a barrel with a rounded top, was completely enclosed within a barbed wire of spines that curled inward at the tips. I stooped and photographed the cactus. I leaned in for a close-up of the ring of plum-shaped fruit. Too close. The cactus, living up to its name, snagged me. One of those vicious barbs ripped into my finger. It took a week to heal. For the native peoples, the flirt with a gash must have a cost of doing business, for the cactus was edible. Not only the fleshy, succulent fruit, but also the seeds, buds and flowers could be consumed.

For those with more extensive appetites, the pale green, pulpy stem could be cooked and eaten. No wonder the cactus needed weapons. In a pinch, the stem provided a reservoir of liquid. But you had to get by those spines!

Flanking Compound B were Compounds C and D. Ahead, to the north, lay Compound E. All were covered with brush and yet to be excavated.

Within only a few generations after its rise, Casa Grande, like other large Hohokam sites of the Classic Period, was abandoned. By the late Twelfth Century, public works projects were no longer undertaken here. Irrigation canals fells into disrepair. Trade routes collapsed. By the mid-Thirteenth Century, it was over. The populations throughout the Hohokam world fragmented and scattered into smaller groups. No one is sure why, though theories abound. In any case, when the Spaniards rode into town over three centuries ago, the Hohokam, as a cultural entity, had disappeared.

Their descendants may still be with us, however. The indigenous Pima Indians and the Papago Indians (Tohono O'odham) claim the Hohokam as their ancestors.

I thought back to Bunny's orientation. The Pioneer Period was followed by the Colonial Period (500 to 900 A.D.), which witnessed dramatic evolution. Canals were dug, so the inhabitants didn't have to rely solely upon rainwater for their crops and personal needs.

The Hohokam still resided in primitive pithouses, huts without windows that were perpetually in shadow during the day. Thus most activities took place outdoors. Under a shading ramada near the pithouse, the inhabitants went about their daily tasks of shaping pottery, grinding corn, weaving textiles, or preparing meals, the cooking being done over large pits.

Their villages became more complex. The Hohokam positioned their dwellings around a large central plaza. A higher level of social organization was emerging. People were working together more as a group. Public works projects become more involved.

The Hohokam expanded their production of clay figurines. Pottery, red-on-gray, became somewhat more colorful. Cotton had been introduced, providing a bonanza for the weavers.

As with the Anasazi and other peoples of the Southwest, the bow and arrow came to supplant the spear as the hunter's weapon of choice.

The Hohokam never developed a written language, but they did express themselves in their art, in which geometric designs were ubiquitous, many still undeciphered. Human forms were also favorite creative icons, as were birds and lizards, often depicted in stylized versions.

During the Ninth Century, the ball courts, a hallmark of the Mesoamerican cultures, proliferated. Though the games as played in pre-Columbian Mesoamerica may have passed the way of the stepped pyramid, they have left descendants, just as Latin has evolved into the Romance languages. Today, in parts of Mexico, evolved versions of the game abound.

Back into the three vans for the ride through the desert southeastward to Tucson. We passed flat terrain framed by low mountains in the distance on both sides of the road. This was nothing like any desert I ever imagined. When I envisioned a desert, I thought of the Sahara: barren dunes, blowing sand, oases, Arabs on camels. While I didn't expect to come across a camel caravan in the Sonoran, I counted on sand, more sand, and an occasional wind-tossed tumbleweed. But the Sonoran satisfies the definition of a desert only by its aridity, averaging less than ten inches of precipitation a year in a climate where moisture has a high evaporation rate. This young desert (10,000 years old) consumes 106,000 square miles of southern Arizona, southwestern California, Baja California, and the northeast coast of the Gulf of California, making it North America's third largest desert, behind the Chihuahuan and the Great Basin. But the subtropical Sonoran is unique among its counterparts in rainfall distribution. The Great Basin and Mojave (smallest of the four) receive precipitation from the west. This winter moisture, which may fall as snow, is steady, long lasting and blankets large areas. The Chihuahuan, to the east, gets none of this precipitation. Its rainfall sweeps in during the summer from the Gulf of Mexico to the east. The cloudbursts generally dump torrents of rain very quickly over localized areas, in stark contrast to the winter storms from the west. The Sonoran gets both! It thus has rainfall patterns in the summer and winter, with brief hiatuses between the two seasons. So it's not surprising that this so-called desert should be carpeted with greenery, and flowers. The Sonoran, though the domain of cacti, is a greenhouse. In the spring, parts of the desert blossom with a kaleidoscope of color.

We were climbing as we crossed Gates Pass in the Tucson Mountains. Fields of creosote bushes spread out from the road, running to the mountains. These shrubs prefer the low, flatlands in the basins between the myriad of short, discontinuous mountain chains of the Southwest. Their range does extend up the lower slopes of the mountains. Averaging three or four feet in height, this rounded, little bush is most useful. It will permeate the air after a rain shower with a resinous pungent aroma. The tiny leaves, which limit moisture loss, contain camphor and have antiseptic and antibiotic properties. Many desert peoples have brewed a creosote tea to treat a wide range of illnesses. Scale insects secrete lac on the creosote stems. The lac can be scraped off, heated and used as a waterproof sealer and adhesive.

With the increased elevation, the terrain became dotted, then saturated, with the tall saguaro cacti, which erupted boldly from the landscape. Their columnar configurations, randomly dispersed, reached above the trees and bushes. Their erect posture reminded me of silent sentinels, like the Queen's palace guards, watching over their domain. A saguaro's roots are shallow, fanning out a distance equal to its height. The individual plants maintained the proper distance from one another, not clustering together.

Like other cacti, the saguaro has developed strategies to cope with the desert's aridity. Its leaves have long since been modified into spines, which serve a triple function of reducing moisture loss, shielding some of the sun's rays from the stem (body), and protecting the plant from animal predation. The cactus also stores immense quantities of water. Waxes, that absorb solar radiation, will build up on the side of the cactus that generally faces the sun.

A fourth device I found most interesting. Although the saguaro lacks leaves, it needs to engage in photosynthesis to feed itself. It does this in the green stems. Plants exchange gases with the atmosphere via stomata. Most plants do it in the leaves. In the saguaro, these pinpoint pores cover the stems and allow the plant to expel oxygen while taking in carbon dioxide. The chloroplasts, which give the plant its green color, use sunlight to make the chemical conversion that produces the plant's food. But when the stomata are open, exchanging gases, moisture is lost. With most plants, it's not a problem. They open their stomata during the day, taking advantage of the sun's energy to undergo photosynthesis. The cacti can't afford to do this. They'd forfeit far too much precious water. So they make their food in two steps. They open their stomata at night, taking care of the gas exchange. The next day the stomata remain closed, but the solar radiation is absorbed. Thus, photosynthesis is completed. It's a tactic also utilized by such succulents as the yucca and the agave. Those clever cacti!

We pulled into the Sonoran Desert Museum in Tucson. Two other scholars, Suzanne Fish and her husband, Paul, joined us for the remainder of the seminar. Once inside the museum, Suzanne discussed the environment. Fortyish, with collar-length white hair, this ethnobotanist was associated with the Arizona State Museum in Tucson. Her soft voice didn't carry well outdoors, but she spoke authoritatively and with enthusiasm. We were partway up a slope of a basin, she said. This basin is typical of those in this Basin and Range Province, which lies between two sets of mountains, the Sierra Nevada on the west and the Rockies on the east.

"Most basins between the mountain chains are fifteen to twenty miles wide, sometimes thirty."

I peered beyond her, gauging the basin that unfurled before us and sloped to the distant mountains. The Province has valley floors at high elevations, often more than 4000 feet. The protruding mountain ranges had been erected through faulting. Most of the ranges have a north-south orientation, with peaks reaching 10,000 feet, and beyond.

"There are two places people tend to live in desert basins because of the presence of water," she continued. "People, of course, want to live along a river. It's easy to understand why. You can have irrigation."

She hesitated to let us digest that. "But with prehistoric settlements, and historic settlements to a large extent as well, you find people living at the base of mountains with no one living on the slope that leads down to the river."

She gestured into the distance.

"With mountains, you get an orographic effect for rainfall. It rains heavier in the mountains. The mountains catch all that water and it begins to run out in the drainages down toward the river. At the edge of the mountains is something we call pediment, which is dead rock that goes out beyond the mountains to some distance and keeps the water high near the surface. So the water actually runs in the drainages after a storm. The mountains have been shedding dirt and rock, and the basins have been filling for thousands of years. So the water begins to pass down beyond the pediment in the drainages. It sinks down to the porous basin fill, and it often doesn't run on the surface at all. Thus the people can't have access even though the water is draining down on the ground toward the river."

Suzanne went on to explain that there are two main vegetation zones in southern Arizona, which are demarcated by what she referred to as the "paloverde-saguaro association" at the boundary where the saguaros cease marching down the mountain slopes. The saguaros are joined by such pod-bearing trees as the mesquite, paloverde and ironwood. So there are edible cacti and leguminous trees in this zone.

Where the slope flattens into the valley floor, the creosote bushes and bursage take over on the fine-grained soil. Small game, such as rabbits and rodents, are available.

"Hunting is best, though, as you go uphill," Suzanne noted.

We were allowed several minutes to roam about the outdoor exhibits at the museum. One building on the looping trail was dedicated to the majestic saguaro. This cactus must be quite important, I mused, to warrant a building all to itself. Indeed it was — and still is — to the native peoples. And to the birds, animals and other wildlife that visit or inhabit it. An entire ecosystem derives from this single plant. Its northern range is generally limited to the Sonoran Desert. A sun worshipper, it will not survive daytime temperatures that remain below freezing. Its water needs are substantial, such that its western range is restricted by lack of summer rainfall. Its growth is slow at first, agonizingly so. Within fifteen years, it only reaches volleyball size. Older plants, some stretching fifty feet into the air, have been around for 200 years. By then, the saguaro's frame must support a huge bulk, over a ton. An internal framework of woody, vertical ribs provides the support.

Woodpeckers and flickers burrow out homesites in the saguaro's body. The cactus seals off these gouges with fibrous calluses.

The lesser bat sips the nectar deep within the saguaro blossoms. Pollen grains, sticking to its fur, are thus shuttled to other saguaros as the bat moves from plant to plant, inadvertently pollinating its saguaro host and ensuring a continued line of progeny for both species — truly a symbiotic relationship.

Native peoples have traditionally harvested the saguaro's cornucopia. The ripe fruits are collected in the summer from the top of the lofty cactus. To reach this ambrosia, a dead saguaro's skeleton is employed. Two lengthy ribs are lashed together. A foot-long crosspiece is attached to the far end at an angle. Standing at the base of the cactus, the collector maneuvers the canted crosspiece to dislodge the fruit into waiting hands.

The fruit is delicious right off the cactus. The seeds and pulp can be separated, as each plays a dietary role. The juice is squeezed from the pulp and boiled, yielding crimson syrup. The juice can be fermented to produce a ceremonial wine. Or the pulp can be returned to the syrup to make a thickened jam.

The seeds are dried, roasted and eaten whole, or ground into flour and cakes, or scattered on the ground for the chickens.

We boarded the bus and rode into Tucson, parking under the stands of the football stadium. What a place for a lab, even a tree-ring lab. I guess they had to stuff it somewhere. It's as though the university regents were trying to hide it. They certainly weren't showcasing it. The head honcho of the lab, Dr. Jeff Dean, casually ushered us into a cubbyhole on the ground floor. Someone had long ago hung a blackboard on the front wall. Presto, instant classroom. Jeff narrated a series of slides. Large-framed, bespectacled, with receding, short black hair, he droned on about the science of dendrochronology. Despite his insipid delivery, I found the topic fascinating.

Water and nutrient availability vary from year to year, thus trees grow at differing annual rates, he explained. The pattern of growth is discernible from the size of the individual rings of a tree. Within a given area, all trees will contain a similar pattern of rings for particular years. Decades ago, one of the pioneers of the science, an astronomer named Douglass, sampled cross-sections of living trees in the area. He wondered if sunspots might affect climate. It occurred to him that tree rings might be related to climate and could be used to construct a sunspot record. He never demonstrated conclusively any such relationship, but he noticed the similarity of ring patterns from tree to tree, like a fingerprint. Since Douglass knew exactly when the living samples were taken, he was able to readily count the rings inward, from the outer ring to the core, thereby stepping back in time. Thus did he trace the growth of these living trees back to their beginnings, in some cases to 500 years ago. The process is complicated in that a tree might not grow a ring during an unfavorable year. During other years, the tree might produce more than one growth layer.

Could the system work beyond the starting dates of living trees? Douglass proved it could. He uncovered the trunks of trees long dead, but which were alive sometime within the past 500 years. The outer rings of those dead trees matched up with the inner rings of the living samples. But the dead trees had rings that extended the characteristic pattern for the area back hundreds more years. When other samples of prehistoric trees were found, the chronology marched further back in time, all the way to 322 B.C. There are samples from bristlecone pine trees that date back over 8000 years, but there are great gaps in the chain beyond twenty-three centuries ago.

Jeff was very emphatic about the certainty of this method, as he held up a cross-section sample. "It will only match in one place. We can then date every ring in this piece of wood back to the year in which it was grown."

The significance of this science to the archeologists is that they can determine precisely when a log last existed as a tree trunk. That, in turn, would closely date a site in which the log was used for construction. The date when individual rooms were erected can even be determined.

Certain sampled trees or timbers can reveal the climate for a particular year of a long-ago century. It's of tremendous benefit for archeologists to know whether a particular time period was dry or wet, cold or warm.

Jeff then led us up to the second floor, where the lab occupied several rooms on one side of the hallway under the stands. The passageways that would lead into the stands during football season were blocked off. Across the hall were the closed booths that would dispense such health-food items as sodas, hot dogs and French fries. Jeff showed off cross-sectioned slabs and pencil-thin core samples, taken from tree trunks. Each yielded valuable dating information. In a poorly lit back room, which reminded me of an attic that hadn't been entered in a century, Jeff led us between stacks of samples, some from distant lands. I expected to see bats hanging from the dingy rafters. Box after box of specimens, each numbered, lined the high shelves. Loose samples were stacked on the floor, or on benches, or just scattered about. I wondered if they could actually find a specific sample if need be. I doubted they ever discarded anything.

In adjoining rooms, students and faculty were busy with computer programs or tree-ring samples. These individuals took this stuff seriously, heeding their work as we entered their labs, smiling politely at our intrusion, muttering some glad tiding or other, then turning back to the task at hand. Still, the lab tour was edifying since Jeff explained what was happening.

More on Bunny's orientation. From the Colonial Period emerged the Sedentary Period (900 to 1100 A.D.). The canal systems became more extensive. The Hohokam figured out that wider wasn't always better. Their broad canals allowed precious water to evaporate too quickly. So they started cutting their channels deeper but narrower.

Burial practices changed radically, from simple interment in a fetal position to cremation and storage of the charred remains in jars. Often slate palettes, shell ornaments, clay figurines and pottery were thrown into funeral fires.

Weavers displayed their skill, forming blankets, breech clouts, kilts, ponchos and sleeveless shirts.

The Hohokam discovered etching — centuries before the Europeans independently made the discovery. To seashells imported from the Pacific Coast or the Gulf of California, they applied a design in organic resin to the back of the shell. The shell was then soaked in a weak acidic solution, probably the fermented juice of the saguaro cactus. The acid slowly ate away the uncoated portions of the shell. When the resin was peeled away — presto, the desired design adorned the shell in bas-relief!

Populations expanded, ceremonial activity increased, trading proliferated. The Hohokam exported raw cotton and cotton textiles. They worked stone, for their own use and as a trade item. They shipped out pigments, agaves and other desert resources. They imported decorated pottery and turquoise. From Mesoamerica came macaws and parrots, copper bells, mosaic mineral mirrors and marine shells. They also bargained for obsidian and quartz, from which spear points, arrow tips and knife blades were fashioned.

* * *

The next morning we were back on campus, where the Arizona State Museum was situated. Paul Fish lectured briefly on the Marana project, a Hohokam site he was then excavating and which we would later visit. He reiterated that the Hohokam irrigation system was most impressive. "It rivals that of Mesopotamia. It's unmatched in the New World north of the Inca."

The Hohokam were also renowned for their stone carvings. "They are really the only people not in Mesoamerica who were carving stone objects," Paul added. He was fortyish, wore glasses and had dark-blond hair being infiltrated with gray. He acted as though he had misplaced something. He reminded me of a likable absent-minded professor. Paul was very knowledgeable and eager to discuss the subject of his life's work.

Several accouterments had been placed on a bench for us to examine. The agave plant was well represented. The natives extracted the fiber from its leaves, to be woven into fabrics. I ran my fingers through a batch of the thread, which was coarse and stiff, but sturdy. An open-weave pouch, hundreds of years old, was in such good repair it could be used today. A gauze-like square of undyed beige textile hardly had the softness of silk, but barely budged when I tugged it by the sides. A stack of rope was coiled and tied together. It appeared to have just come from a hardware store. Its condition was so remarkably maintained I almost expected to see a manufacturer's label. There were fist-sized stones used for pounding or gouging. A flat, wide slate of stone had "ears" at each end. It served as a two-handed grinding implement. Other gray and brown stones, flattened on one end, were used for scraping. Two spindle whorls, thin as soda straws and about as long, were on display. They seemed to be of some sort of wood, with tapered ends. Near one end was a ceramic disc, the size of a half dollar, which had been shaped from a piece of broken pottery.

Paul mentioned that the Hohokam habitations in the Phoenix area were concentrated. The population had access to irrigation from two main rivers: the Salt and the Gila. But around Tucson, along the Santa Cruz River where the Marana site was located, the population was more diffuse since water was less available. Only limited quantities of water could be channeled off from the Santa Cruz, enough to irrigate several hundred acres. The people looked upslope. Floodwater rolling down the slopes was diverted with makeshift weirs formed from brush. Crude as these devices were, they were adequate to funnel streams of water onto thirsty crop fields.

As in other parts of the Hohokam world, the inhabitants of Marana underwent a dramatic reorganization about 1150 A.D. The ball courts were no longer ritual centers. This distinction passed to the platform mounds.

We took to the vans and headed for the platform mounds in what was called Zone 1, for reasons not explained. We climbed through the topography. Floodwater agriculture was practiced here. Alluvial watering was also available in this zone. We parked in a clearing and followed Paul and Suzanne through the site. Students, stripped to the bare essentials, were working the site beneath the stark sun. Domed, two-man tents were staked into the ground under a pair of large trees. Two clotheslines ran between the trees and were fully loaded. In the heat and dryness, the clothes must have dried completely in a couple of hours. Water jugs and picnic coolers were strewn beside the tents. They looked well used.

The area under excavation there was a square, forty feet on a side. The digging had only progressed to a couple of feet into the ground, apparently a recent excavation. Two students in shorts, a male and female, took turns mechanically tossing shovelfuls of piled dirt onto a strainer. Another student in the far corner knelt as he carefully scraped the exposed ground. Two others were loading up a bucket with newly dug dirt. One of them toted it to the dirt pile being strained and poured it on. Though no one was abuzz with frenzied activity, the students seemed generally to enjoy their labors. Some were here for the college credits, some to satisfy their curiosity, others because their friends were here. Regardless of motivations, they appeared, to me anyway, as a team, working together, coordinating the efforts of their individual tasks of the moment.

We passed another excavation pit half a football field away. More students were busy with shovels, whisk brooms, trowels, dust pans, galvanized buckets. Their mined dirt was dumped onto strainers set on wheelbarrows around the perimeter of their pit. Other students picked through the dirt, pulling out interesting objects. Their pit was three feet deep, still shallow. They were uncovering some sort of building. The tops of walls were already popping into view. I wondered how they differentiated the normal dirt for the mud-adobe walls. I asked Paul about this.

"The walls are more compacted," he said offhandedly, as if it was obvious. It sure wasn't obvious to me.

It would take many digging sessions to uncover the walls in that one pit. There would be enough work to keep aspiring archeologists busy for many digging seasons.

The entire site was in a basin packed with creosote bushes, interspersed with paloverde and mesquite trees. Fields, packed with the vivid, ocher heads of wild mustard, gently swayed in the light breeze, painting the countryside in dazzling yellow. The paloverde trees had virtually naked limbs with few leaves. Those leaves that I could find were tiny as a teardrop. But the tree could survive without leaves most of the year. In fact, the bare stems were an adaptation to the desert. The yellow-green branches and twigs of the paloverde contained chlorophyll, which manufactured the plant's food. The natives made good use of this plant. The seed pods from the paloverde (and mesquite) were edible.

I followed Paul and Suzanne to the top of a nearby platform mound. It wasn't much of a hike since the unexcavated, overgrown mound was only six feet high. But despite the minimal rise in elevation, the mound allowed a surprisingly unobstructed view many miles into the distance of the flat terrain. Paul mentioned that the mound probably contained four rooms, one in each corner. The timbers used in the site were manually transported from the Santa Catalina Mountains thirty miles distant, noted Suzanne. The proper wood — fir and ponderosa pine — could only be obtained from trees that grew at altitudes of 5000 feet or so. Obtaining even a single tree trunk and lugging it to the site must have been arduous beyond belief. For the Indians here chopped the tree down without the aid of metal tools, and ferried it home without beasts of burden. They had to haul it with manpower — all without the use of the wheel! And gathering faraway timbers was a constant necessity.

The community that once lived here occupied an area a mile long and half as wide. Suzanne estimated that 400 to 800 persons called this place home. The nearest permanent water source was six miles away, which the inhabitants tapped via a canal. Reservoirs were widely used by the Hohokam, but none had yet been located at Marana.

The site was unusual in its span of occupation. The Hohokam tended to dwell in an area for centuries. Marana was only occupied for some seventy-five years. The area was marginal for agriculture, which may explain the site's limited duration.

"These people exercised lots of crafts besides agriculture," said Paul.

There's evidence of shell manufacture and pottery production. Fiber artifacts, bone implements and projectile points have been excavated. Enigmatic "donut stones" have turned up. These basalt rocks were worked into the shape of a holed donut, their function a mystery.

We strode down the mound and clustered around a third group of students. They too were scooping, brushing, shoveling and sifting the dirt of their shallow pit. Despite the work being dirty, sweaty and tedious, the students for the most part seemed to enjoy their project. One of them proudly handed Paul a thumb-sized figurine he had just uncovered, which Paul passed around. The features were eroded, but it was clearly some type of human effigy, its meaning unknown.

Some of the building walls were reinforced with stone. I noticed one with the two halves of a broken metate imbedded in it. At first I thought of recycling, then remembered the trash heaps extending down the talus slopes, practically out the front door of the living quarters, of so many other Indian sites. No, the inhabitants here at Marana weren't environmentally conscientious, just pragmatic.

We rode to the next stop, a couple of miles down a dirt road. We were in Zone 2, from 2500 to 3000 feet up. Scattered saguaros stood tall above the underbrush, their robust arms thrust skyward like a battalion of surrendering soldiers. Suzanne led us only a few feet from the roadway. She stopped at a bushel of rocks that had been deliberately piled into a cone-shape stack. A young agave plant, only four years old, was defiantly sprawled in the center of the rocks. The runt was barely one and one-half feet tall. Three of its smaller "pups" were clinging to the sides of the rock pile. The landscape for acres around was dotted with these plants.

"Agaves aren't normal for this area," she said.

You could have fooled me, I thought, looking around.

Suzanne figured it an unlikely location to grow any crops. "Certainly not corn, beans or squash. There just isn't any water."

But the natives did cultivate agave. Although an indigent plant, the agave normally grew at higher elevations. The agaves didn't need to be irrigated, but they did need more water than the area usually provided. Thus the rock piles, which retain some of the moisture nature bestowed begrudgingly on this land. Suzanne estimated that 40,000 agaves were growing here at one time.

"In drought years, the agave may grow little or not at all, but it won't die."

Each plant was harvested about every ten years. But the rock piles wouldn't then be bare. The agaves gave birth to "offsets." These baby agaves sprouted in the rock piles around the more mature plants, guaranteeing generations upon generations of these succulents.

Paul joined in. "The agave was put into pits and roasted for hours. It was a staple. Even today, the Mexicans roast and eat it."

Suzanne pointed out ectopic annual flowers that had staked out spots on the piles into which to spread their roots, evidence that the rocks supported a variety of plant life beyond the agave.

More on Bunny's orientation. With the passage of the Sedentary Period came the Classic Period (1100 to 1450 A.D.), which I feel is in some respects a misnomer. To me, a classic period implies a florescence into a more developed and cultured state. Not so with the Hohokam. In many ways, their culture declined during this period.

The ball courts fell into disuse, with the social emphasis shifting to earthen platforms. Some communities discontinued cremations, opting to bury their dead in polished red-ware pottery. Certain crafts and arts went into a tailspin. The making of stone palettes and clay figurines slacked off.

But there was a revolution in architecture in that adobe dwellings replaced the rudimentary pithouses.

At the end of the Classic Period, it all came crashing down.

We rode back into Tucson to the museum. Mike Jacobs, the curator of collections at the museum, collected our group and ushered us inside. He led us to the storage rooms, closed to the public. One room was absolutely packed with a king's ransom of artifacts. Some 12,000 pots, jars, mugs and other samples of pre-Columbian pottery were crammed onto eight rows of eight shelves each. There were examples of not only Hohokam crafts, but of at least Anasazi, Mogollon and Mimbre as well. They so completely filled the room, from floor to ceiling, that we barely had space to stand as Mike showed us representative Hohokam pottery.

Mike, fiftyish, squatty, with a graying walrus moustache, maneuvered around on a cane, seeming to enjoy his captive audience, like a drill sergeant orienting raw recruits on their first day at the rifle range. He held up a plain, smooth pot. Pinpoints of mica sparkled even in the subdued light. Mike explained that the Hohokam used lots of clay with mica during the Pioneer Period. The pot had been burnished with some type of implement.

Someone asked about the charcoal-gray smears on the pot.

"That's soot," Mike said. "This was a cooking pot."

Mike retrieved another pot from the table at his side. From the Classic Period, it dated even later than the previous one. This finely crafted specimen, which would hold about two quarts, had few flakes of mica. Two elongated "lips" were spread along the rim, one on each side. Mike fingered the "vertical polishing marks." It bore several blotches of soot — a cooking pot.

After displaying a litany of pots and other vessels, which enlightened some of us and bored others, Mike digressed to an explanation of archeomagnetism, an important technique for dating ceramics. Particles of iron in the clay have, under certain circumstances, aligned themselves with the then-existing magnetic pole. When a pot was fired, the heat fixed the orientation of the magnetic pole at that moment. The north magnetic pole wanders over time. From in situ, excavated pots, the direction of the magnetic orientation of their iron particles was readily calculable. That direction was easily plotted on a chart of the pole's past meandering, which had been computed in great detail. Thus, the pottery was dated.

I nodded with comprehension. "This only works because magnetic poles wander," Mike was quick to add.

Mike went back to the exhibits, holding delicately in two hands a huge pot, fully five gallons in volume, painted with muted tones of red swirls and parallel sets of lines. When viewed from the top, eight painted points were equally spaced around the circumference of the rim. I immediately thought of compass points. When I queried Mike about this, Bunny piped up from behind me.

"Their sacred number was four."

That didn't answer my question. I still wonder if the eight-sided "star" had any directional significance.

A pumpkin-shaped "squash pot" from the late Classic Period used a different clay to achieve its "red-on-brown" hues. Designs of swirls, cross-hatching and parallel lines adorned its exterior. I noticed there were seven large bulges circumscribing its equator. I couldn't attach any significance to the number. Neither could anyone else.

As if to revive any of us who had lapsed into a stupor from pottery overload, Mike saved the best for last. He gestured toward a three-gallon bowl, painted red on buff, still in place on one of the shelves. A set of some fifty wasp-waisted anthropomorphic figures, with zigzag arms and legs, completely encircled the pot's exterior. Each figure almost stretched from rim to rim. They were joined hand-to-hand like a strip of paper cutout dolls. The figures alternated having one or two "feathers" curling from their heads. Every other head, those with two "feathers," had a series of horizontal, parallel lines through it. Clearly the enigmatic figures had significance to the pot maker, most of which has been lost over the ensuing centuries.

I noticed none of the pieces shown had handles. I asked Mike why not.

"They just didn't," he shrugged.

* * *

Steve Lekson, president of Crow Canyon, had hooked up with our group. He rode in the rear of our van, being piloted by Jim "Road Kill" White, one of the staff members. This was the first tour since Crow Canyon had installed CBs in the vans. The drivers, Jim, Larry and Laurie, would occasionally chatter to each other like marmosets. But the CBs also provided an intercom system, so the persons in the rear of a van could hear a scholar lecturing from the front seat, a definite improvement over the situation we had on the Anasazi trip. And the intercoms extended from van to van such that a scholar in one vehicle could speak to riders in the other two vans. We headed for a Papago reservation.

As we traversed the narrow asphalt strip that split the desert, I noticed crosses and shrines popping up alongside the road at varying intervals. Bunny related sadly that these were memorials to motorists who had been killed in road accidents. We passed dozens upon dozens of these crosses. This road was like a former battlefield, although the casualties were still mounting, I'm sure. Bunny elaborated. The Indians consumed booze off the reservation and made a beeline for home. Some never made it.

We stopped along the road so Bunny could fill us in on the Papago Indians. They were long preceded by other cultures. The Paleoindians, whom Bunny characterized as "elephant hunters," roamed the land over 10,000 years ago. Then came the Archaic people, who were essentially small-game hunters and seed gatherers.

The Cochise culture occupied the territory. Bunny reiterated the speculation about the Hohokam being their descendants. After the Hohokam demise circa 1450 A.D., Spanish influence swept into the region starting in 1539. The lives of the indigenous peoples were never the same.

The Papago had traditionally adopted three lifestyles. Some were hunter-gatherers without a village. Others were true village dwellers, supplementing their hunting and gathering with farming. The remainder was strictly village people who grew at least half their nutritional needs.

With the advent of Spanish presence, the Papago existence changed radically, in some respects for the better. These Indians, in pre-Columbian times, had no domestic animals save the dog. But they quickly took to raising European livestock. Plows were brought in, to be pulled by horses, mules or oxen. Irrigation was reintroduced by the Spanish to supplement the Papago floodplain farming. Metal tools, such as shovels, axes and picks, became highly prized. These tools made it possible to exploit another source of water never tapped by the Hohokam — wells.

Additional food sources became available. The mainstay foods of corn, beans and squash were *summer* crops. The Papago readily adopted the Spanish farming of wheat and barley — *winter* crops.

Building materials evolved. Construction of walls from crude mud was replaced by the use of formed adobe blocks. The Spanish grid system for the village layout became commonplace. Before its introduction, the natives had situated their dwellings in a more random fashion.

In addition to the technology being altered, the culture changed directions. By the 1800s, most Papago had opted for European-style clothing. Spanish music became popular. Many learned to play such Hispanic instruments as the fiddle and guitar. Spanish dances and songs came into vogue.

But, of course, all of these innovations came with a cost. Many Papago traditions were blurred or lost, values changed, religious beliefs become adulterated, as happens when indigenous peoples the world over come into contact with "advanced" civilizations.

Almost all the Papago today occupy three non-contiguous areas. The Sells reservation was combined under one administration with the San Xavier and Gila Bend reservations. The conglomerate

2.8 million acres make it, behind the Navajo, the second largest reservation in area in the country. Some 300 other Papago live on a fourth reservation, Ak Chin, under Pima jurisdiction.

There were eleven political districts. Each district sent two representatives to the tribal council, the governing body. Neither the state of Arizona nor the local governments had any legal jurisdiction on the reservations except as allowed by the Papago or mandated by federal law. Federal laws, however, did apply. Such federal violations as mail fraud, smuggling and counterfeiting were subject to the federal courts. So were major crimes like murder, arson, burglary and larceny. Otherwise, offenses committed on the reservations were defined by tribal laws and tried in tribal courts.

The Papago have shifted to a cash economy from one of subsistence, said Bunny. This has severely handicapped them.

"There's no on-reservation industry, except for a few wealthy cattle farmers," bemoaned Bunny. "The rest of the people are supported by government relief programs. There are no jobs."

He also characterized the reservation as a "rural slum."

Bunny expounded upon this in his book, **Of Earth And Little Rain**. The Bureau of Indian Affairs and the Indian Health Service operated a hospital and clinics within the districts. The BIA ran some of the schools. The tribe administered "a bewildering array" of federal (and its own) funds for "projects involving housing, health care, preschools, senior citizens, alcohol addiction and much, much more."

The tribe did, however, employ some of its people and generate part of its income. It owned the utility authority, which provided power for most of the reservation. There was a cattle herd owned by the tribe. There were range-improvement programs and programs to develop fresh sources of water for cattle and crops. But federal money was indispensable. "If federal funds were curtailed drastically, the results would be disastrous."

We pulled into the Papago village of Gu Oidak (Big Fields), traversed the town square of packed dirt, and parked on the far side of the square. As we alighted from the vans, there wasn't an Indian in sight. The place looked deserted. On that side of the square squatted some sort of community cooking house, unoccupied. Along an adjacent side of the quadrangle stood an unpainted, concrete room that opened onto the square, attached to it a red adobe hut. Both abutted a concrete slab toward the interior of the square. A pole erupted from the center of the slab. Wires ran from the top of the pole to other poles at the edges of the slab. Portable benches took up the space between the poles on three edges of the slab. The opposite side of the square was occupied only by a white-faced chapel with red brick sides and topped by a bell tower with a white cross — a testament to the erosion of the Papago traditional religious beliefs by those of the Spaniards. This was another symbol of the transmogrification of the Papago pre-Columbian culture.

We spread out on the benches along one side of the slab, which served as a dance floor on occasion. The early-afternoon sun drew an unimpeded bead on us. I dug into my day pack for the sun screen as we awaited our host, Danny Lopez.

In a few minutes, Danny shuffled into view, the only Indian here to yet make his presence known to us. Up into his fifties with dark mahogany skin, he leisurely stood before us, the chapel to his back. He wore an eclectic costume of glasses, knit trousers, sneakers, baseball cap and T-shirt.

I expected Danny to delve into the history of his people. He didn't. Slouching before us and looking worn out, he wailed about his tribe's loss of culture and traditions. The Indian kids weren't into tribal customs. They were more interested in "imitating the youth in Tucson and Phoenix."

Danny paused in the hot sun as if in thought. "They do things like wear black clothes, and carry weapons, and take drugs, and things like that."

I didn't get the part about the "black clothes," but the rest sure made sense. It sounded all too familiar.

In his youth, Danny had engaged in more traditional pursuits. He rode horses, or ran barefooted through the brush, or made slingshots, or erected clay fortresses. The girls played with dolls. When young Danny felt mischievous, he "played rodeo" with the calves, for which he sometimes got into trouble. He didn't have "all the things that the kids now have."

He shifted position, looking at us but absorbed with his memories. "I think about the time kids put cardboard in their shoes. When

I went to school, I did not want to put my feet up and have the other kids see the cardboard. So I kept my feet down."

He went on about today's kids being captivated by television and sports. "Stuff like that takes away part of us."

So far has the trend progressed that the Papago children didn't even speak their native language! "I have to speak to them in English," said Danny, slowly shaking his head.

Danny was instrumental in trying to maintain and revive his people's traditions. But it was difficult to cultivate interest. It seemed most of the people, including the adults, had other priorities.

"People just don't have the *time*," Danny groused.

Danny's efforts have yielded only marginal results. The school board was considering requiring the Papago students to learn their native tongue as a *second* language. While most of the younger persons shunned native ceremonies, they could be coaxed into at least an exposure to traditions — if a dance was held. Even the adults wouldn't show up at scheduled ceremonies unless there was liquor. "There's too much alcoholism."

It was intensely quiet as Danny spoke. There were no animal sounds, only an occasional bird chirp. No one else was out. Traces of clouds, high up, blemished an otherwise uninterrupted sky.

Danny was tired from the long struggle, but he couldn't quit. *Someone* had to pass on the culture to the younger generations. He had hoisted the task upon his own shoulders, now stooped. Danny was particularly keen on preserving the songs and dances of his people. He was a tribal story-teller and singer, disseminating history through song and verse. It was now a dying occupation.

Like an identical twin that shares sensations with his distant sibling, I acutely felt Danny's pain.

But Danny loved songs. He'd often sing to himself about "frogs and turtles and people and eagle feathers and sunsets and medicine men." The songs put Danny in touch with his environment and his heritage, which has always been the framework for his world. Danny liked to pensively gaze at clouds in the morning and stars at night. Meditation and prayer were paramount facets of his life.

He related a trip with his wife to Tucson. En route home at night, Danny broke out in song. His wife joined in.

"We sang all the way from Tucson till we got to our yard, and

CLARA LOPEZ'S OUTDOOR KITCHEN

we do that a lot. Songs are special to us."

I was saddened that Papago traditions were slipping through Danny's grasp. I hoped Danny could dam the outgoing tide of his culture, but I feared time was his adversary. Too much culture had already been swept away. But Danny would always have his roots deep into the Papago soil. Nothing could dislodge him.

"The night my father died, I was up at three o'clock, and I was sitting by the window and decided to look up. There was a bright star up in the sky. I remember saying to myself, 'Dad, is that you up there? Are you the new star?' "

We loaded into the vans for the ride to Danny's mother's house, a few miles away. A late lunch awaited us. I didn't expect much of a meal as we turned down the long dirt driveway to the Clara Lopez residence, but I was anxious to sample the native cuisine. The neighboring houses were well spread out, lots of open terrain on both sides — no row houses here. There was a ramada attached to one side of the unpretentious Lopez house. The inside of the ramada was open and faced the entrance to the house. The outside of the ramada had been walled off with oco- tillo stalks. The slender, woody rods, taller than a man, were cut from a living ocotillo and planted in a row. They germinated into a spine-laden protective hedge. The gaps between the stalks

JOAN SAMPLING CLARA LOPEZ'S FOOD

allowed for the flow of air, so the inside of the ramada was cool despite the relentless sun. Light also filtered through. Tables and chairs, put there for our group, took up most of the ramada. The remaining section of the ramada served as the outdoor kitchen. Simmering coals glowed beneath a low grille that was supported by blocks. Blackened pots and kettles rested on the grille. A serving line had been set up between the two sections. A delicious concoction of aromas drifted over us from the grille, stimulating appetites to fever pitch.

Danny's wife welcomed us into the ramada and pointed the way to the food. I didn't hesitate. I loaded up my plate with chili, pinto beans, cholla buds, squash, a tortilla and two pieces of strawberry cake. I didn't have room (on the plate or in my stomach) for the fry bread or upside-down cake. What I did gulp down was delicious. What a serendipitous feast. The cholla buds were a new one on me. They were picked before they bloomed, from the spiny treelike cholla plant indigenous to the Southwest. The

CLARA LOPEZ SHOWING OFF HANDMADE BASKET

green buds were soft with a hint of lemon. Author Clive Cussler, who was part of our group, here to research a new book (now on the market as **Inca Gold**), had his main character, Dirk Pitt, describe the cholla buds as reminding him of okra, in a fictional dining scene based upon this real-life feast.

We got to try one more unusual delicacy, another first for me. A bowl of saguaro syrup was passed around. I dipped my tortilla into the dark liquid. It was very sweet, tasting remarkably like molasses. Everyone raved about the food. Even Dirk Pitt "couldn't recall a more delightful meal."

As I struggled from my chair and waddled out of the ramada, Danny's mother was lining up her handiwork on a bench alongside the house. For decades she had weaved baskets and bowls from native plants. Wearing a loose, Prussian-blue dress bearing an appliquéd cluster of flowers, Clara posed with a basket between her large, deeply bronzed hands. The furrows of her rugged, heavy face deepened as her mouth cracked into a genuine smile. Joan and I each quickly came away with one of her baskets, at bargain-basement rates. White yucca strands were meshed with pea-green fibers of bear grass. Clara mentioned that the bear grass would eventually turn yellow. The top of the basket was ringed with black ribbons of devil's claw. We would treasure Clara's artistry.

We all followed Danny to the "round house" (a.k.a. rain house) across the road. The crude structure squatted in isolation in a field. It was some fifteen feet in diameter and constructed from a framework of mesquite beams and saguaro ribs, filled in with creosote brush. A layer of dirt had been thrown on top. When it rained, the dirt formed mud, which hardened to coat the roof. The hut obviously required an abundance of maintenance. Traditionally, these buildings were centrally located so the town crier could stand on the roof and reach most of the villagers.

Joan and I crawled in through the low entrance that opened onto a ceiling about seven feet high. Dim light squeezed in between the twigs of the wall. Three pits, lined with creosote brush, were scooped into the dirt floor. Though then vacant, the depressions sometimes held jugs of ceremonial saguaro wine, a low-alcohol beverage.

The saguaro wine festival was held annually, the most important surviving aboriginal Papago religious ritual in Arizona, one the Spanish missionaries weren't able to extinguish. The purpose was

DANNY LOPEZ AT CHILDREN'S SHRINE

to bring rain to the desert. The festivities involved singing, dancing, praying, eating and, of course, drinking the wine. The round house and an adjoining ramada were the only structures associated with the ceremony. The ramada that accompanied this round house had collapsed and was stacked like cordwood nearby. Danny was determined to enlist the aid of his neighbors to prop the ramada back up, despite their patent lack of enthusiasm.

Danny followed us as we rode to the Children's Shrine several miles distant. We paused en route for a pit stop at Gu Achi Trading Post, one of the oldest on the reservation. I perused the bulletin board. One notice informed the people of an impending election. It also reminded them of a tribal law that prohibited public dances the night before the election. I guessed that was to prevent voters from boozing it up and being in no condition to vote the next day. Another notice instructed how to apply for social security benefits.

At the shrine we walked with Danny through terrain dominated by creosote bushes. Five minutes from the road we entered a small clearing, lined on two sides by stacks of slender ocotillo twigs, long dead. A two-foot pile of rocks occupied the center of the clearing. The rocks were encircled by four discontinuous sets of twigs stuck into the ground. About six to seven feet long, the tips of the twigs curled inward toward the rock pile. Our group sat in a semicircle in front of this shrine of rock and wood. Danny stood between the shrine and us.

He related the story of a great flood. Even as the waters receded, the people were worried that the waters could rise back up. As an appeasement, the people sacrificed four of their children. The waters then ebbed and disappeared. The shrine was erected as a memorial. Every four years in April, the shrine is refurbished.

The rocks covered pieces of wood, which Danny said symbolized corn or squash. His people visited the shrine and made offerings. I could see earrings and a barrette, but those were hardly the kinds of offerings Danny thought appropriate. He plucked a handful of creosote twigs and leaves, and gently placed them on the rocks. Others of us followed suit with what we could gather from around the clearing.

We bid good-bye to Danny and drove through the reservation to our next destination. The landscape, although devoid of buildings, bore the indelible stamp of human presence. The edges of the asphalt road were blanketed with an assortment of junk as far as one could fling something out the window of a speeding car or truck. Most of it was in the form of broken glass, brown or clear. But hundreds upon hundreds of bottles, mostly beer, lay unsmashed beside the bushes. Carcasses of worn-out tires were scattered about. This makeshift roadside junkyard was disgusting, and deplorable. Finally, the debris subsided with the passing miles.

As we traversed the Santa Rosa Valley en route to Ventana Cave, the picture changed totally. The desert blossomed on both sides of the thin asphalt road. Gobs of desert globemallow, with bright flame-orange flowers, replaced the debris that had lined our route. Delicate stalks of lavender lupine also sprouted along the highway. Batches of marigolds, with vivid canary-yellow heads, grew at the base of majestic saguaros and spiny chollas. Clumps of prickly-pear cacti flourished between the creosote bushes. Paloverde trees added their avocado-green branches to the pageant of color.

Mountains in the far distance paralleled our route. The afternoon sun warmed the dry air. Brittlebushes climbed the slopes of the foothills, dotting the landscape with patches of golden yellow. The stems exuded a fragrant resin used as incense in some churches in Baja California. The terrain was unspoiled by civilization as far as the eye could roam.

We drove off the main road onto what was best described as a wide path that dipped and twisted between trees and bushes. The vans gingerly picked their way along the bumpy trail, jostling us riders. We worked our way up a slope to a clearing, where we alighted from the vans. To the west, a rocky peak of the Castle Mountains rose to meet the sun on its downward course. Its steep slope was carpeted with greenery: saguaros, chollas, ocotillos, and paloverde trees. The ocotillos were just coming into bloom, their crimson tips flashing color onto the landscape. Clusters of yellow flowers were sprinkled throughout the shrubbery.

Joan and I grabbed our cameras and followed the others hiking single-file up to the peak, where Ventana Cave awaited us. We trudged up the face of the peak, pausing to capture the landscape on film. The vegetation abruptly halted as the slope erupted into a gray-brown rocky crest that was its peak. A large gouge in the vertical rocky prominence emerged as we rounded a stack of huge boulders beside the footpath — Ventana Cave. We filed into the opening and spread out on the rocks for Bunny's lecture. The cavern was more like an overhang, some fifty feet high. It extended rearward about thirty feet. Tucked into one corner was a crawlspace that apparently led deep into the cave to a water source. That section was partially walled-off. A small pool of water had leaked through the wall.

Bunny said this cave, along with Russell Cave, provided proof that people inhabited the area 10,000 to 12,000 years ago. The site was excavated starting in the late 1930s by Emil Haury, who studied the stratigraphic sequence in the midden mounds.

Rock art, some of it badly eroded, adorned the rear wall. I could make out a blood-red design in the form of a horizontal zigzag, a foot high and running some fifteen feet. There were parallel vertical lines, white or red, probably of Hohokam or Papago origin. The Papago claimed these were mnemonic inscriptions akin to those formally made for keeping track of the duration of a sickness. Haury felt that "calendrical ideas" were also involved with some of the geometric designs, since the Papago did utilize "calendar sticks" through an assortment of lines, dots and other symbols.

Other faint drawings depicted horsemen, so were obviously made within the past 300 years. Two stylized human figures, one with square shoulders, were probably Hohokam, Haury thought. There apparently was no rock art in the cave predating the Hohokam.

This had been a cemetery of sorts. Thirty-nine complete burials were excavated, almost all of which belonged to the Hohokam. Many were well-preserved though not by any Egyptian-like embalming process. The arid climate naturally dehydrated and maintained the bodies. This was one instance of Hohokam interment, a break from their habit of cremation. Not surprisingly, there was a disproportionate number of infant and child skeletons, indicating high mortality rates for those groups. Three of the male crania showed evidence of artificial deformation, presumably the result of cradling practices.

Bone fragments from lower in the midden mounds were much older than the Hohokam mummies, but Haury wasn't able to assign these fragments to a particular culture. He did say, though, that the bones didn't represent the oldest inhabitants of the cave, who were contemporaries of animals now extinct.

The sun was setting on the Ajo Mountains as we headed toward the Mexican border, fanning oranges and reds through the peaks. Bands of the purple blossoms of owl clover bordered each side of the road. We passed mile after mile of pristine, unspoiled terrain. Finally a truck-stop interrupted the unpopulated countryside. An hour south lay Lukeville, Arizona, where we would cross the border in the morning. As we rolled down the lonely highway through the deserted landscape, the sun slid off the horizon, bursting magenta and purple in a final stupendous gasp.

Lukeville was little more than a couple of motels, a pair of strip stores, a service station and a customs checkpoint. We dropped off our luggage in our rooms at the Gringo Pass Motel.

Joan and I traipsed across the street to a row of stores that housed the restaurant. Spotty lighting from the street lamps, the businesses still open and the customs station, partially illuminated an otherwise black night. There were several unsavory characters milling around this isolated border town. The restaurant wasn't much, but it would have to do. The rest of our group straggled in. We overwhelmed the facilities, backing up the cook and waitresses. Finally we all got served. Joan went outside in search of a public phone. A bunch of scuzzy-looking guys, with dubious intentions, asked her for a ride across the border that evening. She declined, saying she wasn't crossing that night — and hurried back inside the restaurant. When we returned to the motel, we traveled in groups, avoiding the shadows, which were just about everywhere. For a customs official, this had to be akin to service in a Foreign Legion outpost in the Sahara during the Eighteenth Century. You had to really piss someone off to get assigned to Lukeville, I figured.

* * *

We crossed the border early, into the Mexican state of Sonora. Our vans paused just across the line so Jim could get all of our tourist cards and passports checked. As we waited in the vans, I noticed that many of the shops offered insurance or beer. Perhaps the two commodities went hand-in-hand. Teenagers carrying water bottles and squeegees hung around in the street in front of the shops waiting for cars to stop. They immediately approached the vans and started squirting down the windshields, just like back in Miami. They were shooed away from two of the vans. Bunny, in the third van, allowed one kid to clean the windshield and handed him a dollar. The teenager beamed as he strolled off, waving the buck at his buddies, flaunting his entrepreneurial coup.

We traversed the town of Sonoyta, southward through the desert. We were now in the realm of the organ-pipe cactus. The plant's multi-branched, spiny clump of stalks reached upward to six or eight feet. The organ-pipe's presence expanded the farther south we drove. A similar cactus, the senita, also made its appearance. From the road I couldn't distinguish it from the organ-pipe, except that the tips of some of the stalks of the senita were bearded in long spines. The saguaros were still around but slipping from dominance. Craggy hills, with tawny patches of bare rock and blotches of greenery, followed the narrow asphalt road. Globemallows, lupines and brittlebushes splashed color along our route. Chollas, with their prickly arms, were in abundance.

We followed the signs to Quitovac, where there was evidence of human occupation spanning ten millennia. We eased through the dusty Papaguería hamlet and parked at the far edge of town. Originally inhabited by pure-blood Papago, the town's citizens now were often mestizos with a mixture of Indian and Spanish blood. Quitovac has been one of the rare sources of ground water in the region — a spring-fed, five-acre pond clustered with tall reeds. A veritable oasis, it was ringed with perpetually green vegetation. Tamarisk trees, introduced for shade, spread their copious branches over the water. Minnow-sized fish darted near the banks. A spine of hills rose beyond the lake under a blanket of shadowed clouds. One of our gang, Helmut, scanned the reeds with binoculars. He'd been an ardent bird watcher for years. Being in the Sonoran Desert was his first opportunity to spot the magnificent vermilion flycatcher. Coots called from within the reeds. A kingfisher and a pair of ducks hastily took to the air, but no vermilion flycatcher.

The sleepy hamlet now came alive once a year for the Wi:gita ceremony, held in late summer. Papago on both sides of the international border would make the journey. The rite originally commemorated the slaying of a water monster that consumed people. It evolved into a prayer for abundant rain, plentiful crops, good health, and long life. The Papago would parade around in masks. They carried floats depicting water birds, rainbows, lightning and clouds. Gallons of saguaro wine were gulped down. The wine has since been substantially replaced by readily obtainable canned beer. A few years back, Bunny drove into town two weeks after the Wi:gita festival. Hundreds of empty cans of Tecate beer still littered the ceremonial plot.

On the ride back through town, I saw houses of block and of adobe and sticks. Wide-eyed toddlers stared from behind fences, impervious chickens scratched in the yards, tired pickups rusted out front. There were piles of discarded tires, more than the villagers could have themselves worn out. I wondered whether the townsfolk had a use for them, or whether they simply allowed dumping — for a price, of course. Either way, it was a colossal eyesore.

We forded a shallow stream coursing down a much wider, dried river basin. A footbridge allowed pedestrians to cross. We passed a coppice of quince trees and pulled into the rural village of Tubutama for lunch. The sun had whisked away some of the clouds, allowing its radiance to career off the whitewashed buildings and down the narrow streets. A square park, provided with stark-white, wrought-iron, filigree benches, marked the town's center. The church, with its stacked pair of bell towers, rose across the street from the park and dominated the view. I surmised it to be a focal point of activity. On the opposite side of the park was the corner grocery store. A ledge with orange barrel-tile extended over the sidewalk to shield pedestrians. Three teenage girls were hanging around the entrance. Just up the street, three young men sat idly on the curb, hands in their laps, leisurely exchanging conversation. Two men were slouched in the shadows of a nearby building. They returned my greeting. Few other inhabitants were about. Nothing was happening. I figured it was siesta time. Even the dogs were hiding out. I'd have had one hell of a time getting used to that schedule. I couldn't imagine not being able to get things done during the middle of the day.

The road surrounding the square was paved, as were the attached side streets, but only for a distance of a block. From there, the roads abruptly turned to dirt. Two women greeted us in the parking lot of the community hall, a block from the square. (Everything of importance was within a block of the square.) One toted a key, as the hall was, naturally, closed for siesta. The large hall had ample room for our group. We sampled a local gourmet item: quince. This apple-shaped fruit was served as a gelatinous preserve. Its thickly sweet taste blended perfectly with the chunks of pungent goat cheese. After we chowed down, we congregated in the church to hear Bunny's sketch of the town's history.

Bunny related that Tubutama was the nucleus from which an Indian uprising spread in 1695. Spanish troops rushed to the scene, hanging or flogging the instigators. Reprisals by one side begot reprisals by the other. Before the Spaniards suppressed the rebellion, all the buildings in Tubutama (as well as in neighboring Caborca) had been torched, and each side had shed much blood.

Joan and I strolled around the town by ourselves. The streets were practically deserted. I saw only one moving car. A handful of others, unoccupied, were parked along the curb. We could hear people in their houses as we walked the side streets, but almost no one ventured out. When we returned to the square, I spotted Helmut with his face buried in the binoculars. His searching stare darted from treetop to treetop — still no vermilion flycatcher.

We journeyed to the El Camino Motel in Caborca for the night.

* * *

Before heading into the countryside, we paused in Caborca to view another Spanish church from a bygone century. The two-story colonial structure, with a tandem set of bell towers, sat alone at one end of a large park. A horde of teenage bicyclists cut back and forth on the paved plaza in front of the church. Three grade-school boys swung from a set of bars in the adjoining playground.

Then we were off to La Playa. After driving through rural areas, we turned off onto a dirt road that led deep into the boondocks. There were no signs of habitation as we passed through the brush. An endless grove of spinach-green creosote bushes, their tiny yellow buds now blooming, stretched to the horizon. Brittlebushes beamed in tones of gold in the morning sunlight. The tips of the slender rods of ocotillos flashed scarlet. Low-lying clusters of great-desert poppies flaunted delicate white flowers at the bases of the shrubs. Some desert.

In a few miles, we left the road onto an open plain, sparsely populated with vegetation. Low mountains sprouted all about us in the distance. The area was strewn with dark rocks for hectares around. The stones, some with speckles of mica, varied from thumb-size to the mass of a man's fist. Some of the larger rocks, ranging in shade from charcoal gray to reddish gray to brownish gray, were stacked in piles a foot high. These piles were roasting pits, Suzanne Fish explained.

"But we're not sure what they roasted."

Paul Fish piped in. "They might have roasted anything from

corn to agaves, or they might have done kitchen pots."

"In any event," Suzanne continued, "the stones are fire-cracked from thermal stress."

The area had not been excavated, so little was understood about the site. Interspersed with the carloads of stones were thousands of fragments from shell-goods manufacturing. Paul didn't feel the shells from this area got traded to the Hohokam culture to the north. "The Hohokam did their own working of shells. Besides, these shells here were *fresh* water, local snails."

Some of the roasting pits doubled as burial sites, dating to pre-ceramic times, Paul said. There were exposed pieces of human bone at one rock pile I bent over: a mandible fragment with three teeth intact, a small chunk of cranium and a piece of metacarpal. The bodies were interred in a flexed position. The graves, which numbered in the thousands, indicated trade with neighboring cultures. Pottery from Casas Grandes to the east in Chihuahua (not to be confused with Casa Grande in Arizona) wound up with the bodies. Local shell products in turn went eastward.

In addition to the rocks being used for roasting, they served other roles. I picked up a smooth stone the size of an elongated hockey puck, with a malachite-green surface. Paul examined the rock, saying the coloring was a patina from centuries of exposure to the elements. One end of the stone was ragged.

"Oh yes, it definitely looks like a stone that was used to actually chip away at other stones and make other stones into some type of tool," added Paul, peering at the rock as he turned it in his hand.

Someone else handed Paul a stone tool the shape of a jelly donut. He twisted it around in his grasp and pronounced that it dated from a thousand years before Christ. He postulated it was used for grinding, possibly seeds or corn.

Suzanne passed around a flat, dark-brown projectile point, an inch long. I ran my thumb along its edges, noting its rough serrations. It would readily pierce flesh.

Someone got too close to a cactus bud. Its spindly, aciform spines grabbed an ankle. The normal reaction would have been to simply reach down and pull it off. But not with this cactus. It would then lock its needles into a finger, drawing blood. Suzanne clasped two flat stones, placed one on each side of the bud and safely removed it.

One of the staff members related an anecdote about Paul's first encounter with this cactus years ago. When the cactus hooked onto his leg, Paul pulled it off with one hand. Now that hand was pinned to the bud by the spines. So Paul reached in with the other hand. The bud then had him handcuffed. Out of hands, Paul bent forward, bringing his mouth to the rescue!

The area will be tricky for future archeologists to excavate. Erosion has reduced the stratigraphy to a single archeological horizon. As Paul put it, "The place has been flood-washed, so everything ends up on the same level, and you find 3000-year-old artifacts on the same level as a bottle cap that was left here in 1930."

We rode toward the nearest mountains. As we climbed the foothills, the shrubbery gave way to trees: ironwood, mesquite and paloverde. We pulled off onto a trail and parked under an umbrella of trees. We traipsed across a field en masse. Paul led us to a larger rock pile, seventy-five feet in circumference, with creosote bushes anchored into its sides. It had an adobe core and was not a roasting pit. Its function was undetermined. Potsherds littered the ground. I showed a piece, copper-brown with a charcoal-gray center, to Paul.

"This is definitely Papago," he said, fingering the fragment. "The black interior is horse manure, so it's post-Conquest."

Beyond the stack of rocks, erosion had cut deeply into the land, carving out what resembled a miniature mockup of the Grand Canyon. At the edge of an exposed channel of earth, evidence of a human burial poked through the ground. A bleached skull returned my stare.

We retraced our steps, dodging cow chips, to the vans, where we enjoyed a picnic lunch under a leafy canopy. Clive Cussler and I shared the cab of a van as we ate. He told me that for him this trip was to obtain background information about the Sonoran and its cultures for his forthcoming book.

We drove across an arroyo, channeling the diminished waters of the Río Magdalena, and through the town of Las Trincheras, situated at the base of a low peak. The miniature mountain overlooking the town was the location of impressive trincheras terraces.

Paul led the way up the slope, blazing a tortuous trail. We followed, dodged ocotillo and cholla spines, brushing past creosotes, and fastidiously watching our footing on the treacherous rock-strewn incline. We rendezvoused with Paul a quarter of the way to the top. Before us lay the "ball court," now merely an oval depression that nature had fully reclaimed. I probed Paul about the so-called ball court. He confessed that the only indication was the ovoid shape. And even if it was a ball court, there was no indication the game resembled those of Mesoamerica.

A wall on the upslope side of the depression had been reduced to a linear pile of boulders running 120 feet across the face of the mountain. The uncut stones, from the size of a bowling bowl to a bushel basket, were alive with a confetti mottling of brilliantly colored lichens: saffron, tangerine, moss-green, white-green. Downslope, the somniferous town spread out before us in the valley, the locals going about their business.

I turned my attention uphill toward the terraces, some twelve to fifteen of them. Brittlebushes festooned the terraces, their yellow patches demarcating the different levels. The terraces once contained the living quarters of an entire community. I asked Paul about the dwellings.

"At the top of the summit there's a structure that's very much like a compound and, in fact, has been shown to have adobe architecture in it."

I queried Paul as to whether platform mounds existed at this site, Las Trincheras.

"Central sites with platform mounds characterize Hohokam communities that also contain trincheras sites. In Sonora, however, platform mounds are not reported."

Someone asked if trincheras terraces also served defensive purpose, a position promulgated by some archeologists. Paul was skeptical, since the terracing was only on one face of the mountain. "You usually don't have an agreement with your enemy to attack only on one side of the hill."

I tended to concur with Paul's opinion, particularly since there were no hints of defensive walls. I accepted Paul's comment that agriculture took place on trincheras terraces. That certainly comported with what little I knew about terracing in other parts of the world. But what was the evidence?

Paul explained that cold air being dense tended to settle in basins, so winter freezes were fewer on trincheras slopes than at the bases. Minimum temperatures were higher and less prolonged. The frost exposure was limited to one month rather than five months. The daytime heat absorbed by the dark volcanic rocks would be reradiated at night to warm the terraces. Volcanic soils were rich in clay and retained moisture. Analyses of pollen from the sites revealed that corn was grown. Tools to harvest agave and other succulents were found at some sites, roasting pits at others.

The terracing was characteristic of trincheras sites, which extended throughout much of the Sonoran region, even up into southern Arizona. The sites were almost invariably situated on dark volcanic hills. I wondered how long this terracing had existed.

"I think they all date to a time period after A.D. 1100, and the predominant occupation here is between 1300 and 1450."

We only had a few minutes before returning to the vans. But Joan and I wanted to see more. Jim joined us, as we scrambled uphill. We scaled the lower terrace walls. Some of the cobblestones forming the walls had become dislodged, but most were still packed in place. The terraces were discontinuous at some levels. Time wouldn't permit us to reach the summit, but we wanted to go as far up as we could get away with. It was a good thing I wore sturdy hiking boots, as I almost twisted an ankle in my haste. Despite the warm weather, I was also thankful I didn't wear shorts; the bushes would have torn my legs to shreds.

A call from far below cut our climb short. We followed Jim laterally along a terrace, crashing through the brush to the end of the hill. A shrine dedicated to Our Lady of Guadalope had been erected in front of a rocky outcropping there. Steve Lekson popped up. He, too, had hurried up to the terraces. Steve pointed to rock art barely visible in the crest of the outcropping above the statue of Our Lady. I could make out a pair of designs, each a tandem of concentric circles. Steve didn't know their meaning.

A rudimentary trail led us the rest of the way down to the vans.

We stopped at the Hotel San Francisco in Santa Ana only long enough to get our room keys, drop off our bags and wash up. Then we were off to nearby Magdalena.

We parked along the town square, each edge spanning two blocks. The sun raced for the horizon, as the square buzzed with activity. People and vehicles were everywhere this early evening. Pedestrians flocked around a refreshment van stopped in the street. One half of the square was recessed and paved, with a spurting fountain at its center. Stone steps led from a sidewalk down into the recessed level. Groups of young men, feet dangling, were propped along the retaining wall, watching the passing foot traffic, particularly the females. Couples sat below on the benches just inside the wall. Steps led up the opposite side of the lower level into a park that comprised the other half of the square. Walkways, shaded with copious trees, joined this half of the square to sidewalks on its perimeter. Couples strolled the walkways hand-in-hand, or huddled on the benches along the walkways. Others, as singles, couples or families, paraded along the park, some with food or drink in hand. Birds chattered from the trees.

Our group passed by the fountain, ascended the steps, and followed the walkway that led us into a memorial to Father Kino. The open building housed the remains of this Spanish missionary, who brought Christianity to the area some three centuries ago, a mixed blessing at best. The priest's bones were not entombed but on open display behind glass. We paid our respects before setting off in small groups to explore the environs.

The square was surrounded by a swirl of cars and pickups continually cruising its boundary. Most were occupied by young men checking out the action, like young men in any *American* town. Young ladies promenaded along the sidewalks, which explained the young men in the vehicles. The four streets bordering the square were lined on the opposite side with shops and restaurants. One had an outdoor café shielded by a cloth awning. People lounged around its tables, nibbling, sipping, chatting and scanning. We browsed in some of the stores as the lengthening shadows crept across the park.

✳   ✳   ✳

We were joined in the morning by Dr. Tom Sheridan, who presented an overview of Cucurpe, a small ranching and farming community along the Río San Miguel in northern Sonora. Tom, in his forties and slightly built, stood stiffly before us in cowboy attire: scuffed boots, black Levis, white shirt with pearl buttons. His flowing dark-blond locks and white tapered beard reminded me of Buffalo Bill. People have populated the Cucurpe area continuously since prehistoric times. When the Jesuits established a mission in 1647, there was a community of Eudeve Indian farmers tilling the soil. The natives no longer considered themselves Indians or spoke the Eudeve tongue. Their way of life was now a fusion of Spanish and Eudeve cultures. European livestock, crops and farming implements allowed the Indians far greater sources of food than was available to their pre-Spanish ancestors.

Cattle grazing currently took up most of the town's land. Some agriculture acreage was devoted to crops for the cattle: alfalfa, barley and rye grass. The farmers grew corn and beans for their own tables. Irrigation was vital. River water was channeled onto the fields via a system of ditches. Seasonal floods rushed water down the mountains and through the arroyos, carrying nutritious silt onto the floodplain. But what the river fertilized, it could also destroy. In some years the floods inundated the fields, ruining the crops and eroding land along the river banks.

Maintaining the canals was a *comunidad* (community) project. Work parties annually cleaned and repaired the canals and diversion weirs. A committee, selected by the *comunidad*, apportioned water rights. A judge, then appointed by the committee, resolved conflicts over the use of water.

A local *ejido*, a group of landowners, presently had jurisdiction over large tracts of grazing land. Any member's cattle openly grazed this free range. Other grazing acreage was privately owned.

We rode into Cucurpe, with its narrow, swept streets lined with modest, concrete-block houses, some with pickup trucks or satellite dishes. Three boys kicked a well-worn soccer ball back and forth in the otherwise vacant road. There was no downtown, only a few short intersecting streets. In a minute we were in front of the home of Beto Cruz, a local mestizo rancher and friend of Tom's.

Beto, well into his fifties with deeply tanned and lined skin, graciously welcomed us into his home and yard to view the lifestyle of a typical Cucurpe citizen. I doubted Beto was typical. Although he would be considered at poverty level when compared with American ranchers, he seemed glaringly successful by Cucurpe standards. His house was clean and comfortable but not large. A separate building on another side of the yard contained additional rooms. Beto's wife was tending to a garden behind the main house. At the rear of the expansive yard was a pen with three head of cattle milling around. Chickens pecked at the ground near the pen, scurrying at my approach. An adjacent hutch kept a pair of rabbits. Spreading trees interlocked their branches, shading the space like an awning. An orange tree rose from the edge of the garden, its ripe fruit begging to be plucked. A tandem of saddles rested on a sawhorse beneath an open shed. The unused part of the yard was ringed with what I considered junk: battered fifty-five-gallon drums, used truck tires, a pile of rusting horseshoes, empty bottles, an old axle and other car parts, a refrigerator with the door ajar, odd pieces of lumber. Perhaps Beto had a use for it all. Two black hounds, their tongues hanging, had collapsed onto the dusty driveway.

The vans ferried the rest of the group down the street and up the hill to view a church, which sat alone on the low bluff. Bunny had this thing for colonial missions. Joan and I passed on the mission, taking the opportunity to get some exercise. We trekked the short distance up the hill. At its crest we were treated to a sweeping panorama down the side slope to the pastel houses with corrugated-metal roofs that bordered the road running along the base of the hill, to the rows of trees just beyond the road, and out across the arroyo cradling the river, to the hills beyond.

Directly below us a family was at work behind their house. Two clotheslines, completely exposed to the bare sun, were festooned with strips of raw meat. The family members were busily slicing chunks off a pair of hanging carcasses and draping them across the lines, their actions reminiscent of decorating a Christmas tree.

"Jerky," said Joan.

I scooted down the steep slope, setting a minor rockslide in motion and quickly getting the family's attention. When I caught the patriarch's eye, I held up the camera, grinned, and asked permission in Spanish to take pictures. He nodded repeatedly and waved me on. I let them get back to their business before I started snapping the shutter. As I was crouched at the wire fence, my eye to the viewfinder, a pink blur jumped into my peripheral vision immediately followed by a staccato of angry squeals. Fully 300 pounds of pork on the hoof was at the fence, menacingly nosing its way under it toward me! As I was about to backtrack, the chain around its neck yanked the pig to a halt, right at my feet. It screamed in protest, as I kept shooting, just beyond its snout. A white turkey then got into the act, parading defiantly on the far side of the fence, scolding me harshly.

We drove back across the Río Magdalena and set up for lunch on the riverbed. Two smaller tributaries merged to form the river, which was then barely a stream. We relaxed in the overhead sun at the base of the abutting hills, while the staff unpacked the coolers. I noticed Steve hurriedly making his way up the steep incline behind us.

"Where are you going?" I blurted out reflexively before it struck me he might be answering nature's call.

"There's got to be ruins on top," he called down to me, still climbing.

That's all I had to hear. "Mind company?"

"No, come on," he urged over his shoulder.

I bounded after him like an ibex.

Steve was correct. The knoll contained evidence of historic habitation. An adobe structure had been weathered away to a clump of bricks. Steve estimated it dated to the last century. The very existence of bricks placed it post-Conquest. But another, older, pile of stones, arranged in a rough circle, interested Steve. These were definitely prehistoric, he deduced.

"How did you know there were ruins here?" I asked.

"It's a natural place for ruins. You have the confluence of two rivers and a great view."

He pointed up to the higher summit of the next hill. "I'll bet there are even better ruins there."

We racewalked up that hill as the remainder of our party filed through the chow line. We hoped they'd save us something, but this was certainly more exciting than eating, even if it meant missing a meal. Sure enough, Steve was two for two. Eight or nine rooms were once spread over the summit. The walls were long gone, leaving only enough to trace the outlines of the foundations. We crept over the shrubbery-encrusted site, peering at the ground. Steve was amazed at the lack of pottery. I spotted the first piece, handing it to Steve for his assessment.

"It's a potsherd all right," he said, as he inspected it. "Good eye."

We only came upon another half dozen pottery fragments, a mystery to Steve, who figured the place should have been littered with them. We did find a couple of stone manos, so the people had ground something. There was an abundance of flakes from the chipping of stones into tools. This was once a busy place. I asked Steve to venture a guess at the date of the site.

"Definitely before 1450, possibly around 1000 A.D."

Steve and I got back just in time to get the last scoop of tuna salad.

After lunch we all trekked along the riverbed. Puffs of clouds with flat, gray bottoms hung motionless against a China-blue sky. So still was the air that the scene appeared like a painted backdrop on a movie set. We gathered around Tom a quarter-mile downstream, where a diversion weir cut across the stream. Tom explained that the weir, of earth, brush and sticks, bifurcated the running water. Part of it flowed along an ditch chopped into the edge of the riverbed. The remainder fed the stream that also followed the riverbed. Both were diverted or tapped to serve the needs of the *comunidad*. In good seasons, with an abundance of water, both channels flowed freely. When water was scarce, one channel was closed off for a week to allow all the water to course down the other channel. A week later the situation was reversed.

On the way back to the vans, we climbed up to a small overhang above the riverbed. The rear and top of the rocky interior were emblazoned with remarkably preserved pictographs. There were white and maroon anthropomorphs, highly stylized. Stick figures had outstretched limbs bent at the knees and elbows, three toes and fingers to a foot or hand, and a pair of "antennae" curling up from each head. Other figures seemed to be clad in full-length dresses. One repeated design was a rectangle with a redundant geometric pattern painted on each side.

Paul spoke up. "They're prehistoric rock art. They fall outside anything we know for the Hohokam or the trincheras regions, both of which have very distinctive rock styles."

Steve gestured to a faded, unobtrusive, chalky figure shaped like a sea turtle as seen from above. "I'm really interested in this figure. It looks like a masked dancer. In southern New Mexico this is used as evidence that part of pueblo life so characteristic of the Southwest actually comes from Mexico." Steve conceded this point was still debated, however.

I was impressed not only about the rock art but that the place hadn't been vandalized. Not even any graffiti — a rare blessing nowadays.

We picked up Beto in the vans. The two black dogs, large as German shepherds, came to life and trotted along as Beto showed us the way down the road to his agriculture. We followed him between fields to the river at the boundary of his property. I didn't see any tractors or other machinery. Livestock still plowed the fields. Irrigation from the river supported crops of beans, chili peppers and barley. An orchard of guava trees abutted the end of one field. Beto shunned the use of pesticides and artificial fertilizers.

His crops had been ruined and the fields eroded by floods. He had reclaimed his land from the river, and even intruded onto the riverbed as far as he dared. A row of live fenceposts, of willow and cottonwood trees, had been planted parallel to the river's course, on Beto's side of the river. Brush was packed between the trees. As the fence grew, it attenuated the impact of future floods, allowing the onrushing water to seep, rather than surge, over the fields. The alluvial silt that spread over the fields further augmented Beto's property.

Beto, under a white Panama hat, pointed to a smaller row of live fenceposts several feet closer to the river. They had been planted in the years since the previous row. Beyond the second row stretched yet another line of thinner trees, the most recent of the rows. Thus had Beto in stepwise fashion maximized the dimensions of his fields.

As we filtered back to the vans, indefatigable Helmut was at a tree line, binoculars in action. This time his gaze was fixed, not scanning. The object of his focus was a solitary bird posing in the open on a fence post. Helmut's attention vacillated between the binoculars and a bird field guide. He leafed through the book, stopping to study a certain page, then shifted back to the bird. Its plumage was magnificent: ebony for the wings, tail and eye bands, accentuated by a head and belly of brilliant vermilion. Yes, vermilion.

"A vermilion flycatcher!" gleefully blurted Helmut. It was the high point of the trip for him.

We were back in the vans heading across the countryside along dirt roads. Cattle grazed the rangeland. The dogs, similar as a pair of bookends, raced beside us, occasionally disappearing over an adjacent rise and reappearing along the road farther ahead. They knew the route. We dropped into a tight arroyo and bouncing down its course, the mutts tagging along. The dry channel flattened out under overhanging trees before ending at an intersecting stream. A

PREPARING *CARNE ASADA*

BETO CRUZ AND FRIENDS

carne asada awaited us in the opening. Some of Beto's neighbors, the welcoming committee, sat and stood along the banks of the arroyo. They mostly kept to themselves, but did exchange friendly bits of conversation with us when we approached them. Two women and a young girl worked over the grille, packed with sizzling meat and heating pots that filled the air with the saliva-producing perfume of a scrumptious meal in the making. I got in line, coming away with a plate of roast meat, fried beans and a wafer-thin wheat tortilla wide as a pizza for six. An ice-packed cooler held the beer.

We ate around the folding tables and chairs set out for us, as Beto broke out the guitar. Over roasted meat and chilled beer, we were serenaded with *norteño* music: folk ballads of northern Mexico. The delicious fragrance of charred meat wafted over the tables. Beto played on, the dogs camped in the dirt at his feet. Beto enjoyed the performance as much as did his audience. I tilted my chair back and sighed, a cool beer at my lips.

* * *

It was off to San Ignacio, where another gracious local waited to serve us a typical Sonoran breakfast. The unpretentious home of Chata Gallegos sat on one end of a rectangular park in a mostly residential neighborhood. The backyard was lavishly sheltered with foliage. A low retainer wall segregated the property from the dense thicket beyond, which resembled an arboretum. Our host, who was heavy set, reserved, in her forties and eager to please, stood in dappled shadows at the block stove near the wall, stirring the contents of the pans heating on the grille. As we filed by her, she doled scoops of chili peppers, meat and beans onto our plates, then tossed on a folded family-sized tortilla.

We sat around tables or along the wall, shoveling the tasty repast in, washing it down with thick, robust coffee, just the kind I like. Strings of garlic buds were for sale. Some of the ladies stocked up. The aroma of roasting meat, simmering chili peppers and raw garlic converged over us to create an olfactory symphony. I drew in deep breaths as I sipped through a second cup of macho java in the shadowy yard. Life in Chata's backyard was oh so sweet.

But before I got too comfortable, I abandoned Chata's hospitality to stretch my legs and have a look around the neighborhood. An open pavilion squatted in the center of the unoccupied park half a block from Chata's front door. A horde of birds had claimed the rafters as a nesting site. They swept in and out, chattering as they went. A white church with a stacked, double-bell tower stood across the narrow, deserted street. Down the block two senior citizens strode in the neighborhood *abarrate*, grocery store. I strolled across the park and down a couple of side streets. A stream of excited laughter led me around a corner. Elementary kids were at recess. Only one moving car came by as I roamed. It seemed out of place. Very few inhabitants were out on this warm, sunny day.

After saying good-bye to Chata, we headed north. We crossed the international border at Nogales with no hassle. Next stop was in Patagonia, Arizona, for chow. As we dug into our bag lunches while stopped in a park, the first droplets of rain during the entire trip sprinkled onto us. In minutes the air was dry.

Then on to Sonoita, Arizona, to visit the home and studio of Paul and Laurel Thornburg, potters who produced reproductions of Southwestern pre-Columbian ceramics. They copied authentic Hohokam and Mimbre artifacts. Sometimes a vessel was reconstructed from only a single potsherd.

Their Mongolian yurt, much of it solar powered, stood on a knoll of their wooded, isolated homesite. There were no other houses in sight. The Thornburgs obviously liked seclusion. The living quarters in the yurt were partitioned off, leaving the remainder of the round structure for an office and showroom. Juniper trees bearing light-green berries and manzanita trees with burgundy bark shared the knoll with the house.

The yard served as a workshop, as the pottery was made outside. All the ingredients were collected or made by the Thornburgs. They scoured the countryside for just the right clay and pigments. Even the temper was handmade: shale-like slabs of stone were ground on a metate.

Laurel gave a demonstration of fashioning a pot. As we sat along benches before her, she stood over a table, wedging a wad of battleship-gray clay. Like kneading dough, she twisted and pressed it, homogenizing the chunk and forcing out any air bubbles that could expand and shatter the pot during firing. Emulating Hohokam potters, she formed the bottom of the incipient pot by molding it over a completed pot. From there, she spiraled coils of rolled clay upward to complete the sides of the vessel. She obliterated the seams with a stone scraper. Then the paddle-and-anvil technique further smoothed the surface while thinning it out. The lip was shaped as Laurel pressed circles of clay, between her thumbs and fingers, around the top of the pot. The plain pot was ready for firing.

But most of their pottery was decorated, so Laurel discussed their painting methods. She showed off bits of rocky minerals with a variety of dull tones. But the colors came alive when Laurel went to work. She scraped the "iron stone," on a palette with water, yielding a vivid scarlet slurry. The other stones revealed their richness when rubbed: black, yellow, teal, saffron. The ground, red mineral would be mixed on a secondary palette with clay and mesquite sap. The sap held the iron in suspension.

Even their paintbrushes were natural. Grasses were bundled

on a stick and used to sketch thick lines and scrolls. The fibers of yucca leaves were split and chewed to produce skinny brushes perfect for drawing fine lines.

Paul was behind us, firing up the tinder in a slit trench in which some of Laurel's unfired masterpieces had been delicately placed. Two other firing chambers, an adobe kiln and a stone-lined pit, were nearby. As the inferno grew, wind-whipped flames snapped out at Paul.

"Watch out!" Laurel shouted to Paul.

We gathered around Paul as he reached into the trench with a probing stick to make adjustments of the glowing logs. He had to allow sufficient air to reach the pots to properly oxidize the pigments. These Hohokam replicas were gray with red designs when placed in the trench. The gray had been converted to buff. But the red had turned black. Laurel was concerned the red shade wouldn't return. Paul assured her it would. Slowly the red came out as the pots cooled, yielding characteristic red-on-buff pottery. These pots were sold, even before they cooled off, to members of our group.

So realistic was their work that the Thornburgs built in a safeguard to prevent the vessels from being sold as authentic. A tungsten ore, acting as a fluorescent tracer, was incorporated. The ore glowed under ultraviolet light. In fact, Paul and Laurel used a black light to search for the ore at night.

We congregated in the yurt's showroom where Laurel sold several pieces to our group. I noticed a squash pot on display. I counted the bulges around its middle. Sure enough, seven — just like the one Mike Jacobs had shown us at the museum in Tucson!

That evening our group relived the trip at the farewell banquet in Tucson. I didn't fly home with all the answers I had originally sought, for many of the answers weren't yet available. There was still debate about the origins, florescence, decline and disappearance of the Hohokam. More questions surfaced that I hadn't anticipated. Where did the Papago come from and what was their connection with the Hohokam? But despite the lingering questions, I came away from the field trip with a surfeit of information and a wealth of understanding about the Southwest and the Sonoran Desert, and of those peoples who made their homes there. I added another piece to the puzzle, as I had done when I undertook the Anasazi trip.

MOUND BUILDERS OF THE LOWER MISSISSIPPI

The rain had already started as we quickly filed off the bus and followed Dr. Joe Saunders, quick stepping, down the rutted, narrow, dirt road into the hardwood forest. Beneath an ominous gray layer that blanketed the sky from horizon to horizon, some twenty of us intrepid souls trailed behind Joe as he cut off the road into the brush. The rain was picking up, the sky getting darker. Once we were into the dense foliage, the daylight, what little of it that existed, was further soaked up by the leafy canopy. We followed Joe single file as he snaked his way along, dodging trees and bushes, as though he were leading us to the Promised Land. If he was on a trail, I sure didn't see any sign of it. In fact, all the subdued light allowed was the amorphous form of the body moving ahead of me, more shadow than substance. The rain beat into the branches overhead. The wind, increasing audibly like a jet engine winding up, lashed through the trees. I scurried along faster than caution dictated in this rugged terrain, lest the body ahead of me that I could barely see be swallowed up forever by the darkness, leaving me without direction. I stumbled on a root, cursing loudly as I caught myself. I could hear others behind me groan as they bumped into something or other, or were smacked across the face by a released branch from the person ahead of them.

After what seemed an hour, but could only have been a matter of minutes, we were there. Joe stopped, allowing the rest of us to catch up. We straggled in, most of us rain-soaked to some extent, and gathered round him in the gloom on an overgrown, conical mound, some twenty-five feet high. We had arrived at the Promised Land — this chunk of earth known as Mound A. It didn't look like much, just another mundane topological variance in a featureless jungle. But this hump, and others like it, for which we were braving the elements (tornadoes and winds in excess of 100 miles an hour were moving our way), had once been part of a village over 5000 years ago. An Archaic Period (8500 to 500 B.C.) culture thrived here for centuries in what was now northeastern Louisiana. Joe was an archeologist studying the site. The rest of us (counting those dilettantes who refused to venture from the sanctity of our bus in this storm) were on a field trip, sponsored by the Archaeological Conservancy. Over the course of a week we would visit several mound-builder sites along the Lower Mississippi Valley.

Watson Brake, as this site was now known, had once been home to a hunter-gatherer society. Agriculture had not yet come to this region. It would be at least another millennium before this quantum leap in food technology would arrive here. But the people here were "manipulating the plants," said Joe. They were using certain plants that would later be domesticated. Over time, some food plants would become larger; seed coats would become thinner.

We followed Joe en masse in the negritude down the mound, to rush through other parts of the site. "Watch out for armadillo holes," he shouted. *Oh great, something else to trip over.* We made a whirlwind visit to Mound D, noticeably lower than Mound A. Archeologists labeled mounds alphabetically, from highest to lowest. This mound, overgrown with trees and brush like the rest of the site, was built in three stages, said Joe. Although there was debate over whether Watson Brake was constructed all at once or in steps, Joe subscribed to the "serial construction" theory. Which supported his opinion as to the population of the site, another debated issue. He favored the idea of a "smaller group" occupying the site, some 100 to 200 individuals.

Then it was off to Mound C, scurrying through the foliage to the drumbeat of the distant thunder, becoming louder by the minute. From the summit of this mound, Joe, talking above the incessant rain slapping against the leaves, pointed toward another hump, Mound B, that was connected to Mound C by a ridge. In all, there were eleven, maybe twelve, mounds here, mostly clustered around a huge plaza, 300 by 285 yards. The people here lived on the ridges and the mounds or just beyond the perimeter of the site. The mounds were not used for burial purposes, unlike mounds from much later periods. There was no evidence of occupation in the plaza, which may have served as a gathering place or a ceremonial center.

Watson Brake, like the other mound-builder sites we would visit — and apparently like such sites in general — was now devoid of houses and other buildings. Gone, for the most part, were the wood and mud and thatch structures, placed throughout a site, that would flesh out the mounds and plazas. There were no magnificent multistory, masonry complexes of room blocks and kivas, like those at the Anasazi cities of Pueblo Bonito and Mesa Verde. No coursed-adobe monoliths, as existed at the Hohokam village of Casa Grande. No towering pyramids, such as the Temple of the Sun at Teotihuacán. Not even incised, stone stelae and altars as used by the Maya to record important events and powerful rulers through a blend of portraits and hieroglyphs. In fact, there were no writing systems whatsoever, so the mound builders left no written record. The archeologists have thus turned to the mounds for answers — and to the artifacts.

The people at Watson Brake hunted with the atlatl, the bow and arrow being then unknown here. By about 300 A.D., long after the site was vacated by the original inhabitants, this advanced weapon would make its appearance in the area, probably being passed along by the Plains Indians. The Watson Brake hunters used what is known as an Evans projectile point on their spears. The point was unusual in that its base bore a flange along each side just above the stem. The point is a godsend to archeologists, as it's highly diagnostic for middle Archaic cultures from Louisiana and Arkansas. Joe told us that no one knew the reason for the Evans design.

The Evans point, whatever its engineering advantage, brought down deer and smaller animals. Fish, especially drum, constituted another important part of the diet, as did snails. The trees around us, that were partially sheltering us from the thunderstorm, were the same kinds that grew here five millennia ago, said Joe. They provided the inhabitants with such delicacies as acorns and hickory nuts.

Beads and drills, fashioned from stone, had been recovered from the site. Harder stones were used to drill through softer rocks, such as jasper and soapstone (steatite), to create the decorative beads.

Before sites like Watson Brake were discovered and analyzed, it had been assumed that mound complexes could only have been erected by societies with agriculture. For agriculture would have rooted the inhabitants to a permanent residence. And would have allowed the populations to explode, with sufficient time on their hands to engage in massive public-works projects. That myth had now been shattered. These hunter-gatherer peoples, some of them anyway, somehow found the time and manpower to construct impressive complexes of mounds and earthworks, many of which endure even today.

The thunder moved in, now booming like cannons exchanging salvos. My rain jacket kept me dry only above the waist. My jeans were soaked through, rivulets of water streaming down into my loose-fitting rubber boots that I had purchased only an hour ago at a bait-and-tackle shack; I had made off with the only pair they had left. Still, I was riveted on Joe's lecture, not anxious to abbreviate the tour of this site despite the crescendoing winds and rain. Joe was as wet as anyone, but the rain didn't dampen his spirits. About forty and boyish, he clearly enjoyed his life's work and was eager to share his knowledge. His enthusiasm was contagious.

Enigmatic clay blocks had been found here, he said. Roughly fist-sized, their function was still speculative. But Joe had a theory. Chert, a fine-grained, tough rock, had been placed in a sand-lined pit with scalding stones. The chert, once hot from the stones, could be easily shaped into a desired form by whacking flakes from its edges. But the stones in the pit heated the chert unevenly, complicating the fracture patterns and thus the working of the stone. Which is where the clay blocks came in. They spread the heat throughout the chert. The blocks, like the Evans points, were a blessing to archeologists, for they narrowed their origin to seven or eight sites, including Watson Brake, in northeastern Louisiana. Unlike the next site we would visit, Poverty Point, the stones and rocks here, whether raw or worked, all had a local derivation. Inexplicably, trade was virtually absent at Watson Brake.

Lightning was now flashing through the canopy, the wind throttling the trees. The already attenuated light was fading fast. Time to leave. We quickly shuffled out of the forest in a disorganized horde, hopefully in the direction of the dirt road that would lead back to the bus. No time to worry about armadillo holes. My homing instinct was working, taking me straight to the road. Everyone eventually made it, though some by very circuitous routes. I teamed up at the edge of the road with Carol, a former teacher and, like myself, a perennial student. We racewalked down the road ahead of the rest of the pack, which was spread out in twos and threes for over 200 yards. By now the lightning was overhead, its angry bursts intermittently illuminating the road like a strobe gone mad. We dodged the puddles, now coalescing into streams. Carol stayed to the edge of the road, seeking protection from the trees. I informed Carol that since I was from the lightning capital of the world, Florida, I knew that trees were no safeguard from a lightning strike. A bolt can strike a tree and zap anyone near it, as many a golfer can attest

"I wish you hadn't told me that," said Carol, half-smiling.

We were stepping it out in the downpour as though we were sprinting toward the finish line in a marathon-walking event. Finally the bus came into view in the murk. The bus driver, seeing our approach, opened the door for us from his comfortable seat. Dripping water, we filed down the aisle to our seats, past our dry comrades not willing to sacrifice their comfort for a chance to visit this seminal Archaic site.

Someone seated on the aisle asked me if the visit to the site had been worth getting caught in a thunderstorm. The questioner obviously wanted me to confirm that he had made the right decision in staying dry and comfy on the bus. I, of course, was not about to give him that satisfaction.

"Without seeing Watson Brake, there's no way to appreciate the rest of the sites on this trip," I lied.

Over the next ten minutes or so, the others straggled to the bus. Then we were off to the next site, before the tornadoes and two-inch hail could overtake us.

* * *

An hour's drive eastward took us away from the thunderstorms and into Poverty Point, another Archaic site. It flourished much later than Watson Brake, from about 1700 to 700 B.C. Unlike the raw site we had just visited, Poverty Point had been cultivated by the state of Louisiana for public use, replete with a visitors' center, movie theater and resident rangers. Unfortunately, before the site became an archeological landmark, it was partially destroyed by private use. Plantation owners of the Nineteenth Century had plowed the earthen embankments, for which Poverty Point was noted, down to mere nubs.

Dennis LaBatt, the site manager, treated us to an audio-visual presentation, then took us on a walking tour of the 400-acre site. As Dennis was marshalling our group for the tour, I quickly climbed the wooden tower outside the visitors' center, which provided a commanding panorama of the site spread out across a paved road 150 yards away. Beyond the road, which ran north and south, I could see more than half a mile of mowed grass extending westward to a huge tree-covered hill known as Mound A. The grass field was interrupted with wide, arcing rows of tall, red clover, averaging 100 feet apart, standing a yard or so above the grass. The clover, brightly though it shone beneath the grayish sky, wasn't there for decoration or for fodder. It demarcated the locations of the plowed ridges that once rose to heights of five to ten feet. Now the ridges, only a couple of feet high, barely rose above the flat terrain. There were six concentric rows of clover, arranged in a semi-circle and split by four aisles into five pizza-like sections, hovering around a central plaza. The outer ridge spanned a diameter of three-quarters of a mile; the inner, 2000 feet.

As we followed Dennis across the road and through the bands of clover, I bemoaned that the ridges, seven miles of them, had been sacrificed for modern agriculture. But the plantation owners had priorities other than preserving antiquity. Still, it would have added greatly to our understanding of the Poverty Point people had the archeologists been given the opportunity to analyze the site before the ridges were violated. For we don't even know why the ridges were constructed. Although based upon speculation, Dennis felt the ridges served, at least in part, as residential platforms. I asked about the evidence, since no houses had been uncovered on the ridges.

"Cooking pits have been found, on the (truncated) tops and on the sides. And projectile points."

I could envision the inhabitants living on those concentric ridges around a central plaza, where meetings and festivities might have taken place. I imagined that the houses, huts really, would have been formed from a foundation of vertical posts, connected by a latticework of sticks, all held together by mud and capped by a thatched roof. The wide swaths between the ridges could have functioned as alleyways, allowing ready access to the rows of houses. But whatever their purpose, the building of the ridges constituted a massive investment in man-hours. Some 586,000 cubic yards of dirt was hauled into place for these embankments, said Dennis. "Enough for a modern skyscraper!" It was truly a Herculean effort considering that instead of backhoes and bulldozers, the people here dug with sticks, shells and hoes, hauling the dirt in wicker baskets and animal hides. Even draft animals and the wheel were unknown to these people — and apparently to the entire Western Hemisphere before European contact. Which makes sites like Poverty Point all the more incredible. Even among prehistoric villages noted for their impressive public-works monuments, Poverty Point stands out. During its tenure, it was the governmental and commercial center of its time. In its heyday it housed the largest, most elaborate earthworks anywhere in North America.

When in existence, the ridges, perched on Maçon Ridge, opened onto a bluff overlooking a body of water, possibly a lake, that was part of the Mississippi River floodplain. Poverty Point was strategically located with access to a vast riparian system that fostered an extensive trade network. This site, like the older Watson Brake, was erected and inhabited by a hunter-gatherer culture, before the advent of agriculture to the region. Yet food was plentiful. Though corn, beans and squash, the universal triumvirate of agricultural societies in North America, were as yet unknown here, there were abundant wild plants for the taking. Including a preponderance of such nuts as pecan, acorn, walnut and hickory; and fruit such as persimmons, grapes and berries.

The people here hunted with the atlatl, to fell mainly deer but also rabbits, raccoons, opossums and squirrels. The power of the atlatl was enhanced by affixing a stone weight to its shaft, thereby increasing the momentum of the thrown projectile. Dennis later demonstrated the effectiveness of this weapon back at the visitors' center. He had practiced for months with his handmade contraption and had become somewhat proficient in its use. While we gathered around him, he loaded up the atlatl with a spear, cocked his arm, and heaved the spear with only a half-hearted effort toward an imaginary target. From my limited exposure to the atlatl at the Crow Canyon headquarters in Colorado, I knew the spear would fly. And fly it did, as though propelled under its own power like a rocket. It raced above the ground like an arrow when released, gaining altitude, flying over a set of small trees, and onto a field beyond, attaining far more distance and speed than could have been achieved from even the strongest unaided arm. Many in our group, who had never before witnessed the flight of an atlatl spear, were awed.

"That's nothing," said Dennis.

He gestured to the road. "I've thrown it across that road before."

Quite a feat, considering that the spear, had it been a baseball, would have traveled far enough to clear the fences for a home run at most major-league ballparks. Dennis, who appeared in his thirties, may have been in good shape, but he didn't impress me as a decathlete. So his accomplishments with the atlatl were a tribute more to the weapon itself than to his athletic prowess. I couldn't begin to imagine the distance and accuracy that must have been achieved with the atlatl by the hunters here three to four millennia ago. For they would have become acquainted with the device in childhood, and their very likelihood would have depended, at least in part, upon its efficient use.

The people here wove fish traps and nets, which put gar, bream, bass and catfish on their menu. Turtles were plentiful and easily collected, as were frogs and snakes. With a bit more difficulty, alligators were taken.

The hunters also employed a rather unusual weapon to bring down birds and small game. Bolas, which I had thought were confined to the Argentinean pampas, were manufactured, with leather cords connecting to four or five stone weights into an octopus-like configuration. One weight at the end of a leather cord was held in the hand of the hunter, who then swung the rest of the weapon in ever-accelerating circles above his head, as though winding up a sling for a shot. When the overhead portion of the device was at maximum rotational velocity, the hunter released the bola, firing the whirling mass of leather and stones at the potential prey. If thrown accurately, the bola would entangle the legs of the prey, bringing it down.

Stone implements were also utilized to prepare the food. Animals were butchered with hefty, bifaced cleavers and sharp knife-like flakes. Nuts and seeds were pounded into flour by rocks.

We continued our trek westward across the grassy field. We traversed the outer band of clover along an aisle of grass and were immediately at the base of Mound A, the famous bird-effigy mound. Or so it's thought. It took a bit of imagination for me to conjure up the outline of a bird in the topography of the mound. But Mound A was roughly shaped like a poorly molded bird with outstretched wings and a long fantail. Measuring 640 feet from wing tip to wing tip and 710 feet from head to tail, this had been another prodigal construction project, one that required 286,000 cubic yards of fill. It obviously took a sizable population to undertake and maintain such an effort. Between 2000 and 3000 inhabitants, figured Dennis. The food resources were certainly sufficient here to support such a populace. The name of the site, Poverty Point, cast no aspersions on the ability of the mound builders to meet their needs here. The appellation derives from more modern times when farmers and other settlers were unable to sustain themselves.

From the tail end we scaled the long mound, which was loosely overgrown with trees and brush. Squirrels scampered away at our approach, though we posed no threat to them. But in another time, they would have been fair game. After gaining seventy-two feet in altitude, we were at the summit, near the bird's head. The mound had once been higher, said Dennis.

"Probably close to one hundred feet when built."

I queried Dennis as to the basis for the accepted belief that the mound was shaped like a bird in flight, since that never would have occurred to me had it not been pointed out. He mentioned that there was "bird symbolism" here.

"Such as?" I probed.

"Pot-bellied owls."

The stone owls were sculpted from jasper, and came in three sizes, "from the great-horned owl all the way down to the screech owl." They were carved locally and may have been exported. Unlike their earlier counterparts at Watson Brake, these people did engage in trade.

Dennis pointed out a gaping depression to the west, beyond the head of the bird. A "borrow pit," said Dennis — a fourteen-acre quarry from which the dirt for Mound A had been excavated.

The original inhabitants must have been constantly at work on one project or another, for there were earthen features throughout the site. Our guide gestured in other directions, toward structures not readily visible from our observation point due to the foliage on the mound. But the Poverty Point people would have had a clear view to the north, to Mound B, almost half a mile away, since Mound A was then bald. Mound B, a domed hill, was much smaller, rising to only twenty feet. It's thought to be a tumulus, since charred human bone fragments have been excavated from an ash bed within the mound. It was the only evidence of a burial within the entire site, posing a conundrum as to how these people disposed of their dead. Perhaps cremation was practiced, but if so then more charred remains should have turned up. Or maybe there was a cemetery somewhere as yet undiscovered.

A mile north of Mound B stood Motley's Mound, thought to have been an incipient bird mound. With a borrowed pair of binoculars, I descended partway down the north face of Mound A, to where an opening in the foliage allowed an unobstructed view over to Motley's Mound. It took a tremendous leap of faith to make a bird mound out of what I saw — an unimpressive hump of earth in no particular shape. A guidebook claimed that because the mound "had only a slight bulge where the bird's tail should have been, it was believed to be unfinished." Such a belief borders on the religious!

About 600 feet to the south of us was a small hill, Ballcourt Mound. The name was a misnomer, since there was no evidence of ball games played there. No one seemed to know what function

Ballcourt Mound served or how it came to be named. Farther south, a mile and a half beyond Ballcourt Mound, rose Lower Jackson Mound, another enigma. This may not have been part of Poverty Point, and may have antedated the site by at least a millennium. If so, that earlier society is a complete mystery.

However, much is known about the Poverty Point people, not just from their earthworks, which alone would guarantee them a place in the archeology books, but from the magnificent implements and other artifacts they created. They imported and worked stones and minerals — chert, flint, soapstone, magnetite and copper, among others. Accomplished craftsmen, they fashioned not only spear points and knives but also adzes and drills. They polished stones into celts, for axe heads; and into plummets, for bola stones and net anchors. And carved beads, pendants and animal figures. From the softer rocks, such as soapstone and sandstone, they sculpted jars and bowls as storage and cooking vessels.

Hand-molded, fired-clay "cooking objects" went into their cooking pits by the dozens to evenly distribute the heat. These lumps of clay varied considerably in shape, from spheres to spirals to more amorphous forms. Whether the differing configurations were the result of the artisans' creative efforts or served the more pragmatic function of modulating the temperature was still anyone's guess. Toward the end of their occupation here, the Poverty Point culture somehow came upon pottery. Of course, they never knew of the potter's wheel, yet they formed durable, thick-walled vessels reinforced with palmetto fiber and Spanish moss.

Like the other North American cultures, the Poverty Point people left no written record. Many facets of their existence thus remain a mystery. Their political structure, for instance. "It's unknown whether they were theocratic or democratic," said Dennis. There were other options, of course, which likewise couldn't be ruled out.

It's doubtful the Poverty Point people engaged in, or were subjected to, warfare, the guidebooks informed me. But how did they know? Remains of houses — or of any building, for that matter — didn't exist here. So how did anyone know whether the houses were torched, in an act of war or civil unrest? And there weren't nearly enough human remains to deduce whether large numbers of individuals died a violent death, from warfare or sacrifice.

I wondered why, with such a thriving culture, having built massive earthen monuments, having established extensive trading networks, having sustained their numbers from the land, the people of this site had not endured. Why had they just disappeared? Then it occurred to me that they hadn't simply come and gone like fly-by-night scam artists. They *had* endured. For a thousand years — at least. *Our* culture should do so well.

As we retraced our steps down the bird mound, again scattering the squirrels, I asked Dennis why the site had been abandoned. He ventured his theory.

"They opted for a simpler way of life."

I tend to seek more complex reasons for a society's decline or disappearance — like tribal conquests, civil war, depletion of resources, overpopulation, extended drought or combinations thereof. But perhaps the answer lies in Dennis' simplistic explanation.

※　※　※

The Archaic Period was immediately followed by the Woodlands Period (500 B.C. to 900 A.D.). Pottery became more pervasive, plants were being cultivated, and the bow and arrow made its introduction toward the latter part of the period. We pulled into Toltec, a late Woodlands site in central Arkansas, where we were greeted by Dr. Martha Rolingson, the resident archeologist. Beneath a clear, pastel sky blemished by only a few cottony puffs, Martha led us along a trail through Toltec, now a state park.

The site name was a blatant misnomer. A Nineteenth Century owner of the property somehow got it into his thick head that the Toltecs from Mexico built this place. He was dead wrong. The Toltecs never came anywhere near this area. Perhaps the landowner, like the misguided individual who inaccurately named Aztec Ruins in Colorado, figured such elaborate constructions could not have been the product of local indigenous ingenuity.

The 100-acre site was contained on three sides by an earthen embankment shaped like a flattened semicircle and bordered on the outside by a ditch. The semicircle opened onto a pond that constituted the fourth boundary of the site. As we trailed Martha around the site, it was readily obvious that many of the manmade features were missing. There had once been eighteen dirt mounds. Few of them remained. The locations of most of the others, which had been razed or eroded to ground level, were each now marked by a short pole with a red pennant bearing the letter assigned to that mound. From my vantage point at the top of the semicircle, I scanned the site, a mowed-grass field stretching to my left and right. A few tree-covered mounds popped up here and there, interrupting an otherwise flat terrain. The lettered pennants dotted the field in both directions. They called to memory a golf driving range with flags denoting distances from the tee. The mounds, both the visible ones and those now marked by pennants, had once been clustered around two large plazas, which were now merged into the grasslands.

Martha, blithe, about fifty, and shaded by a straw hat, smiled and stepped with alacrity as we made the rounds, pausing from time to time, hands in pockets, to discuss some feature or other. She pointed out the embankment and the ditch, or rather where they had been, since modern farming had ravaged them almost into oblivion. Only tatters of the embankment, which once rose to ten feet and stretched for a mile, still survived. As with Watson Brake and Poverty Point, it took an abundance of imagination to form a picture of what Toltec must have looked like in its glory days, from about 600 to 1050 A.D.

The embankment-and-ditch construction was a rarity for sites in the Mississippi Valley. It occurred to me that this combination would have made a formidable defensive system, especially if the ditch were filled with water. I asked Martha about warfare.

"There's no good evidence of much warfare during this Woodlands phase, at least not here."

So much for that brainstorm.

In contrast to Poverty Point, Toltec was not a population center. Rather, it served as a political and religious hub. The occupants, referred to as the Plum Bayou culture, resided in scattered villages and farmsteads in the surrounding area.

We stopped in front of Mound C, at twelve feet tall the third highest mound, at least of those still in existence. The earthen dome was a burial mound, said Martha. Two human graves were excavated there in 1966. Surprisingly, no funerary goods were found with the bodies. If the mound had been erected as a tribute to those buried within it, I would have expected the deceased to have been members of the ruling class, or at least of the elite. As such, dedicatory objects, of ceramic and stone perhaps, should have been placed in the graves. Then again, maybe the mound represented a convenient spot to dispose of the bodies. After all, the supposedly sophisticated Anasazi were known to have dumped their corpses in refuge heaps. Martha did note, however, that there had been reports of pot hunters (read: thieves of history) finding pottery in the mound. Of course, the pot hunters, not being motivated by academic concerns, didn't turn their finds over to archeologists for study. So whatever they uncovered from Mound C probably wound up in private collections. Those artifacts could have told archeologists something about those buried in the mound, and probably about those who did the burying. But those artifacts will not be allowed to speak, restrained by a gag-order imposed by their current (anonymous) owners.

Martha gestured toward Mound B, off in the distance at the edge of the farther plaza. It was a rectangular platform mound, thirty-nine feet in height that once was the foundation for a residence, supposedly for a member of the elite.

"This was a chiefdom society," Martha told us. "But the chiefs weren't held to god status as in later societies." Which I took to mean that the political hierarchy here had a tighter structure than that of the egalitarian society of the Anasazi, but less than that of the totalitarian theocracy of the Aztecs.

Cotton was grown on Mound B in the late Nineteenth Century. The owner at the time reported coming across pottery shards and bones during the plowing. Pottery, widely used here, was more utilitarian than ceremonial, usually being unpainted, rarely being incised. Some of the vessels were monochromatic, coated with a red tint, vastly inferior in an aesthetic sense to the polychromatic works of art from contemporaneous cultures in Mesoamerica and South America.

While the real Toltecs of Mexico didn't venture into the Mississippi Valley, I wondered whether one of the hallmarks of Mesoamerican cultures — the ballgame, which had religious significance — reached here. No, said Martha, there was no evidence of that.

The trail took us to the pond. Martha explained that food was available to support a fairly large population, but the people chose to reside outside the compound.

"I don't see any large population here," she said.

Someone asked the basis of her opinion.

"There are no thick midden deposits that would indicate a high population density."

Yet, game and plants were here for the taking. The inhabitants foraged for nuts and berries. They grew "native grasses" such as barley, amaranth and may grass. Squash, an imported crop, had reached the Southeast by then. And there was "some corn only." I asked about beans, knowing they were a late addition to the diet of the cultures of the Southwest.

"There were no beans in eastern North America before 1200 A.D."

From the remains of long-ago meals excavated at the site, it was apparent that the mound builders enjoyed a variety of animal protein. Over fifty species of meat were available. White-tailed deer were taken in large numbers, now that the bow and arrow had replaced the atlatl. Turkeys constituted a major portion of the diet. The pond provided fish and turtles. Other fowl, particularly those that ventured near the pond, wound up on the dinner table. Interestingly, hundreds of bones from passenger pigeons, a bird that became extinct early in the Twentieth Century, have been uncovered. The area was a way station on one of their migratory routes.

We followed Martha along a boardwalk that skirted part of Mound A at the pond's edge. Tall bald-cypress trees with copious interlocking branches lurked in the shallows, shading our route. These trees, though conifers, were noteworthy in that they were deciduous, shedding their leaves annually. They were felled and scooped into dugout canoes, as were pine trees, by the Plum Bayou people. Other trees, not so partial to a watery environment, enveloped the mound.

One of the men in our group lacked sufficient bladder capacity or control to make it back to the visitors' center. So he ducked behind a wide tree, one surrounded by short plants with a most distinctive leaf pattern, which he failed to notice. As he was streaming blissfully on the far side of the tree, apparently in very close proximity to these other plants, someone called out a warning to beware of the poison ivy.

"Oh shit!" he blurted — inaccurate as to the bodily function he was exercising but descriptive of his amusing (to the rest of us) predicament.

When he reappeared from behind the tree, a telltale dark stain on his pants told of his panic when greeted by the revelation.

This modest hill of earth before us, the largest here, peaked at fifty feet. Remarkably, it had never been excavated. Its purpose, therefore, remained unknown. When probed about future plans to dig into Mound A, Martha expressed a lack of interest, mentioning something about not wanting to expend the resources and about leaving something for later archeologists. That response sure didn't square with the enthusiasm about the site that Martha displayed on our walking tour. Had I been the resident archeologist here, you can bet I'd have found a way to get a shovel into Mound A, one way or the other.

As we continued our trek, Martha pointed toward certain mounds (or their current representatives, the pennants), noting that patterns of cosmic alignments have been discovered along some pairs of mounds. For example, Mounds A and H lined up with the equinoxes. Mounds H and S collimated with the winter solstice. And so on. The people here, despite their limited reliance on agriculture, were keeping track of the seasons for some reason.

The Plum Bayou people did trade, but only on a limited basis. A single piece of unforged copper, probably part of an ornament, was uncovered. Some of the metal made its way to Toltec from the Great Lakes region, to be cold-hammered into shape here. The process of smelting and forging copper was not discovered here or anywhere else in North America in prehistoric times. In fact, metallurgy of any sort was completely unknown on the continent until the arrival of the Europeans.

Interestingly, effigy owls were carved here, reminiscent of the practice at Poverty Point, though the two sites were separated by some 300 miles and more than a thousand years.

For some reason, almost a millennium ago, the site fell into desuetude, the people fading away. The destination and the fate of the Plum Bayou people remain a mystery.

✳ ✳ ✳

The Mississippian Period, which ran roughly (depending upon the geographical area) from 900 A.D. until the Contact (by the Spaniards), followed on the heels of the Woodlands Period. This era was characterized in part by a proliferation of truncated rectangular mounds and more extensive agriculture. Winterville, a D-shaped collection of mounds and plazas, situated on the western border of Mississippi, was a classic site of the period, enduring from around 1000 to 1400 A.D.

We exited the bus, cut through the miniature museum, and filed along a trail that circumnavigated the site; that is, the eighteen acres of it owned by the state. The remainder of Winterville was in private hands, the archeological features having fallen to the plow. Most of the state's site was groomed, including many of the truncated mounds. A leaden sky threatened rain but mercifully held off until we finished our tour of the site.

Alan Gruber, a regional director of the Conservancy, guided our stroll. The first structure we encountered was Mound A, the Great Temple Mound, and the highest at fifty-five feet. It stood at the approximate center of the site, with the other mounds arcing around it. In terms of size, it wasn't impressive. Some 80,000 cubic yards of earth went into its fill, a pittance compared to the huge volumes of dirt it took to complete the massive earthen monuments at the much earlier site of Poverty Point. The mounds here differed in another respect from those at Poverty Point, and the other earlier sites we'd visited as well. In keeping with the times, these were all flat-topped, in contrast to abundance of domed and conical mounds of the previous sites. It's true that Ballcourt Mound at Poverty Point was flattened, but that was exceptional for that site and for the Archaic Period. And Mound B at the Woodlands center of Toltec also was a platform mound, again unusual for that period.

Only thirteen mounds remained at Winterville, from the over thirty that probably once existed. According to Jay Mitchell, the site's manager, two of the thirteen actually dated to a previous culture, the Coles Creek, which was in the area hundreds of years before the Mississippian people arrived on the scene. The Coles Creek group, a warlike tribe, was eventually displaced or assimilated by a more peaceful, commercially oriented society from the north during the beginnings of the Mississippian Period. It was this latter culture than erected the additional mounds and other features.

Winterville, like Toltec, was a ceremonial, rather than a population, center. The mounds, many of them anyway, were platforms for temples, another characteristic of these times that varied from the earlier Woodlands Period. Chiefs probably lived in some of the structures atop the platforms, said Alan.

He gestured to the south, toward Mound B. A midden deposit had been uncovered there, which would usually be indicative of an extensive or an enduring occupancy. But this place only housed a couple of hundred residents, at most, at any one time. So how, I asked Alan, could so much have been built here by so few workers. Oh, there were thousands of inhabitants in the area, but they lived out in the countryside, beyond the borders of the site. When not busy with farming or household duties, they devoted some time to their ceremonial center.

I had noticed discoidal stone artifacts in the museum. Shaped like hockey pucks and polished to a smooth finish, they varied in size from a couple to several inches across. I asked Alan about these enigmatic objects. They were used in the game of chunkey, he told me. In one version of the sport, a chunkey stone was rolled along the ground. When it came to rest, players hurled spears at the stone, the winner being the one who came closest. Sort of a cross between lawn darts and shuffleboard, I guess.

There were about four plazas when the site was inhabited. A causeway that then connected Mound A to Mound D was all but gone now; only a low grass-covered bump was left to bear witness to its former grandeur. There was no evidence here of an embankment or of a ditch, as had existed at Toltec. Nor was the site ever palisaded for defensive purposes. So the place was never a fortress.

The museum displayed samples of the multitude of the tools available to the industrious site builders. From quartz, chert and flint, they fashioned axes, chisels, adzes and hoe blades. They shaped bone into awls and needles, a necessity for weaving cloth, making baskets, and working leather.

The Winterville people had the benefit of corn, which by then had come to dominate their diet. To their detriment, thought Alan.

"Their diet became less diverse."

The increased reliance upon corn for calories "caused nutritional problems," he added. "Their overall height decreased a couple of inches. There were more deaths in childhood."

It's ironic that a crop that became so widespread, which allowed populations to blossom, could also have been deleterious. The people here used "too much corn," said Alan, which substituted for a well-balanced diet, thereby leading to many diseases.

But the people weren't dying, at least in droves, of deficiency diseases. And their numbers apparently weren't being depleted by warfare. So why did they leave? Alan wasn't sure. Archeology hadn't yet come up with an answer.

Jay, however, had a theory. There was a fire in the 1300s and again in the 1400s, he told me. The people rebuilt after the earlier fire, but not after the later one. Excavations revealed that no mounds were erected after about 1350 A.D. It was about that time, Jay figured, that the nearby Mississippi River changed course, perhaps over several years. The people then just drifted away, probably to a neighboring village — a simplistic solution, but one that sounded plausible.

*   *   *

We finally got to glimpse a prehistoric site complete with a plaza, buildings and mounds. Chucalissa, tucked into the southwestern corner of Tennessee, was a reconstruction, but it gave the visitor an idea of the layout of a Mississippian town. Between 1000 to 1550 A.D., the modest twelve-acre site was occupied, abandoned and reoccupied several times. It derived its name from the Choctaw word for "abandoned house." The population peaked at close to a thousand individuals.

Our guide, Dr. David Dye, led us to the site from the interpretive center via a modern, underground passage. It had been recently emblazoned with a harlequin rattlesnake zigzagging along one wall for several feet. The painting was derived from an engraved water bottle excavated at the site. Rattlesnake motifs, symbolic of the Sun God, were common in late Mississippian times in the Southeast. The design was reminiscent of the feathered serpent of

RECONSTRUCTED FAMILY SCENE AT CHUCALISSA

Mesoamerica and the horned serpent of the Southwest. Although the snake motif could have arisen here independently, I did notice what appeared to be a short horn on this snake's snout, perhaps implying a connection to the serpent of the Southwest.

The passage exited at a corner of a square plaza, about the size of a football field. Houses, of dignitaries and craftsmen, recently built of course, were arranged around the plaza, as they would have sat in the Fifteenth Century. Along the southern perimeter stood a pair of thatched-roof huts. Too inquisitive to follow along on the tour, I played hooky from our crowd and ducked into the closest hut. Such a structure would originally have been constructed from a framework of posts, with walls of cane mats plastered with mud that was reinforced with grass. This reproduction, meant to endure for decades, was built of sturdier, more modern materials.

Life-sized mannequins, scantily clad, depicted a typical Indian family at work in the single-room hut. A man, supposedly the husband, was intently affixing a stone point to an arrow shaft. His wife was engrossed in her weaving. An older woman, perhaps a grandmother, was preparing a meal of shellfish, while keeping an eye on an infant. Other children were playing nearby. Furs, a valuable trade commodity, were draped and hanging within the hut. Bear skins were spread around the room, for comfort and warmth. A woven fish trap sat on an overhead loft beneath the steeply pitched, high roof. Gourds, to be later cut and cleaned for use as containers, dangled from the edge of the loft. I was beholding a moment of time frozen and sectioned for scrutiny under a microscope five centuries later. So lifelike was the exhibit that I felt like a voyeur. Though not one riddled with guilt. I gawked like a youngster surreptitiously witnessing, for the first time, an adult couple frolicking in a romantic embrace.

I shuffled past the other hut, its entrance shielded by a wooden ramada. The ramada's open framework would have allowed a breeze to cool the Chucalissa occupants who carried out some of their domestic chores outdoors.

On the eastern edge of the plaza stood a small rectangular mound, once a platform for a seigniorial residence. The mound was now bare. I wandered around to its backside, still able to avoid the crowd that was just now all trying to squeeze into the first hut. I was at the crest of a bluff overlooking a floodplain of the mighty Mississippi River — a magnificent view. But the erection of Chucalissa on this spot was more for self-preservation than for sightseeing. For the Mississippian Period was characterized by rampant warfare, unlike earlier times. While this western flank of the settlement was virtually inaccessible to hostile approach, the opposite side was most vulnerable to attack. So it was almost certainly protected by a stockade wall.

Farther along, at the northwest corner of the site, stood the shaman's thatched-roof hut. A pivotal figure in an aboriginal community, the shaman employed a smorgasbord of herbs, chants and dances, reinforced by the vigorous shaking of rattles, in the perpetual struggle to ward off evil spirits and to appease the gods. A peek into the hut revealed the mannequin shaman engaged in a curing ceremony, an herbal potion simmering on a nearby fire. Dried plants, hanging from the rafters, constituted part of his pharmacy.

Along the northern side of the plaza rose the chief's house, elevated above the surrounding terrain on a platform mound of its own. A stairway led up to the high-peaked, thatched-roof dwelling, easily twice the volume of the huts of the less noble that sat across the plaza. Even to the casual observer it was obvious that this structure was special, conferring elite status upon its residents. The exhibit inside confirmed my suspicions.

The chief, regally attired to reflect his high status, was sitting majestically on the fired-hardened earth, holding court. From top to bottom, he was the embodiment of royalty, starting with the feathered headdress, resembling a Plains Indian war bonnet, and the copper head ornament. Two pendants dangled across his chest — one of hammered-copper ornaments, the other of Gulf Coast shells. He was wrapped in a feathered cloak and was clutching a stone war club. Three advisors waited intently behind him.

The chief's attention was directed to three other men, none from his village. These strangers, clad in loincloths, were passing through the territory and, in keeping with the consuetude, stopped to pay homage to the chief. And bear him gifts. A tortoise-shell rattle was being presented. As was a soapstone pipe bowl mounted to a wooden shaft, an excellent device for smoking one's way through a wad of tobacco.

I bid the chief farewell and slipped out without interrupting his important meeting. Down the mound I hurried to the eastern side of the site. A corn crib, perched high off the ground, held the inhabitants' stash of the crop that had by now become a mainstay in the Indian diet. The legs of the structure were kept polished to discourage mice and other hungry critters from raiding the crib, for they too had developed a fondness for corn, nutritionally deficient or not.

A patch of ground adjacent to the crib was reproduced to depict those crops cultivated by the villagers. Beans by now had arrived, supplementing the existing staples of corn and squash. Sunflowers and tobacco were also grown.

And game abounded, especially deer and turkey. The bow and arrow, in use for centuries, had replaced the atlatl. It had also essentially superseded the blowgun, a weapon I hadn't realized existed in the pre-Columbian Western Hemisphere north of South America. The blowgun here, used mainly during the Woodlands Period, differed from the version I had toyed with while in the Amazon Jungle. That blowgun was laboriously fashioned from two long strips of wood, which were lashed together. A channel was then reamed out down the center of the strips, using a stiff rod coated with a mixture of sand and water. The task was labor intensive and time consuming.

The Indians near Chucalissa had it easier. Cane was readily available. If a tube of cane was not perfectly straight when harvested, it could be made so by heating and bending. Once cooled, the cane retained its heat-induced straightening. A channel could then be quickly reamed out through the cane, since most of its length was hollow.

The center of the plaza was recessed and served as an arena for sporting events. By now the crowd had caught up with me. Which turned out well, since our guide launched into a discussion of the local pre-Columbian ballgames. Chunkey was then still around, but no longer was it the only game in town. Games of dice were popular, and gambling was legal. The stakes could be high. Sometimes one's entire possessions rode on a toss of the cube.

Dave pointed to the two towering, wooden posts, resembling telephone poles, shoved into the ground at opposite corners of the arena. They were the "goals" for stickball, which had come to proliferate throughout the Southeast. There were two teams, each defending a goal. The object was to hit your opponent's post with a deerskin-covered ball, while preventing the other team from doing the same thing to your post. The first team to amass 100 points was the winner. Games could last for a couple of days, or more.

"What about rules?" someone asked.

"Rules?" There weren't any other rules, said Dave. Just about anything went.

Not any more. The present-day Indian residents of the area, the Choctaw, now play a remarkably similar game, one with a set of rules. The players today, like their predecessors, wear no pads; some wear no shoes. Despite the modern rules, meant in part to curb rampant injuries, many players have to take a time-out to visit an emergency room.

❋   ❋   ❋

In 1539, Hernando de Soto and his expeditionary force of 700 men disembarked on the Florida peninsula at what is now Tampa. With some 500 soldiers, 225 horses, dozens of craftsmen, priests and servants, and a herd of 300 pigs, he set off to explore the Southeast. His incursion would form a foundation for the Spanish colonization of the region. Its purpose was also to confer the benefits of Christianity upon the misguided indigenous heathens. And, most importantly, to relieve those very same heathens of any gold they happened to have hanging around. For de Soto was well familiar with the ruthless but lucrative exploits of Cortés in Mexico and Pizarro in Peru. In fact, de Soto had served under the brutal Pizarro in the campaign that destroyed the Inca empire.

Gold!

It was de Soto's mantra as he meandered through the Southeast fervently seeking to emulate the triumphs of his illustrious conquistador forebears. To heap untold riches upon the Spanish crown — and upon himself in the process. To find the equivalent of El Dorado here as his contemporary, Coronado, was doing in his search for the famed (but mythical) Seven Cities of Cíbula in the Southwest. But, like Coronado, de Soto was destined to fail. His quest for gold would be a will-o'-the-wisp, forever eluding him as the Fountain of Youth would later elude another Spaniard who set foot on Florida shores, Ponce de Léon.

De Soto's trek has been labeled "one of the most devastating military invasions in Southeastern history." Sherman's infamous March to the Sea centuries later would make de Soto's expedition seem like an Easter Day parade, but for its time de Soto's escapades constituted a reign of terror. For despite having overwhelming numbers most of the time, the Indians' were almost invariably defeated in armed conflicts. Their stone-age weaponry was completely outclassed by modern implements of war levied against them by the Spaniards. The Indians, who had never been assailed by metal weapons, were slashed to ribbons by iron swords. And ripped by metal bullets. Their return fire, from arrows, spears and clubs, was grossly ineffective, as that very same metal that decimated their ranks, iron, also shielded the Spaniards. And then there were the mounted soldiers, many of them battle-hardened from other wars, the likes of which the Indians had never seen. Their first glimpse of horses — and of Europeans — was to portend dire consequences for them.

It is estimated that de Soto's men killed 3500 Indians, at least. And took many others captive. Despite subsisting in part on the swineherd, the Spaniards, in accordance with their game plan, lived off the land. Which usually meant consuming the food supplies of natives along their route, sometimes from gift, at times by purchase, occasionally through confiscation.

In village after village, de Soto inquired about the shiny metals — gold and silver. His interrogation methods at times would have earned him a nomination for Inquisitor General back on the Continent. The Indians were understandably only too anxious to rid themselves of their unwelcomed guests. So they invariably sent the Spaniards off in the direction that would take them to their pot of gold at the end of the rainbow. The rainbow always seemed to end over the next hill. And there was always one more hill. I wonder if de Soto ever caught on.

In 1541, his travels took him to Casqui, an Indian village in what is now northeastern Arkansas. At the time, Casqui was engaged in centuries-old hostilities with its imperialistic neighbor, Pacaha. De Soto himself experienced the truculence of the Pacaha as he prepared to ford the Mississippi River. During the month it took for his men to construct four barges, to transport troops, animals and supplies across the river, they were harassed daily by 250 canoes full of warriors. Upon crossing the river, de Soto passed up the chance to pay a social call on Pacaha, opting instead to drop in on Casqui. What transpired survives today thanks to the accounts of the Spanish chroniclers on the trip. For the Spaniards' lust for gold was matched by their obsession for history — they were meticulous record keepers.

The Spaniards encountered a complex of platform mounds in Casqui. The village was heavily fortified with a wide moat and a palisade of logs. Garcilaso de la Vega, a Spanish historian, described one of the mounds:

> *"[The chief's] dwelling was situated to one side of the town on a high mound, where there were in addition ten to twelve large structures that housed the chieftain's entire family of wives and his numerous servants."*

The initial encounter between the Spaniards and the Casqui was cordial if not friendly. De Soto managed to avoid a confrontation with this group of Indians. Despite the lack of aggression from the Casqui, de Soto declined an invitation to house his men within the village and instead camped in a nearby orchard. At the time, the Casqui were suffering through an extended drought. They sought help from their strange visitors. In a gesture of assistance, the Spaniards erected a huge cross on a mound overlooking a river. Some 15,000 natives looked on in wonder from across the river. As dumb luck (or divine intervention) would have it, it rained the very next day. The cross was left in place as a gift to the Casqui, who constructed a cane fence around it.

By now the Casqui and de Soto were allies of sorts. They combined forces to settle the score with Pacaha. The Casqui amassed an army of 5000 warriors and 3000 bearers to accompany the Spaniards. The Pacaha were caught completely off guard by the invasion and fled to an island sanctuary. I can imagine the shock of the Pacaha at suddenly seeing their traditional enemy, joined by the very Spaniards they had recently harassed, swooping through their village in an all-out assault. The hellish scene must have been beyond their worst nightmares.

The Casqui raiders themselves were horrified as they came across the severed heads of their countrymen, formerly killed or captured, mounted on lance points at the Pacaha temple doors. Other Casqui captives, taken in previous skirmishes, were released. Pacaha was then sacked. But sacking wasn't retribution enough for the past sins of the Pacaha. The Casqui defiled the sacred temple that housed the bones of the ancestors of the Pacaha chief, a sacrilege of biblical proportions.

The Casqui were unable to dislodge the Pacaha from their island retreat, but enough damage had already been inflicted. Now it was the Pacaha who sought retaliation. According to de la Vega, the Pacaha chief said to the Casqui:

> *"Remember well what you are doing and what you already have done, for when these strangers (the Spaniards) have departed, then we shall see what manner of men you are in battle."*

But it never came to that, at least not while de Soto was still around. He made peace with the Pacaha, and even brokered a détente between the two tribes. Then he sent scouting parties into the countryside searching for gold. Finding none, he moved on.

De Soto never finished the expedition. He died along the way in 1542, the cause unknown. He was buried in the Mississippi River. His men, their numbers greatly worn down, worked their way down the Mississippi, eventually reaching Mexico later that same year. Only 311 men made it. The hogs fared better. In spite of consumption by the Spaniards, gifts to and thefts by the Indians, and occasional escapes, there were 500 hogs when de Soto died.

The historical record of the region fast-forwards more than a century to 1673, when the French explorers, Marquette and Joliet, passed through. They didn't encounter the thriving towns of mounds and plazas and houses that the Spaniards visited, or the thousands of industrious inhabitants in each town. Not even the war canoes loaded with archers that bedeviled the Spaniards. That was all gone. The towns and villages were, for the most part, deserted. The populations had all but disappeared. A pall of silence, devoid of civilization, had been cast over the region. For the Europeans, including de Soto's men, who preceded the Frenchmen into the area, had left more than the trappings of their culture. They had left a legacy of death!

Smallpox, influenza and measles, unintended gifts from the Continent, decimated the indigenous tribes who had no immunity to such diseases. Entire villages and cities were depopulated even by 1673. Smallpox, and other foreign infections, continued to take a heavy toll of the Indians even into the Nineteenth Century. Marquette and Joliet never did get to meet the Casqui. Whether the Casqui succumbed to these diseases or were vanquished by another tribe, the Quapaw, that later moved into the area, is still unknown. Perhaps their demise was the result of a combination of the two.

Over three centuries after the Marquette and Joliet adventure, our intrepid gang disembarked from the tour bus and followed Dr. Jeff Mitchem through Parkin, an unrestored archeological site. The seventeen-acre state park was bordered on one side by a river. Jeff led us across a footbridge that spanned a muddy ditch that curved around the site to form the rest of the boundary. Parkin has been worked by archeologists, including Jeff, in recent decades. It was reputed to be the remains of Casqui.

We paused along the trail at a "floatation tank," currently out of use. Jeff explained that when soil was dumped into the tank, plant material would float to the top. The slush was filtered through a screen to remove the debris, which was then sent to the lab for analysis by the ethnobotanists.

Continuing along the trail, we passed swaths of brilliant red clover bordering our route and extending off into the fields. Hundreds of monarch butterflies flitted over the clover, pausing to sample the nectar. I had never seen so many monarchs — or any other species of butterfly — in such masses. Jeff explained that the monarchs were on their migration route from Mexico, headed north, possibly to the Great Lakes region. They were magnificent in their Halloween costumes of orange and black, sprinkled with white dots. It was doubtful that any of these butterflies would ever see home, as it takes longer than a single generation to make the round trip. Monarchs are capable of very lengthy flights, but to complete the return trip, the relay baton would have to be passed down the line to a few more generations. Each butterfly travels only part of the route home, then it loads up on nutrients, breeds, and passes on, allowing its offspring to continue the journey. The route is essentially the same from year to year, yet it is a new trail to be blazed for each butterfly. But it is a trail unerringly followed, the butterfly being kept on course by its genetic GPS that has been programmed over countless generations.

The monarch's vivid coloration does not go unnoticed by birds always on the lookout for a tasty morsel. But the ostentatious color pattern that would seem to doom the monarch is in fact its very salvation. For this butterfly dines heavily upon the milkweed, a plant possessed of toxic substances that usually fend off even the hungriest of herbivores and insects. Not only has the monarch figured out a way to ingest the milkweed safely, but also it can even divert the plant's toxins into its own armament to ward off avian, and other, predators. Its bold pigmentation, like that of such other toxic animals as poison-arrow frogs and the lionfish, is a warning that any assailant dare not ignore twice.

The viceroy butterfly, though not closely related to the monarch, bears a striking resemblance to it. So striking in fact that the viceroy, which is *not* toxic and is quite edible, avoids being consumed solely by virtue of evolution having endowed it with this protective coloration. You might not be able to fool Mother Nature, but you certainly can fool her predators.

Jeff led us by a platform mound, now overgrown and greatly eroded. It once supported houses that, for some reason, had a square floor plan thirteen feet long on a side. Any evidence of such houses had long since vanished. Waving his hand across the expanse of the site, Jeff mentioned that: "This is by far the largest village in this region." He estimated the population at 2000 at any one time. It was the "capital," which "ruled over a province."

Many pottery vessels have been found at Parkin, some as grave goods. The clay here was tempered with shell flecks, another characteristic of Mississippian cultures. The shell was imported from the Gulf coast and worked into ornaments, the discarded chips being mixed with clay for molding into jars and bowls. Jewelry was also fashioned from bird bones, fired clay and perhaps copper, which was rare at this site.

One distinctive set of artifacts from Parkin was the human-head effigy pots. As the name implies, each pot was shaped into a human head, somewhat smaller than life size. The heads varied in their features as though they were individual portraits. But they differed significantly in some respects from the life-like portrait vessels I had seen from other cultures; such as from the Moche of Peru, who were master craftsmen. The Parkin effigy heads all had holes punched in an arc through each outer ear, apparently as decoration. But it was other features that caught my attention: they had closed eyes, and the mouths were drawn tight with the lips curled back, as though in death. Jeff figured these were trophy heads, clay depictions of enemy heads taken in battle. The actual heads would have decayed after a short time, said Jeff, but the effigy pots would survive to commemorate the victories.

* * *

The bus disgorged us at the base of a huge platform mound, the second largest in the United States. Located in the southwestern corner of Mississippi, Emerald Mound was under the auspices of the National Park Service. It was now carpeted with trimmed grass and sprinkled with a handful of trees. Behind our guide for this site, Dr. Jim Barnett, we traipsed up the path to the flat-topped summit of the eight-acre, rectangular, earthen mound. Which was not its highest point, for there was a pair of secondary earthen mounds, also well groomed, set atop the base mound, one at each end. The site was built and occupied between 1250 to 1600 A.D.

We scaled one of the secondary mounds on this warm, sunny day. Its peak was only three and a half stories above the ground underlying the site, but much of this structure had eroded away over the centuries. Jim gestured around the site, noting its dimensions of greater than 700 feet in length and 400 feet in width, about as large as eight football fields. It had risen sixty feet into the air when totally intact, a lofty prominence in those days. Its sides were oriented according to the cardinal directions, said Jim. This was another prodigal public-works project carried out with primitive, but effective, tools of wood, bone and stone. Dirt was laboriously lugged up onto the mound in wicker baskets and animal skins, a tribute to the industriousness of the inhabitants. And to the persuasiveness of their leaders. General Norman Schwartzkopf characterized a leader as someone who could get those under his command to do *willingly* what they would not otherwise do, even to the point of endangering their own lives. Clearly the leaders here, and at other mound-builder sites, had that ability, whether by political or religious means.

I scooted down this secondary declivity, across the top of the base mound, and over to the other secondary mound, for a view from the opposite end of the site. This mound was not as lofty as the one I had just left. Six other platform mounds had once rested on the summit of Emerald Mound. Erosion and modern plowing had eradicated them completely. The secondary mounds had served as foundations for temples or other ceremonial structures. All the temples and other buildings were unfortunately long gone by now.

For a time, Emerald Mound was the political center of its region, influencing the daily lives of its neighbors for miles around. But that eventually changed. The population drifted away, abandoning the thriving site. It neighbor, Grand Village, long relegated to being a satellite of Emerald Mound, then rose to prominence.

When queried about the reason for the exodus, Jim expressed his belief: "Perhaps this part of the royal family for some reason lost status, and relatives over there (Grand Village) gained status."

With that, we set off to see the village where those other relatives had gained status.

* * *

Jim led us through Grand Village, as the sun was breaking through a patchy sky. The Natchez Indians occupied the place from about 1200 to 1730 A.D. Since the site was inhabited into historic times, there were written records, at least as to the last two centuries of the Natchez's existence here. The Spaniards under de Soto, and later the French explorers, chronicled the life of these Indians, preserving a part of a culture they essentially destroyed. Like Emerald Mound, this site was well groomed like a golf course. A trail that circumnavigated the village took us past a vast field. Though it now resembled a fairway of a par-three hole, it was once a prehistoric ceremonial plaza.

Farther along the trail an equally expansive, elongated plaza spread out before us, another short fairway. Two mounds, one at each end, were set on the plaza, their summits a soft chip shot above the field. The nearest structure, the Great Sun's Mound, now bare, once supported the chief's dwelling. When the chief, also known as the Sun, died, his journey into the afterlife wasn't a solitary one. His wives and retainers were ceremonially strangled in hopes they would accompany their chief to his post-mortem destination, where they would be expected to continue serving him, I'm sure. It seems that even death didn't free these poor souls from servitude. Supposedly, though, many of these sacrificial victims accepted their fate willing, even eagerly, convinced that their death served a noble purpose. Once the chief and his entourage were on their way to the spirit world, his royal manor was torched and his mound raised to new heights to accommodate the newly erected residence of his successor.

The other hump, Temple Mound, at the far end of the plaza,

sequestered the remains in baskets of previous Suns, along with their wives and retainers. It was on this mound where funeral rites were conducted when a chief died. A sacred fire perpetually burned there, a symbol of the sun from which the royal lineage descended. The fire was maintained by selected attendants who guarded it with their lives — literally, for if the fire died, so did they.

A French ship's carpenter, Jean Penicaut, stopped at Grand Village in 1704, when it was still occupied. He jotted his impressions of the place in his journal:

> We paid a visit to the Natchez, one of the most polite and affable nations on the Mississippi. The Natchez inhabit one of the most beautiful countries in Louisiana (as the area was then called). It lies about a league from the banks of the Mississippi, and is embellished with magnificent natural scenery, covered with a splendid growth of odoriferous trees and plants, and watered with cool and limpid streams. The nation is composed of thirty villages, but the one we visited was the largest, because it contained the dwelling of the Great Chief, whom they called the Sun, which means noble.

The following year Penicaut again recorded his observations for posterity:

> The Great Chief of a noble family can only marry with a woman of plebeian race, but the children born of this race, whether boys or girls, are noble.

Jim elaborated on this strange matrimonial practice. The nobility selected their mates from the hoi polloi, but the offspring of these unions were deemed royalty. The society was matrilineal (common among the peoples of the Southeast at the time), with the women owning the property and the family name. Even though it was a king who sat on the throne, it would be his sister's son (rather than his own son) who would succeed him upon his death.

Natchez domestic concepts were also unusual in that there were no illegitimate children. Regardless of the identity of the father, a child always took the mother's family name.

There was a sharp division of labor between the genders. The men hunted with the bow and arrow, bringing home deer, smaller animals and birds, and occasionally bison, a prized bonanza. They also built cabins, cultivated fields, dressed animal skins, cut firewood, and made weapons, tools and dugout canoes. The women performed the more domestic tasks of making clothing, molding pottery, weaving baskets and nets, and generally keeping house.

It was not all work and no play for the Natchez. They liked their holidays. Each new moon was occasion for a feast. And, despite their agrarian existence, they were stylish. Both genders painted their faces in red, black, white and blue. Tattooing was commonplace, especially by warriors wherein it was a badge of honor. Like other prehistoric (and even more modern) cultures, the Natchez favored head-shaping. At birth a baby's head was slowly flattened as it grew, resulting in a beautiful profile. Blackened teeth were the rage, a feature easily accomplished with ashes. The women adorned themselves with earrings of shell and necklaces of shell and beads. The men were equally decorative with iron or brass wires (in historic times, obviously) through their ears, and bracelets of deer rib along their forearms.

The Natchez, festive though they could be, were not as hedonistic as the Romans of Pompeii in 79 A.D. But the two groups shared a common destiny. For the Natchez, Mt. Vesuvius took the form of French soldiers. During the early part of the Eighteenth Century, the French and Natchez maintained diplomatic relations. But the situation deteriorated, culminating in the Natchez storming of the French stronghold of Fort Rosalie and the massacre of most of the inhabitants. (Jean Penicaut was one of the few who escaped.) The French, not willing to turn the other cheek, retaliated in kind, obliterating the Natchez as a nation. The Indians, those who survived, became refugees. Some were adopted by neighboring tribes. But their history came to an abrupt end.

PUEBLO PEOPLES OF THE RIO GRANDE VALLEY

Eighteen of us archeology enthusiasts rendezvoused for dinner in Albuquerque, complements of Crow Canyon. All but two of us were veterans of these excursions. Surprisingly, Joan and I recognized one other participant. Jean, a teacher from Virginia, had been with us on the dinosaur dig in Montana. She was also a veteran of Crow Canyon trips and was currently on a year's leave of absence, so she could hurry from one archeology seminar, or dinosaur dig, to another. She was a compendium of interesting experiences, wearing neat T-shirts that bore tribute to her excursions. At breakfast each morning I would search her out to see which of her trips was represented in cotton that day. Jim White, one of the Center's staff members, would be the trip leader. Ever friendly and helpful, Jim had the ability to organize these trips and keeps things flowing smoothly. Jim bore a superficial resemblance to actor Chuck Norris, but there the similarity ended. Whereas Chuck (in his movie roles) wouldn't hesitate to bash in the dirty teeth of a bad guy, Jim would offer the guy a toothbrush. Two scholars, both archeologists, would accompany us throughout the venture.

Using extensive hand gestures, Vern Lujan was the first of them to make his presentation. He was in his thirties, I would guess, of medium build, with chestnut skin, ebony eyes, a rugged nose, and a single braid of black hair stretching to his waist. He apologized for his shyness. A Taos Indian, Vern had left the pueblo life so his family could enjoy the comforts of modern living, though he maintained strong ties to that traditional lifestyle. Taos Pueblo staked claim to being the oldest continuously inhabited city in the country, having been occupied for at least 600, and maybe as long as 900, years. (St. Augustine, Florida, founded in 1565, which boasted of this distinction, wasn't even close.) But the pueblo also existed now very much as it did early in the Second Millennium A.D. The adobe apartment-like structures, reaching four and five stories, were still without electricity. When we later visited the pueblo and I asked Vern if they had running water, he replied, "Oh sure, there it is," as he pointed to a brook that burbled through the village. And the situation wasn't going to change anytime soon. The pueblo council recently reaffirmed the pueblo's cement-like bond with the past by voting down a suggestion that the adobe homes be brought into the Twentieth Century.

Vern's people were descendants of the fabled Anasazi, now extinct as a culture, who migrated in pre-Columbian times from the Four Corners region into the Rio Grande Valley. His village was the northernmost pueblo along the Rio Grande. Other pueblo peoples in the Southwest also asserted an Anasazi heritage. The traditional leader of the Taos Pueblo was still the "war chief," a post Vern's dad currently held. The Spaniards, who first appeared in the area with Coronado in 1540, installed the additional office of governor.

* * *

After breakfast the next morning, the other scholar, Carol Condie, took the podium before we headed for the field. Seemingly fiftyish, with burnt-umber locks, Carol was more comfortable and composed speaking before an audience than Vern had been. She informed us that the earliest New World sites of human occupation dated back 14,000 years to a location in Chile. Some archeologists insisted people were in the New World between 20,000 and 30,000 years ago, she said. If primitive humans had migrated across the then-existing Bering land bridge, why weren't the oldest sites found in and around Alaska, she wanted to know. The Paleoindians were the first to traverse the land bridge, Carol said. Their presence was noted by Clovis, and later by Folsom, sites. The people for whom these sites were named fashioned "beautiful points" for their spears. In fact, the distinctive structures of their points was a major factor in defining these two groups, from each other and against any other cultures. The Clovis people followed herds of big game such as the mammoth. Later, the Folsom people hunted species of camel and bison that are now extinct. I have since read that such peoples may have been largely responsible for the demise of the big animals, though climatic changes have also been implicated. What is clear is that within 2000 years of the Clovis people's arrival in the New World, numerous large animals somehow went extinct, including the mammoth, ground sloth, saber-tooth cats, dire wolf and camel, among others.

"These people also ate plants, tubers, roots and seeds," Carol added. "But that was not their main focus."

I glanced around. Although I was the only one taking notes, the others were all riveted on Carol's interesting lecture.

"The Paleoindians continued until 6000 B.C. in some areas. The Archaic Indians followed, and sometimes coexisted with the Paleoindians."

The warmer and drier climate that followed the Pleistocene Epoch (which ended about 10,000 years ago) contributed to the gradual demise of the large animals taken by the Paleoindians, Carol told us. The Archaic peoples thus sought smaller game. Plants then played a greater dietary role. The Archaics did roam, but not so far as the Paleoindians.

"The Archaics became very knowledgeable about plants, soils, rain and sun in an area. They eventually got domesticated seed from Mexico. Agriculture happened over centuries and millennia."

By 300 to 400 A.D., there were permanent villages. The people "committed to agriculture," but continued to be hunters and gatherers. This was true even today.

Carol pointed out that there had been three main influential cultures in the Southwest, all of which have passed into the history books. One was, of course, the Anasazi, centered around the Four Corners region. The Hohokam ranged throughout southern and central Arizona. The Mogollon extended from southeast Arizona to southwest New Mexico.

"They were all village people," Carol said. "They grew corn, beans and squash. Some also grew cotton." The three vegetables were each deficient in at least one essential amino acid. But eaten together, this group of victuals added complete protein to the Indian's diet. And the crops benefited from being grown together. Corn required an abundance of nitrogen, which beans supplied through the nitrogen-fixing bacteria in their roots. The beans in turn used the cornstalks as beanpoles.

Then it was into the vans and off to our first stop, El Rancho de las Golondrinas (The Ranch of the Swallows), which billed itself as a "living museum." It was noteworthy as having been a *paraje* (campsite) on El Camino Real (The Royal Road), which stretched 1200 miles from Mexico City through Chihuahua to Old Santa Fe in the 1700s. During much of its tenure, from 1598 to 1821 A.D., this highway was the longest and most significant in North America. An Eighteenth-Century placita house complete with a *torreón* (defensive tower) was now preserved on the ranch. The property also contained a Nineteenth-Century home and numerous outbuildings. Although the 200-acre property's theme was to depict Spanish colonial life, later heritages were evident as well.

Our gang traipsed through the *zaguán* (immense entrance) and into the fort-like placita. High walls surrounded a rectangular courtyard. Rooms were connected end to end, by small portals, along the inside perimeter of the rectangle, like railroad cars. Each room also had its own door opening directly onto the courtyard.

Three oxcarts with log frames and wooden wheels rested in a row along the wall outside the main entrance, waiting patiently for their next hauling assignment, which would never come. There weren't any oxen on the ranch anymore. In keeping with Spanish tradition, the museum had yoked the oxen by the horns. When an ox broke a horn, it was no longer capable of hauling a cart, and the team of oxen was sold.

Our group split up. I ducked through the low portals and strolled from one dimly lit room to another, working my way around the rectangular enclosure. The dirt-floor rooms were small and sparsely equipped by our standards, but were probably deluxe to the original inhabitants. The size of the rooms was determined by the length of the roofing timbers the colonial occupants were able to haul from the mountains with their oxen. The outside walls were thick, being several feet in width in places — good insulation. Two weaving rooms on the east side of the rectangle proudly displayed their large, machine looms with bolts of woven fabric in situ. An Indian loom stretched from floor to ceiling. These were not simply museum pieces but were currently in use. The ranch's sheep were still being sheared. The wool was washed and carded before it went to the dye shed on the premises. Once tinted, the wool was returned to the looms to be woven.

A room on the south edge of this enclosure led to the defensive tower, which provided a commanding view of the scattered outbuildings and surrounding fields. An approaching enemy could readily have been spotted and fired upon. The living rooms and bedrooms were stocked with period furniture, kept in excellent repair. The rooms were inviting, though the furniture was diminutive and uncomfortable by modern standards. There weren't any king-sized beds or stuffed sofas to be seen.

The room at the northwest corner housed the kitchen, complete with original implements, which were perfectly suitable for preparing a meal even now.

A modest but welcoming chapel was built into the northeast corner. Dark woods, rich in color and texture, were liberally used in the construction of its interior. An enormous, decorative panel of Christian iconography embellished most of the wall behind the altar. The patron saints, whose images were skillfully carved and brightly painted onto the panel, were chosen to reflect the agrarian and pastoral lifestyle of the Spanish colonials. Saint Isidro was of particular significance and was called upon to bless the fields, livestock and ditch system.

A covered drinking well pinpointed almost the exact center of the dusty courtyard. Two beehive, adobe *hornos* (ovens), an Arab invention introduced to the Southwest by the Spaniards, squatted along an interior courtyard wall waiting for their next baking assignment, which could come at any moment. In the event of attack by bandits or Indians, the original occupants of the ranch would have bolted the *puertón* (sturdy gate), and sequestered themselves and their livestock within the compound. The fortress was heavily

WORKERS REPAIRING ADOBE WALL AT
RANCHO DE LAS GOLONDRINAS

stocked with provisions. The well furnished the water needs, while the ovens churned out loaves of bread. Thus they could have withstood a prolonged siege.

I ambled out the rear gate to an adobe house just beyond the walls of the compound. Two smutty workmen were repairing an exterior wall of the house. One of them mixed a mud concoction and shoveled it up to his helper, positioned on a ramshackle scaffold, who troweled the muddy mixture onto the wall. The foreman, Santos, stood beneath the unshielded sun in the dirt plaza in front of the house. A throng of us sightseers clustered around him, as he explained the repair process. Clad in worn jeans with a matching shirt, construction boots and a straw cowboy hat, the crinite foreman ambulated about as he showed how adobe blocks were made. He displayed a well-used metal box-mold.

"The mud adobes here are not sun-baked. They're sun-dried," he emphasized. "It takes about two weeks before they're dry enough to use."

The blocks formed the walls of the house, which was then coated with a protective layer of mud. Rain slowly deteriorated the walls. Thus repairs were constant.

"What's the composition of the mud?" someone called out.

Santos explained how that was determined. A jar was filled with dirt and water, then allowed to settle overnight. The mixture separated into layers.

"You want fifty-fifty clay and sand. The stratification tells you what the percentage of soil is. Add what's necessary for a fifty-fifty ratio."

Santos was enjoying his captive audience. His dark eyes, set in weathered, tanned skin and framed by salt-and-pepper mutton chops, moustache and beard, flashed as he made a point. By design, the buildings here had no sharp corners or plumb lines.

"We don't want square walls."

A peahen was startled when the crowd got too close. She scurried, chicks in tow, along the edge of the plaza to join her prancing peacock. They looked out of place and did not represent the ranch's original fowl population. The birds had recently been donated to the ranch. A pair of roosters strutted beneath an expansive cottonwood tree that shaded one corner of the plaza. In an adjacent corral, a burro looked on with disinterest. A pair of geese picked at the ground between its hooves.

Carol rounded us up and led us along a footpath that meandered through the countryside, linking the outbuildings and fields. The molasses mill, though worn, was still in use, but only for harvest festivals. To actuate the machine, a burro was harnessed to one end of a long, wooden lever arm, the other end of which was connected to the stationary milling apparatus. The animal trudged around and around in a circle, thereby operating the mill's grinding mechanism. Workers fed sticks of sorghum cane, grown on the ranch, into the grinder's teeth near the stationary end of the arm, while the animal plodded along on its journey without a destination. The resulting syrup was then boiled down in a nearby shed. One of the museum's employees assured me it was still "the best damn molasses around." But since it wasn't festival time, I didn't get to judge for myself.

We crossed *Acequia Madre*, merely a ditch in which brownish water lazily flowed. I paid it little notice until Carol informed us that this seemingly insignificant rivulet was listed in the National Registry of Historic Places. Seeing the surprise on our faces, Carol said this was the original *acequia*.

One of our group cast a suspicious eye at the thick, dirty water. "This must be the original *water*, too," he quipped.

The path continued past the wheelwright shop, constructed of logs and planks and containing two open bays. Tired buckboard wagons slouched out front, their long, slender, wooden tongues dragging on the ground. Despite their antiquity, the wagons were glaringly more sophisticated than the oxcarts. These wagons sported iron-rim wheels and a metal undercarriage. And a surprisingly advanced suspension system with both leaf and coil shock absorbers.

Fields of maturing corn, wheat, chili and squash sprouted adjacent to the trail. Rye, beans and pumpkins were also grown, as was alfalfa, which fed the livestock. Beyond these fields was the apple orchard. Besides sheep and burros, the ranch kept horses and goats. Ahead on the right sat a log cabin with an attached ramada over the door. The building contained a water wheel that once turned a milling device. Water still flowed by, but the gears had long since rusted into immobility.

The blacksmith shop still saw plenty of action. Blacksmiths were regularly called in by the museum to tend to the ranch's need. The smiths also fashioned metal wares they sold to the visiting public.

On a shunt off the main trail rose the two-room schoolhouse, built in 1878. One of the spaces was the classroom, the other the teacher's office. The school once claimed a student body of some fifteen pupils and was only used for two years.

This detour led to the vineyard and winery, which were now relegated to history. However, with the advent of wine production in New Mexico, the ranch intended to re-initiate viticulture. Wines from New Mexico? Did I hear that right?

There was even an herb garden, still producing such seasonings as sage, rosemary, basil, oregano and thyme. The Spanish also made ample use of medicinal herbs. Boiled roots of the Apache plume supposedly dissipated a persistent cough. Its leaves were dried and ground, then mixed with native tobacco to produce a soothing rub for arthritic joints. Cockscomb provided treatment for such divergent maladies as heart trouble, tuberculosis and jaundice. Also, the plant's crimson juice was smeared on the faces of the Spanish ladies as a sunscreen. The powdered root of the coneflower would soothe an aching tooth. Mullein was a tobacco substitute. Its inhaled smoke would ameliorate asthma. A beverage made from its leaves acted as a mild sedative. Sagebrush tea diminished high blood pressure. A poultice derived from the verbena plant relieved aching backs. Wild tea, a member of the aster family, was an excellent laxative. Field marigolds, chewed raw or brewed into a tea, were good for stomach complaints. This impressive selection of plants constituted a virtual pharmacy. Mark Plotkin, a Harvard-trained ethnobotanist stated the obvious in his book **Tales of a Shaman's Apprentice:** "The plant kingdom has long served as humankind's primary source of therapeutic compounds." Plotkin's field experience was primarily confined to Amazonia, but his observations were universal. He could just as well have written about the reliance of Southwest cultures upon their flora.

Colonial plants had additional functions. A soap, suitable for washing raw wool or a person's hair, was fabricated from the root of the yucca. Wild tea provided a russet dye for wool. Spearmint came in handy as a perfume. It was also used to impart a green tint to wool. Segments of the scouring rush were formed into whistles for children. Rabbit-brush flowers yielded a vivid yellow dye, and a yellow paint when mixed with guano.

I returned to the main trail and set off toward a large, vertical water wheel attached to the side of a mill, *El Molino Grande de Sapelló.* This was a reconstruction of a mill house that had originally been erected elsewhere. Its adobe walls prevented it from being transported to this ranch when the mill was purchased by the ranch's owner at that time, thus the replica. The original milling equipment, still in use, was incorporated into the mill. The water wheel delivered about twenty horsepower, allowing the mill to grind 100 pounds of grain in less than an hour.

As I followed the trail back to the placita house, I passed another mill, *Molino Barela de Trunchas.* This one was smaller and operated via a *horizontal* water wheel. The mill was originally built elsewhere in 1873. It was taken apart there and reassembled at the ranch. When I stopped by, the mill was the only functioning Spanish colonial-style gristmill powered by a horizontal water wheel in the entire country. Unfortunately, it wasn't running at the moment.

The basic blueprint for this horizontal water wheel was developed by the Greeks during the First or Second Century B.C. The Romans (who also developed the vertical water wheel about the same time) refined the design. Mills then spread throughout the Roman empire.

The ranch was initially acquired by purchase from the Spanish Crown about 1710 by Miguel Vega y Coca. He would be proud at how well his homestead has endured.

The vans next took us to Pecos Pueblo, vacant since 1838, when the last few inhabitants drifted away to nearby villages. We enthusiastically trekked up the long, sloping trail that led to the top of a broad ridge. The ruins of the pueblo occupied much of that vantage point. As we approached, a low stone wall demarcated the site from the open terrain in the foreground. The wall continued around the rear of the ridge. Carol mentioned that this was not a defensive wall. "It's too low." Rather, it defined the pueblo's space, serving as the "city limits." During the day, visiting Plains Indians came inside to conduct business. When night fell, the city was off limits to outsiders. Upon attaining the summit of the ridge, I was disappointed at the lack of visible ruins. The site had been partially excavated during the second and third decades of this century, but then had been backfilled. The site's magnificent North Pueblo compound was completely buried. Weeds and shrubs now blanketed this complex. Only grassy mounds hinted at the delitescent ruins below.

The North Pueblo complex once contained clusters of rooms, some reaching four stories, that enclosed a rectangular courtyard pitted with ceremonial kivas. Unfortunately, none of this was visible to us. A tandem of kivas had been dug into the earth just outside the complex's east wall. One remained unexcavated. The other had recently been reconstructed. An artist's rendition depicted this complex of the pueblo with wooden ladders leading down into the kivas. Ladders were also used to gain access to the above-ground rooms. In the event of outside hostilities, the ladders were hauled up, denying the enemy ingress. The rooms on the first floor were usually for storage or refuse. The living quarters began on the second floor, like the modern hurricane-ready homes in the Florida Keys (but for a different reason). Wooden ramadas extended from the rooms to provide shaded areas for work.

The site overlooked the Glorieta River, source of life-giving water so vital to survival in this area of limited rainfall. When the Anasazi migrated to this region, they constructed their villages along these rivers. Even prior to the Four Corners exodus, there was pithouse occupation dating to 800 A.D. in the Pecos area. Populations were small. But around 1200 A.D., populations suddenly expanded. Pithouses gave way to more permanent dwellings composed of coursed adobe. To erect a wall, successive courses of mud were poured into a movable wicker basket. After a poured segment of mud hardened, another wet course was placed on top of, or adjacent to, the hardened segment. When that hardened, other wet sections of mud were added until the adobe wall was incrementally completed. This was tedious work, to be sure.

By the Rio Grande Classic Period, 1325 to 1540/1600 A.D., architecture had taken a quantum leap forward. Buildings of stone set in mud mortar supplanted coursed-adobe construction. Vertical timbers, incorporated into the wall masonry, provided added stability. All the neighboring sites, except Pecos Pueblo, were abandoned by 1450.

These Indians of the Classic Period still relied upon their centuries-old livelihood of hunting and gathering. Elk, deer, antelope and smaller game were taken. But they also cultivated crops. Irrigation allowed them to achieve the yields necessary to feed the burgeoning populations, which exceeded 1000 persons at some pueblos. Pecos Pueblo was home to about 2000 souls during its golden age. The pueblo could field 500 warriors. It was at the pinnacle of its power and influence for a century, from 1450 to 1550.

Pecos Pueblo was a focus for Indian trade fairs. Plains tribes — mostly nomadic Apache — brought slaves, buffalo hides, jerked meat, flint and shell to swap for crops, pottery, textiles and turquoise. The Pecos Indians acted as middlemen. They later traded with the Spanish and the Comanche.

The ridge I was standing on formed part of the Glorieta-Pecos Corridor. Mountain streams had eroded a thirty-mile-wide passage between the Sangre de Cristo Range (southernmost extension of the Rocky Mountains) to the east and Glorieta Mesa to the west. Since prehistoric times, travel and commerce between the peoples

AUTHOR ENTERING KIVA AT PECOS PUEBLO

of the upper Rio Grande Valley and the Great Plains had taken place through the strategically located Glorieta Pass within the Corridor.

I joined others from our group who were scrambling down the ladder into the reconstructed kiva. The ladder allowed access through the only entrance, a square hole cut into the log roof, which was at ground level. The subterranean, pill-shaped room was the size of a modern-day dining room, though with a circular wall. Two vertical support beams ran from the dirt floor to the timber roof. A crossbeam, set perpendicular to the vertical beams, rested horizontally across the tops of those two beams. It in turn held up other smaller, horizontal timbers, which comprised the roof. The sun's rays slanting in through the roof opening provided the only light in the chamber. There was a noticeable drop in temperature within the kiva, a welcome respite from the hot summer day. The musty smell of raw earth was actually pleasant. The kiva possessed the features I had seen in other such chambers throughout the Southwest. A fire pit, fortunately not in use, was scooped into the ground directly beneath the roof opening, which doubled as a chimney. A rectangular ventilator shaft was carved into the wall at floor level. It burrowed into the surrounding earth, made a ninety-degree turn, and headed straight up to the surface, thereby providing an alternate source of fresh air. Between the ventilator shaft and the fire pit stood the obligatory deflector slab. This stone block, set vertically into the floor, kept the air that was sucked down the shaft from extinguishing the fire. An imaginary straight line drawn on the floor from the ventilator shaft, through the deflector slab, then through the fire pit, led to the sipapu, near the opposite side of the room. This softball-diameter hole, cut into the earth, symbolized the people's initial emergence from the underworld. Many pueblos still regarded the kiva as a model of their universe, with the sipapu representing the "below," the kiva floor indicating this world, and the roof entry serving as a metaphor for the "above."

This was an average-sized kiva, dwarfed by some I had seen at Chaco Canyon and Aztec Ruins. Those enormous kivas needed roof support from four, thick, vertical beams. And those kivas were ringed internally, at least in part, by a stone banquette (bench), a feature absent from this Pecos kiva. An antechamber, present in those monstrous kivas, was likewise missing here.

Upon exiting the kiva, I continued along the trail. Trash piles, also excavated and backfilled, once accumulated the remains of the pueblo. They were repositories for broken pottery, table scraps, cooking-fire ashes, floor sweepings and worn-out tools. They also comprised the village's cemetery. But this did not evince disrespect for the dead. The Indians were, in part, being pragmatic; it was easier to inter the bodies in the softer trash heaps than to dig anew into the hard-packed ground.

A guide brochure informed me that I was standing amidst the quadrangle of what had been a multistory compound. In the 1400s, it had contained over 600 rooms. The tops of the grass-blanketed mounds were now at the level of the second story. The upper floors of this complex had crumbled or eroded before being concealed with layers of earth during the ensuing centuries.

The trail took me past cholla bushes, juniper trees and rabbit brush to a prime lookout perch. One of the two nearby sources of year-round water, the Glorieta Creek, ran along the base of the escarpment. The other, the Pecos River, flowed a mile to the east through the Pecos Valley, with its rich farmland. Spanish observers also reported springs and reservoirs near the pueblo. The commanding view from the ridge alerted the villagers to anyone approaching from the Rio Grande Valley or the Great Plains.

With an elevation of 7000 feet, frost came early to this site. The principal crops of corn, beans and squash were, therefore, squeezed into an abbreviated growing season. Planting continued throughout the spring, so a late frost wouldn't kill all the crops. Hundreds of single-room "field houses," scattered in the upper valley, allowed the villagers to keep constant watch over their agriculture. The plantings were accompanied by ceremonies to insure a decent rainfall and bountiful harvest.

The solar disc beat down on me. I was protected with sunscreen and a floppy hat. Despite hiking in the heated air, I never broke a sweat. The lack of humidity kept my skin dry. But we had been cautioned to consume copious amounts of liquid, lest we be lulled into dehydration. The ridge top was quiescent except for occasional tattered bits of conversation drifting by. I continued south along the trail. Ahead rose the remnants of a Spanish mission. The Spaniards, with the tandem goals of finding wealth and subjugating the indigenous populations to the authority of Spain, arrived on the scene permanently at the close of the Sixteenth Century. Franciscan priests, accompanying the soldiers, sought to convert the native "heathens" to Christianity. The priests constructed their mission structures adjacent to the pueblos, so the priests could readily interact with the Indians. The Pecos church was initially constructed in 1625. It must have been an impressive structure, consisting of 300,000 adobe bricks weighing some forty pounds apiece. The altar stood half the length of a modern football field from the entrance. The bases of the Goliath walls were twenty-two feet thick in places. The church, with its rows of exterior buttresses, white-washed walls and six bell towers, took center stage at the mission compound. This church survived for fifty-five years. During the Pueblo Revolt of 1680, the Indians set fire to the roof and toppled the massive, but vulnerable, walls.

The uprising drove the Spanish out of the area for a dozen years, after which they returned with a vengeance. The church was rebuilt in 1717, but on a less grandiose scale. Over the years, wind, rain and vandalism had reduced it to a shell. It therefore fell to my imagination to reconstruct the church's architectural grandeur, for all that greeted my eye was the unadorned foundation with some bare, lower sections of the walls.

I roamed through remains of the *convento*, where the priests carried out their daily lives. An adobe multi-room appurtenance to the church served as the Franciscans' living quarters. Only the lower portions of walls and other structures still stood. Some of the rooms had fireplaces, and were either bedrooms or workshops. Sections of the *portería* (porter's lodge) were evident. It was the mission's first business office and reception. In the 1600s, a visitor was greeted by a *portero*, usually a newly converted Indian. The *portero* guarded the *convento* at night.

Interestingly, a circular kiva, dug into a plaza within the convent, still remained. During the missionaries' early efforts at converting the natives, the Indians accepted the Christian god into their pantheon of deities. But they refused to accord exclusive status to this god and to abandon their traditional religious beliefs as the priests had demanded. When New Mexico suffered drought, famine and disease in the 1660s, the Pueblos thought the natural order of their universe had been upset by the Spaniards. Native ceremonial activity accelerated with a passion. The former conquistadors tried to stomp it out with force. A mistake. In 1675, after fifty of the Indian's religious leaders were punished, the pueblos began organizing in secret. The Pueblo Revolt went into the history books as one of the most successful rebellions by native peoples against Europeans. When this church was gutted, as part of the rebellion, the rebels cannibalized the adobe bricks from the mission and used them to construct their kiva. It was purposely placed within the *convento* as both a symbol of defiance and to restore the natural order. Upon the Spaniards' return, the priests buried, but did not destroy, the kiva. It has since been excavated.

✳   ✳   ✳

We kicked off the day with a lecture by J.J. Brody, whose academic background blended art history and archeology, an unusual, but valued, combination. Short of stature with a balding pate, a salt-and-pepper moustache and a large nose, both of which added to his presence, dominated his countenance. Standing before us in baggy safari pants and worn sandals, the enthusiastic J.J. launched into his summation of ceramics and architecture with the commanding bearing of a general briefing his troops for a forthcoming battle. He acknowledged Anasazi presence but emphasized Mogollon influence in the Rio Grande Valley. The red-ware pottery was an example of the Mogollon "flavor."

He glanced around to be sure we were paying attention, then went on. "Architecture and painted pottery are two main markers for determining a culture's sophistication. The Rio Grande pottery was not pretty. The buildings were of adobe or rubble block. Few places had pretty stone for buildings. There's no sandstone in the Rio Grande Valley."

I took a hit off my second cup of coffee, as I feverishly scribbled in my spiral notebook.

"There's no neat ruins now in the Rio Grande Valley as in the Four Corners," J.J. continued. "So Rio Grande Valley architecture looks regressive."

During the Pueblo III period, Anasazi pottery had a tendency to "draw patterns with a fair degree of precision" and to "organize designs." There was "neat execution." Not so with Rio Grande pottery, which J.J. characterized as "sloppy as hell." But the artist in J.J. could not let that accusation stand without mitigation. The sloppiness had an explanation: "It's spontaneous."

From surrounding areas, a diversity of cultures flowed into the

Rio Grande. "Between 1100 and 1300/1350, every village simply picked up and moved — the Great Migration. The Rio Grande area became the new heart of the Pueblo people. It was an agglomeration of people."

Another slug of coffee.

"But in Acoma, people were there for centuries."

We would visit this mesa-top pueblo during the trip. Still occupied after nearly a millennium, it also claimed the distinction of being the oldest continuously inhabited city in the country.

J.J. accompanied us to the vans for a visit to the state museum.

We were allowed access to the museum's archives downstairs, off limits to the general public and kept under lock and key. J.J. foraged through the metal shelves that ran from floor to ceiling, row after row, throughout the humongous storage room. The shelves were crammed with ceramic artifacts representing a multitude of Southwest cultures. J.J. wiggled his fingers into spotless white gloves, like a Marine drill instructor about to conduct a barracks inspection. J.J. then delicately cupped his hands around a red-ware clay pot coated with yellow slip and outlined with a black glaze design. It had been discovered south of Sante Fe and dated to the "late prehistory," somewhere around the early 1500s.

He extracted a narrow-necked vessel, capable of holding about three gallons, and held it aloft. This *olla* was a water container. Its tawny background likewise bore runny designs of black glaze.

He continued foraging through the exhibits, selecting specimens to show us. There were large *ollas*, flat canteens, squat cylinders, bowls of various sizes, all fashioned from clay and fired into permanence. Some had black ticking along the rim, suggestive of Mesa Verde influence. Most were embellished with linear and geometric patterns drawn in black. Birds, feathers and dragonflies were amply represented. An angular, serpentine design was also frequently depicted on these vessels. It represented a highly stylized snake, a common feature in the Southwest and Mesoamerica. From this serpent's head protruded five "feathers." Or were they fingers? J.J. wasn't sure. Many of the figures and designs were obtunded with the passage of time.

J.J. showed an example of pottery-making technique. Pots were originally built by coiling. Eventually the Indians discovered a short-cut. The lower portion of the vessel in J.J.'s hand was shaped within another bowl, which acted as a mold. When the pot's foundation was thus formed, the upper portion of the pot was completed by coiling the clay.

Textiles were next. Not many had been preserved. One specimen was a Hopi tapestry woven early this century. The blanket-sized fabric was richly embroidered in a dazzling array of blue, maroon, red, green, gold and black. Its cotton backdrop had already yellowed, but it was a magnificent piece of art nonetheless. An anthropomorphic figure occupied most of the middle third of the textile. It was a fertility and harvest symbol. On either side of this figure a three-lobe cluster of clouds was outlined in green, gold and red. Straight, black vertical lines dangling from the clouds depicted rain. Red and green zigzag lines reaching up diagonally from the clouds exemplified lightning.

Then on to another set of ruins.

Our loaded vans paused at the entrance gate to the Puye ruins as a somber, swarthy Indian policeman in uniform checked our tickets. His shoulder patch identified him as a member of the Santa Clara Tribal Police. The current dwellers of Santa Clara Pueblo considered Puye to be an ancestral home. They spoke the Tewa tongue, a branch of the Tanoan language tree. Vern spoke a related dialect, Tiwa, and could understand many Tewa words, like an Italian speaker can somewhat comprehend Spanish. A quick ride took us to the base of a steep precipice. A trail cut back and forth across its face and led to the summit, where ruins awaited us. The upper part of the ridge was bare rock sprinkled with shrubs. From the base of the sloping terrace that led to the ridge, I could readily make out craters pockmarking the rocky face of the upper ridge. Even from this distance, the site looked "very awesome," said Joan. It was even more awesome up close. Joan and I led the way, as a handful of us set out along the trail. The rest of our group opted to ride to the summit in the vans. Too bad, as they missed half the show.

The climb was facile despite the 7000-foot elevation. A wooden, homemade ladder provided a shortcut, connecting the upper and

JOAN IN CAVE HOME AT PUYE

lower segments of the trail. The craters turned out to have been living quarters of the ancestral Indians. These Spartan abodes, generally consisting of but a single room, reminded me of animal dens. To create one of these homes, an entrance had been hacked into the rock at the side of the trail. The soft, porous rock, composed of tuff (compacted volcanic ash and froth), was easily worked.

I had to duck my way into one of the rooms. Once inside the confining quarters, I couldn't stand straight. The roof, chipped and scraped by hand, was a foot above my head. But the room was very small, enclosing no more space than one of our vans. A fireplace had been gouged into the base of the wall at floor level directly across from the doorway. The upper walls and ceiling were heavily blackened, evidence that the fireplace had been well used. At this altitude, I'm sure it got chilly at night. There did not appear to have been sufficient ventilation to allow the smoke to escape freely. It must have been suffocating in this chamber when the fire was roaring. Perhaps at bedtime the blaze was allowed to simmer down. The glowing coals would have provided some warmth. That, augmented by what the stony walls would have re-radiated at night, might have been enough to allow the inhabitants here to get through the night without coughing their lungs out.

The caves had other advantages. During the summer months they offered relief from the relentless sun. And they provided an unobstructed vista across the countryside below, although the view on top of the ridge was superlative.

Numerous scooped-out chambers lined the trail as we made our way to the crest of the ridge. Joan and I popped into a few of them. All were diminutive. All had a fireplace. Some had other recesses dug into the walls above the packed-dirt floor — cupboards without doors, I guess. At least the occupants didn't have to heat much space. Despite the ease with which the volcanic rock could be hollowed, it must have taken some effort to construct one of these pre-Columbian cave dwellings without the aid of metal tools, unknown then in the Southwest.

In a couple of the cave-homes the rear wall opened into another chamber. Apartments?

At first I assumed the caves were randomly situated. Perhaps these inhabitants wanted privacy. But then I came upon a line of portals, separated from one another by the width of two of the dwellings, hacked into the cliff beside the trail. Each portal opened into its own dwelling. It was reminiscent of modern row houses and must have been sort of a community. I noticed a horizontal band of evenly spaced holes drilled into the rocky face just above the portals. Postholes immediately came to mind, although there were no remnants of wood in the apertures. Clearly the holes were manmade. Did the posts support roofs? If so, had there been rooms in front of these caves, such that the houses were multi-room? Or did the holes signify ramadas, which would have provided badly needed shade? I was undecided until I scanned right and left to survey more of the cliff face. There were additional lines of horizontal post holes similarly situated, one story up from the trail. Then I saw the smoking gun. Other horizontal lines of holes, yet another floor higher, ran above and parallel to these lower holes. Clearly, there had been buildings of at least two floors there. And I spied a pair of adjoining stone houses, two stories tall, like town houses, tucked against the cliff face. Even some of the roof timbers were yet in place. I returned my attention to the row of portals in front of me. Had there also been stone houses built out from the cliff here? Other than for the postholes, there was no evidence of that. But if there had been town houses (or single-story villas) here, then why was the fireplace put in the cave, which would have been attached to the rear of the house? Such an arrangement would have caused the smoke to flood through the house to escape — not a likely scenario. Perhaps the earliest settlers had used the cave as just that, a cave. Then later dwellers might have constructed multistory stone buildings and used the attached cave for storage. Or maybe the postholes were for ramadas after all. I didn't come up with the answer.

We finished our ascent. High-altitude clouds were smeared across the sky, intercepting some of the solar penetration. The riders were milling around the vans or drifting though the summit's ruins. A police car (actually, an all-terrain wagon) was now parked under the trees at the edge of the cliff. The tribal cop was strolling around, keeping an eye on things. I pored over the site, backdropped by the Jemez Mountains in the distance. There had to be hundreds of rooms in the complex, almost all of which had been reduced by the ravages of time to ground floor, low walls. The rooms were small and had been fashioned from volcanic stone blocks, which were roughly hewn. Mud mortar held the stones in place. Smaller stones were embedded in the mud between rows of the blocks. These chinking stones added additional support to the walls. I cornered Carol, who informed me that most of the rooms here were for storage. She dated the site to 1300 to 1600 A.D.

"Looks typical Pueblo IV," she said.

There were two structures, each at opposite ends of the site that still consisted of more than low walls. They had a few intact rooms on the bottom floor of what had been multistory buildings. I could discern perhaps three floors. Fewer rooms were evident on the second floor than on the first floor. Rooms were diminutive. The third story had almost eroded away. Many of the roofing timbers were intact. Doorways between the rooms were petite. I had to stoop to pass through them.

Time to go. Joan and I passed up an offer to ride down in the vans. The hike back down the trail gave us another opportunity to quickly view the cliff dwellings.

Then north to Taos, where we would spend the night. John, a young professor from Nebraska, currently sitting shotgun, was responsible for dispensing drinks from the cooler during the ride. In the next row rearward, the window-seat occupant, in this case, Mary, had the duty to dispose of the trash into the plastic baggie at her left elbow. Joan and I took up the next row to the rear. The goodie box was at our feet. We were barely underway when someone wanted M&Ms without peanuts. I snatched a package of cheese crackers for myself and passed the box around. John doled out the drinks. As the countryside passed, we nibbled and sipped, chattering like squirrels. We later passed the cans and wrappers to Mary, whom we dubbed "Midden Maiden."

*   *   *

Affable Mike Adler greeted us at the day's first stop. Young, clean shaven, good looking, with short, dark hair, he would lead us around the uninhabited Pot Creek Pueblo. Mike had his Ph.D. in anthropology. He was the head archeologist at the site, which was currently being excavated under the auspices of Southern Methodist University. Mike was casually attired in a baseball cap, shorts, T-shirt and sneakers — without socks, of course. He looked more like a spring-breaker at Daytona Beach than an archeologist in the Southwest, but Mike was no slouch. He took his task seriously despite his relaxed attitude. We followed Mike along a dirt road to the excavations. He explained that people had been here for at least a millennium.

"There are carbon-14 dates from the 1000s, 1100s and the 1500s."

The pueblo had been merely a hamlet at first. By 1260 A.D., it had grown to become a "major village" with some 200 occupants.

It survived until shortly after the year 1320. Hummingbirds darted and hovered among the roadside bushes and flowers as we passed. The site had access to vital water from nearby Pot Creek. This creek converges with the Little Rio Grande, which in turn merges with the "big" Rio Grande. I asked about irrigation.

Mike wasn't sure. "But some archeologists think there's an irrigation canal here," he offered.

The site contained ten room-blocks. Present-day Indians in the area regarded it as an ancestral village. The terrain consisted of natural rises supplemented by mounds of buried ruins, most of which had not been excavated. And wouldn't be. Someone asked if they would uncover the complete site.

"We don't excavate an entire site," Mike said. "It's too redundant, and there's no sense in unnecessarily excavating pristine sites."

The groups of rooms were built in stages. "There were three or four room-blocks in 1260," Mike mentioned. "In the 1280s, there was a construction gap."

Mike slowed and waited for the stragglers to catch up. "In the 1290s, it may have been abandoned," he continued.

Apparently the pueblo was later re-occupied. Dendrochronology discovered that the years of 1300 and 1301 were important "cutting dates." No such dates have been found from later than 1319 A.D. Mike gave the pueblo another five years of occupation after that.

The road terminated at a clearing. Piles of fresh dirt were stacked around an excavation pit. Strainer screens temporarily lay on the piles. A team of archeologists and students was working the site. I'm sure they could have done without our intrusion, but we descended on the site like Genghis Khan's hordes. Mike stood at the edge of the pit and lectured as we gathered around. Two men working in the shadows at the bottom of the pit, twenty feet down, paused in their digging to look us over.

"It's all adobe," said Mike, sweeping his hand across the pit. "It degrades easily."

Coursed adobe, in sections of twelve to eighteen inches, formed the walls here. There were separate room-blocks with plazas in between. This contrasted with what we would see at Taos Pueblo that afternoon, Mike said. Each room-block at Pot Creek had its own midden mound.

"Trash and bodies were buried there," noted Mike.

One of the women in our group shook her head at that one.

"These were sacred areas . . . *not* landfills."

As with other sites we visited, the ground-floor rooms here were generally for storage. The living space began one floor up.

I noticed what looked like a tape measure strung vertically from the top to the bottom of the pit. I asked Mike about it.

"That's a pollen column. It gives us a pollen profile through time."

Most of the digging team was congregated at another pit, much smaller and shallower, a few feet away. I moseyed over for a look. One of the team members was spraying water onto one of the dirt walls of the pit. Four other young members, apparently students, held a tarp high over the hole to shield out the sun. Yet another of the team was in the pit, focusing a camera at the wetted dirt. The tarp kept glare from washing out details on the resulting photos, he said.

In an intermediate-size pit, located between the smaller and larger pits, two dark-complected men, both archeologists from Egypt, were absorbed in their digging. They conversed with themselves in another language, presumably Arabic, and paid us no heed. Their demeanor did not invite inquiries from our group. The obvious question, of why these guys would want to excavate such a meager site when they had the pyramids, came up. Mike explained that the Egyptians were here to learn techniques they could use in their native country. Egyptian archeologists, with ready access to giant monuments and much treasure, tended to overlook smaller, less valuable artifacts. It was these other artifacts that could provide important archeological information, Mike said.

A woman, dirt caked on her pants, sat on the ground between the pits, a notebook in her lap. She would take a sample of newly excavated dirt, wet it, compare it to other samples on a color chart, and then make a notation in her notebook. She was keeping a log on the dirt samples, recording what was scooped up from various parts of the site.

Mike and the rest of our group assembled around the smaller pit. If any human bones were dug up, the coroner was called, Mike said. If an archeologist determined the bones to be prehistoric, the coroner lost interest and left the scene. But then the state archeologist had to be contacted. In turn, that archeologist put out a notice to all the Indian tribes in the state of the unearthed bones. If any Indians had a legitimate "ancestral interest," the burial portion of the site was avoided.

Across the highway from the site stood the reconstructed Fort Burgwin, originally in use from 1852 to 1859, when it was abandoned as being impractical. It now saw duty as the classroom, lab and living quarters of the archeologists. Mike took us for a tour of the lab. Every artifact was categorized here. Forms were filled out and data entered on computers. "Within forty-eight hours, an artifact goes from the ground to the computer," said Mike. Then the artifact was curated in an adjoining room.

We filed into the vast storage room. Shelves were stacked with what looked like pizza boxes. But these boxes held the likes of pottery shards, plant material, stone tools, cooking-fire charcoal and bits of wood.

Then we loaded into the vans for the short trip to the Pot Creek Cultural Center.

Our guide, Richard, a middle-aged Picuris Indian, met us at the Cultural Center. His nearby pueblo claimed an ancestral link to the area. At one time the Picuris Pueblo had a population in excess of 3000, then making it one of the largest pueblo "metropolises." Now it was down to 250 inhabitants. They spoke Tiwa, so Richard and Vern were able to converse in their native language.

Richard, dark-skinned and solemn, wore a blanched shirt, black jeans and a cream cowboy hat with a beaded hatband. Scraggly hair bedecked his leathery face, and twin braids stretched below his collar. He led part of our group along the wooded trail that looped through the site. The remainder of our group followed in a few minutes, led by another guide.

First stop was a reconstructed ceremonial chamber consisting of a single room. Vertical timbers, anchored into the dirt floor, held up the crossbeams that formed the roof. The requisite fire pit, deflector slab and ventilator shaft were in place. The musty, circular room was about nine feet in diameter and somewhat cooler than the outdoors. It was large enough to accommodate our party. There were no windows. The only door was the rooftop entrance, a foot or so above my head. The walls were of coursed adobe, both originally and as reconstructed. I noticed straw embedded in the walls.

"What binding material did they use here originally," I asked Richard.

"No binding, except occasional ash and pottery shards."

I pointed to the wall. "What about this straw?"

"The Spanish introduced the straw."

"So the reconstruction is *not* totally with pre-Columbian materials."

"Right."

We exited the chamber and returned to the path that cut through the forest. A reconstructed pueblo with eight ground-floor rooms was next along the trail. We climbed a log ladder to reach the roof of the structure. Another such ladder, ends poking through the small, square roof opening, allowed us to enter a rectangular, one-room chamber, which I estimated to be fifteen feet long and ten feet wide. Again, there were no windows, and the only way in was through the roof, seven feet above the dirt floor. Richard pointed out that the ladders were withdrawn in the event of an attack by marauding Indians — Ute, Apache or Navajo. A rectangular masonry slab, set lengthwise into the floor to form a low wall, caught someone's eye.

"That's a turkey pen," said Richard.

Blank looks.

"The people raised turkeys," he explained. "They kept the turkeys penned up there."

Four or five families lived here, Mike informed us. They grew the ubiquitous mainstays: corn, squash and beans. This pueblo was their "summer home." The ground floor was for storage, the second floor the work area. The living space occupied the third story. The top floor served as a lookout. I didn't recall seeing any upper floors on this building when we had climbed in. I queried Richard about it.

"This is a *partial* reconstruction."

One of the ladies in our party wondered how the elderly Indians negotiated the ladders.

"The people here only had a life expectancy of thirty-five to forty years," Richard remarked. "So there were few elderly that had to fight the ladders."

Some of the more senior members of our group shook their heads and exchanged disapproving glances.

Back on the narrow, tree-shaded trail. The air was redolent with the perfume of juniper, piñon, sage and cedar, all blending together to create an olfactory symphony. Richard stopped and pointed into the woods. I didn't see anything noteworthy. But our guide informed us that the slight bumps, carpeted with grass, in the wooded terrain hid a pueblo containing ten rooms.

There was evidence just off the trail of a check dam, used by the Anasazi when they migrated to this area. Water was trickling along the altered course. Other check dams and irrigation channels ran through the site, carrying and diverting water from adjacent Pot Creek. Bear, eagle and bison were once hunted. Richard, who had yet to smile, mentioned that the original settlers here always had a pot of beans cooking. That set off my appetite. I couldn't wait to get back to the van and raid the goodie box.

Pottery was widely used. Clay for the pots could be found two miles away. Crude corrugated pots were utilized for cooking. But storage pots were painted. The Indians used yucca leaves as paint-brushes. The end of the leaf was chewed to the proper consistency. Black paint was derived from the bee plant or from ground iron ore. A placard along the trail extolled the uses of the sagebrush. The plant was crushed and rubbed on the skin as a deodorant by the Indians. Tea was brewed from the leaves. A strong potion would dry up a mother's milk after weaning. A natural tinder, the bush also got campfires started.

At another point along the trail, Richard drew our attention to a pile of stones. These were utilized for the hearth, he said. A few yards ahead, he paused again and gestured toward a large flat stone embedded in the ground. This was a metate upon which corn was ground. Then fishing around in the dirt near the metate, Richard came up with a smooth, fist-sized rock. It was a broken mano. After displaying the mano, Richard re-buried it, as he glanced warily around. It was the first — and only — time I saw Richard crack a grin.

The site was occupied for some 200 years in prehistoric (pre-Spaniard) times. Around 1150 A.D., there was a severe drought that endured for two decades and followed on the heels of a population explosion. Resources vanished. "They overworked the land," Richard said. The people drifted away in spurts to nearby pueblos. Many wound up at Picuris and Taos.

Once back in the van, I made good on the promise to myself to get into the snack box.

We cruised onto the Taos Reservation and pulled into the driveway of a modern single-family house set on a huge lot. Vern's mother-in-law lived here. We had been invited for lunch, after which we would ride to the nearby pueblo for the renowned Corn Dance ceremony. Picnic tables, draped with tablecloths, were placed end to end in the yard under a cherry tree that was laden with fruit. A pair of *hornos* hunched near a fence. They had seen lots of action. Fields and pasture surrounded the homestead. There were no neighbors in sight. A dense layer of slate-gray clouds was creeping up on us. Carmen, Vern's demure wife, was our gracious host. Like Vern, she possessed attractive Indian features, but with shorter hair.

Our ravenous gang took our seats at the tables. Carmen and her mother transported the mountain of food from the house to the tables. Vern's well-mannered, ten-year-old daughter, with big black eyes, helped out. We feasted on chicken verde spiced with chili peppers, red chili with chucks of lean beef, hominy, potato salad and elbow macaroni. All washed down with tea or coffee. I prudently saved room for cookies and bread pudding. But not enough room. I hadn't counted on the three helpings of pudding that I wolfed down. What can I say? It was delicious.

Vern's and Carmen's other child, a boy of about six, was also well behaved. It was so different from the way kids behaved back home in the big cities, and even in suburbia. So refreshing. I don't know the derivation of the expression about unruly kids acting like wild Indians, but it didn't come from this reservation. The shy lad was so cute, with his big expressive eyes and shiny black hair, that some of the ladies kidded one another about stealing him.

We genuinely thanked Carmen and her mother for the sumptuous feast. Vern briefed us about the Corn Dance. It was held at least once a year, as a prayer for ample rain and a bountiful corn production. The black clouds had moved in and were now sprinkling us, as though anticipating the dance. The first group to dance would consist of young men and women, Vern said. "The adults dance later." The participants had to dance a round before they got fed. Then they were served rabbit, obtained from a recent hunt. Vern explained that the men took to the hills and fields after the rabbits. The hunters mainly used bows and arrows. Some used clubs.

"How could a man chase down a darting rabbit with just a club?" I wondered aloud.

"There are so many people there that a rabbit might pass near you, and you can club it," offered Vern.

The light rain subsided. As we were leaving, Vern's father, Virgil, pulled into the driveway. We greeted him en masse. Spattered with soot and wearing a firefighter's helmet, he had just come from the woods, where he was leading a group of Indian firefighters tackling a wild blaze. He possessed an authoritative bearing. I could easily envision him as a leader of men. Virgil now had to quickly clean up, change clothes, and get over to the pueblo. As war chief of the tribe, Virgil had to be present for the festivities. Vern stood by quietly as we chatted with Virgil. It was readily obvious that Vern accorded his dad a great deal of esteem. Parents and elders were respected here, unlike the society I was used to. Virgil beseeched us to enjoy the dance and reminded us firmly about the ban on picture-taking.

Our vans parked in a makeshift lot within the pueblo grounds. We traipsed down a narrow dirt road toward the central plaza, merging with the gathering crowd of other sightseers. The rain was holding off for now, but the clouds hung around. At least the brief shower had cooled things off. Cars, wagons, vans, jeeps, pickups and pedestrians jammed the grassy lots and crowded the dusty roads. This was a major shindig. There was a variety of license plates, mostly from California or the Southwest. I entered the vast plaza area, which was bisected by a shaded stream. The entire plaza, except that portion by the stream, was a carpet of barren earth — no trees, shrubs or grass. Two clusters of unpainted, mud-coated "skyscraper" pueblos, four and five stories high, rose abruptly from opposite sides of the plaza. Each superjacent floor contained fewer rooms than the floor immediately below. Wooden ladders rested in place against the exterior walls, allowing the inhabitants to ascend and descend from floor to floor. The pueblo shops were closed by decree during the dance. Dusty dogs, their tongues hanging, lounged in the shadows.

I traversed the plaza toward the farther pueblo group. Near the base of that pueblo complex, the plaza was alive with noise and people. Most of the sightseers were flocked around costumed Indian dancers. I could hear the drums pound and the singers chant as I approached. But I couldn't catch a glimpse of the dancers until I broke through the dense barrier of tourists.

There were about thirty dancers, males and females, almost all of whom were in their teens or preteens. An older (in his twenties) male dancer seemed to be the conductor. The girls apparently took their cues from two of the older (in their thirties) female dancers. Set apart from the two rows of dancers was a dozen of the male elders: the tribal council. One elder pounded a large drum as others chanted.

The female dancers were clad in multicolored skirts, some with floral patterns. They were bedecked with necklaces, bracelets and earrings of turquoise and silver. Feet were encased in white, leather, knee-high "moonwalker" boots. They toted clusters of flowers in each hand.

The male terpsichoreans were bare-chested. Each wore a kilt. A fox pelt dangled from the rear of a waist sash. Beaded moccasins covered the feet. An eagle feather adorned the back of the head. Like their female counterparts, they were adorned with bracelets and necklaces (but not earrings) of turquoise and silver. They held gourd rattles, which they shook as they stomped around the dusty plaza to the cadence of the thundering drum.

Boom! Boom! Boom! ... Boom! Boom! Boom! Boom! Boom! The deep bass tones of the drum, mingled with the wailing chant of the singers, surged across the plaza, drowning out any other sounds that had the audacity to invade the sacred rite. The dancers scuffed up tiny puffs of dust as they stomped around and shuffled about to the heavy low-pitched tattoo of the drum.

Boom! Boom! Boom! Boom! Boom!

When the dancers finished their routine at one location in the plaza, they worked their way to another nearby spot. The elders led the way. The drum beat on. I anticipated the movement of the dancers and picked out a choice viewing position before the herd of tourists swamped the next dance site. I had an unimpeded vista. As the dancers migrated to this new location, they went right into their routine again. The drum banged out the cadence.

Boom! Boom! Boom! Boom! Boom! . . . Boom! Boom! Boom!

I stood in awe as the primordial dance again unfolded. I was witnessing a ceremony that had endured for countless generations. The dance ushered me back in time. If I mentally blocked out the tourists, I could have been back in the 1700s — or the 1400s. I tried to imagine what it must have like being a dancer here during a bygone century. But that was too remote in time and culture for me to really grasp. I could only conjure up tidbits of what had been. Yet the drum's incessant pounding stirred my soul. If asked, I was ready to shed my white-man's trappings, don native garb, and take my place in the dancers' lines.

I wasn't asked.

Boom! Boom! Boom! . . . Boom! Boom! Boom!

The dance participants were absorbed in their task, seeming not to heed the enveloping crowd of tourists. The serious-faced boys, in particular, were all business, high-stepping and jerking, bobbing their heads, shaking the rattles to the beat. The girls' movements were less vigorous. And I caught a couple of them smiling and whispering to each other as they shuffled their feet and waved their flower clusters. The rain clouds loomed overhead, but nary a raindrop fell despite all the commotion.

The dancers performed by my unobstructed fifty-yardline seat for ten minutes before wandering, with their tourist entourage, to another part of the plaza. The drums beat on. I remained at the nearby pueblo complex to look about. Few Indians were around here now. Many were indoors avoiding the sun — and possibly the crowd. Others were watching the festivities from rooftops or doorways. Some mingled with the sightseers. Many of the drab pueblo dwellings were incongruously decorated with brightly painted doors or window frames. Turquoise was the dominant color, but there were doors of red or blue or green. I separately asked two of the villagers whether the colors had any significant. No, the colors were only a product of a homeowner's desires.

I caught up with Joan, who was roaming around on her own. One of the Indian merchants surreptitiously let us slip into his shop, despite the tribal mandate that the stores be closed now. We came away with some interesting postcards. One of them bore a photo, taken in 1935, of the Corn Dance. The costumes were only slightly different from what we had just witnessed.

I trekked across the plaza to the other high-rise pueblo complex. Many of the ground-floor, adobe rooms had been converted into boutiques. The doors, with attached plaques containing the names of the businesses, were padlocked during the festivities. Some of the dwellings were vacated or possessed only part-time occupants. Yet the rooms appeared to be well maintained, at least from the outside. We never got a chance to view the insides. By now the dancers, and the trailing throng of sightseers, had caught up with me on this side of the plaza.

Boom! Boom! Boom! Boom! . . . Boom! Boom! . . . Boom! Boom! Boom!

I watched the dancers strut their stuff again before they shuffled off to another spot. Another group of dancers, composed of the adults, would take to the plaza later.

A couple of the villagers strolled down a narrow lane within the complex. The passageway seemed to lead to the rear of the building. Curious, I followed them. I didn't get far. Some pudgy, disgruntled Indian teenager loudly hailed me. He curtly informed me that I was out of bounds. The boisterous, self-appointed sergeant-at-arms escorted me back to the plaza. I sarcastically thanked him. He grunted, probably wishing that the scalping of white men was still fashionable.

By then it was time to head back to the vans.

❋   ❋   ❋

We rendezvoused with our guide for the day, Tim Maxwell, in a parking lot across from the post office of the San Juan Pueblo. Unfortunately, we wouldn't be visiting this active pueblo. We would be on our way to the Rio Chama sites. Tim, a tall, boyish-looking doctoral candidate, briefed us. The peoples of those long-deserted

ROAMING THROUGH TAOS PUEBLO

sites spoke Tewa. Tradition indicated that the Tewa speakers in this region originated from southern Colorado, but this had not been confirmed archeologically. The abandoned pueblo sites on our itinerary were ancestral villages of the present Tewa people. The Tewa forebears, in turn, had an Anasazi heritage.

The Chama River Valley was initially occupied by Archaic Indians some 4000 years ago, he said. By the time of Christ, these people had disappeared. The region remained abandoned for 1200 years.

We piled back into the vans. The first site was Poshu-ouinge. This Tewa pueblo bordered the Rio Chama. There wasn't much for us to see. We scaled the rock-strewn hill behind the abandoned site. From our vantage point, amidst juniper and piñon trees interspersed with rabbit brush, we looked down onto what seemed to be only grassy fields. It was another site that had been excavated early this century, then backfilled. No ruins were visible. But the general layout of the site could be deduced from the terrain. A weed-covered depression had been a kiva, Tim noted. The outlines of two plazas, as extensive as present-day soccer fields, were evident from the low, linear, grassy mounds that ran through the site. The rooms here were arranged differently than in Mesa Verde.

"Here there were room-blocks," said Tim.

"How many?" I asked.

"There were two multi-level room-blocks."

"How many rooms?"

"It's estimated there were seven hundred ground-floor rooms."

"What were the walls made of?"

"Stone or coursed adobe."

Buzzards soared high above the hill. A smaller bird with a different silhouette floated on the thermals, emitting a shrieking cry. A hawk, said Tim.

Tim continued with the lecture. Plazas started being constructed in this pueblo about 1250 A.D. The villages in this area generally were large, and were erected on terraces above the river and its tributaries. These villages, including Poshu-ouinge, flourished for two centuries, until 1300 to 1400. Within a generation, they were abandoned. When the Spaniards arrived in the 1500s, the Tewa people had moved downstream to the confluence of the Rio

Chama and the Rio Grande, and to other locations within the Rio Grande Valley.

Then Tim gestured to the right of the plazas, to other vacant fields. "Those were probably for agriculture."

"What did they grow here?" I asked

"Pollen has been found for corn and cotton! . . . but there's no evidence of beans and squash."

As we rode to the next site, leaden clouds swept over the landscape. When we turned off the highway and bumped along a dirt road, the lightning started in the distance. Like artillery fire, the flashes intermittently lit up our gray background. Seconds later the thunder rolled over us. We pulled up at the edge of an escarpment and climbed out of the vans. The wind was kicking up. The air had cooled off. Droplets were starting to pelt us. The hill was strewn with juniper trees, cholla bushes and rabbit brush. No one else was around, although there was ample evidence of recent human presence from all the discarded aluminum cans and glass bottles. The nearest building was a mile away. Mountains ringed the hill.

Tim pointed to several arrangements of rocks embedded in the ground. These were "rock gardens." We were standing in a "rock field." The Indians had placed the rocks within their gardens. Although the gardens have been unused for centuries, the rocky outlines remained. The rocks captured the sun's rays during the day, allowing these stones to re-emit heat to the garden plants after sunset. Corn needed a temperature of at least seventy degrees to produce properly. This nocturnal heating added an hour or two of warmth each day to the corn. The rocks also conserved moisture that otherwise would have slipped out of reach of thirsty roots.

"Water lasted three times longer," said Tim.

The stones provided protection against frost, thereby lengthening the growing season. But there was a drawback.

"Organic material can't get back into the soil. The pores in the soil get clogged, and water can't enter anymore. So the rocks may have been good for only a year or two."

Apparently, the stones then had to be replaced. Tim drew our attention to large dimples in the terrain. These had been pits from where the rocks were gathered.

The lightning continued to crack, growing in ferocity. It occurred to me that we were standing on the highest elevation in the immediate area. We stood as tall as the tops of the stunted juniper trees. The rain held to a sprinkle. We loaded back into the vans and bounced down the deserted road to a nearby site.

We quickly hiked through the roadside brush to a vast pasture perimetered with trees and shrubs. It was another of those sites that had been previously excavated and backfilled. Again, there were no ruins to be seen. The clearing was demarcated into square or rectangular segments by differences in the color of the grass, most of which was light brown. But long, straight lines of green grass, intersecting or meeting at right angles, cut through the pasture. Some of the segments were also outlined by long, low mounds of grass. We were standing on Sapawe, considered by some archeologists as the largest prehistoric pueblo in the Southwest. Cattle now grazed over it. Tim explained that the grass was green wherever there was adobe beneath the ground.

"The adobe retains moisture."

The menacing clouds blanketed the sky, dispensing only sprinkles now but threatening a downpour. Thunder competed for our attention. Our group dispersed to quickly roam over the huge site. I tracked the perimeter of the walls by walking along the low mounds. Although only a foot high, these mounds covered the second story of the underlying ruins. The layout indicated the presence of expansive plazas, now buried. As I strolled around, I had to dodge the numerous prairie-dog holes that dotted the landscape. None of the animals was in sight. Either the weather or our presence kept them underground. I was mindful that where there were prairie dogs, there were probably rattlesnakes. I kept a wary eye out for them, but I suspected the weather drove them for cover, too.

The site was littered with pottery shards. Some were painted inside and out, some only on the exterior. I found an unpainted sample and asked Tim about it.

"That's corrugated, washboard, micaceous pottery," he said offhandedly, as though anyone would know what the hell he was talking about.

"Oh yeah," I nodded.

We took to the vans before we pushed our luck too far.

* * *

We rolled along a dirt track that bisected deserted fields in the Galisteo Basin. Ahead jutted a spine of hills, interrupted by Comanche Gap, so named for the Comanche who passed through in a bygone century. There was hardly a cloud in sight this morning. We were on private property at the moment. We would soon cross onto government land. Crow Canyon had written permission to be here. A pickup truck trailed us as we trundled toward the hills. Jim, in whose van Joan and I were riding this day, commented that it was probably the owner of the property checking us out. No sooner had we pulled up at the base of the hills, when the driver of the pickup, clad in soiled and worn cowboy duds, confronted Jim. The cowboy scratched his head, as Jim politely displayed the letter he had from the land's owner. Satisfied, our inquisitor drove off.

Our guide for this day's venture was Helen Crotty, a rock-art expert. Her husband, Jay, who was adept at searching out petroglyphs, accompanied her. Helen, a senior citizen, explained that the art here started around 1300 to 1350 A.D. Most of what we would see dated from at least the 1400s. The narrow, rocky crest of the hills, the result of a volcanic dike, carried the label of "Devil's Backbone." It seemed a fitting appellation. As we set off to follow Helen up the steep, boulder-strewn face of the escarpment to the summit of the hills, Jay spoke up.

"Watch out for rattlesnakes. This is when they're out."

All eyes immediately switched to the ground. Helen led the way. Joan and I were in the vanguard of our group that followed Helen. As I picked my way over the boulders to the crown of the nearest hill, I scanned the rocks warily before placing a foot. The naked sun was warming up the rocks, which would soon become choice lounging spots for the cold-blooded reptiles. The footing was treacherous. And we had to dodge the tenacious needles of the cholla bushes that dotted the hillside below the crest of the hill.

Petroglyphs abounded on the boulders at the top of the hill. Some of the rocks were coated with desert varnish. Much of the art was carved into this encrustation. A veldt, of vast bare fields, stretched out from all sides of this backbone of hills. We scrambled over the boulders here, and worked our way over to another hilly crest also loaded with rock art. Many of the rocks bore a stylized human face, with a circle for the shape of the head, smaller circles as eyes, and an open mouth with pointed teeth.

The horned serpent was represented, with a zigzag body that was filled in with stippling, a round eye, and a forward-facing "horn" on the head. There was speculation in the reference books that this figure may have also symbolized lightning. Numerous four-pointed "stars" were scratched into the rocks. I wondered if the stars represented the planet Venus, which formed a pivotal part of the Mayan cosmos. Helen thought it possible. One figure seemed to be a combination of a four-pointed star and a human face, some sort of planetary anthropomorphic, I guess. Two circle eyes were set in the center of the star. The bottom point of the star contained a turndown, open mouth with sharp teeth, as though the face was snarling. To the left of this figure was another petroglyph, a clockwise-circling line that spiraled inward to the center of the design. To its left was another four-pointed star carved above a sinuous reptile.

A standing human figure, the outline of its back arced into a bulge, was apparently blowing into a musical instrument. Kokopelli?

Jay pointed out several impressive petroglyphs etched onto a stack of rocks at the very pinnacle of the hill. I clambered over the underlying boulders and squatted on a precarious perch, as I viewed and photographed the iconography. A misstep on my part would have started a minor avalanche, of which I would have been an integral part. I immediately recognized a large cloud-terrace. The vertical lines extending downward from the base of the design depicted, of course, rain. Was this glyph a prayer for rain?

A large "shield " figure caught my eye. I guessed it to be a frontal view of a warrior. The oversized, round shield dominated the icon and totally obscured the torso of the "warrior." The head was separated from the shield by a thin neck. A pair of inward-pointing "horns" arose from the top of the head. The figure's scrawny legs, extending from beneath the shield, were both bent to the left.

The sun was arcing up from the horizon. There was merely a hint of high-altitude clouds. Another enigmatic shield figure on a nearby boulder got my attention. I scrambled over to it. The massive, circular shield also totally covered the warrior's torso. The frontal silhouette of the head was devoid of facial features. The legs and feet were in profile and faced to the left. The shield was fringed with a continuous row of solid points. The design on the shield differed from the one I had just seen. Here there was a pair of "eyes" — a thick dot within a thick circle — near the top of the shield, set off from the rest of the shield to form a "mask."

Other rocks contained outlines of human figures, one of which had two head "feathers." Another was holding a spear. Zoomorphic

depictions were represented. An outline of the pro- file of an animal only showed two legs, both of which had long claws. The tail stuck straight out. A long, out-of-pro- portion "feather" extended from the head to beyond the tail. On a different rock face, a bird was etched in fron- tal view, wings ex- tended. The avian head was turned to the right. The legs were splayed, tal- ons bared. Yet an- other boulder de- picted the outline of a bird in profile.

Our allotted time for this site over, we carefully hiked back down

SHIELD WARRIOR AT COMANCHE GAP

to the vans. No one saw a rattlesnake.

We drove through the barren New Mexico countryside to the
next stop, Pueblo Blanco. This site was buried. But we came mainly
for the rock art. The petroglyphs were incised on the sandstone face
of the low bluff overlooking the unexcavated pueblo. We parked
beneath juniper trees near the base of the bluff. The site was overgrown also with piñon trees, cholla bushes and thistles bearing vio-
let flowers. No one else was in sight. The solar globe was approaching its daily zenith. Scarcely a cloud patch was present to diminish
the sun's blistering gaze. It was getting hot out. As soon as we stepped
from the vans, we came upon pottery shards. The ground was littered with them. We trailed Helen and Jay up the bluff.

The designs and figures here were not so easy to make out as at
Comanche Gap, probably because these rocks were not generously
coated with desert varnish. Helen pointed out the outlines of human faces, some of which she characterized as "masks." These figures generally had circles for eyes. The mouth was usually in the
shape of a rectangle, with rows of sharp teeth. One wore some sort
of headdress that contained "feathers," "horns" or whatever. I
couldn't get a definitive answer about it. Helen drew our attention
to "masks" that utilized natural holes in the rock as part of the
figure's face.

Helen led us to her favorite petroglyph: a twenty-one-foot serpent — she had measured it — which zigzagged horizontally above
our heads. It had a forward-pointing "horn," upon which Helen commented.

"The horns go forward here. Up in Bandelier, the horns go backward." There was no explanation.

There was one life-sized outline of a zoomorphic depiction that
was carved onto desert varnish and was, therefore, readily discernible: a bear. The beast was shown in profile. Small ears were drawn
on the head. There was a nub of a tail. All four legs were visible.
Each foot showed bared claws. The animal appeared to be standing
still. It was a magnificent piece of rock art. Unfortunately, it had
been defaced with modern graffiti.

An Indian artist placing his hand on the rock and spraying (possibly with his mouth) red pigment over the hand and surrounding

rock had left a handprint on a rock. When the artist then removed his hand from the rock, the red pigment remained on the rock, forming an outline of where the hand had been. This might have been the artist's signature. It mimicked handprints sprayed onto caves by Australian aborigines millennia ago.

The outline of a human figure, in frontal pose, had the legs akimbo, with the arms bent and raised to shoulder level. It had circles for eyes and an oval for a mouth.

Time for lunch. Jim had a buffet table set up for us under an expansive juniper tree. We lounged under the trees, hungrily munching on sandwiches, salad and Oreo cookies (which didn't last long).

Before we could even think about napping, the scholars led the way to the buried pueblo. In the Galisteo Basin, which included Pueblo Blanco, there were some 2000 pueblo rooms. The site was inhabited from the early 1300s to the early 1500s, just prior to the arrival of the Spaniards. By 1520, all the pueblos in the Basin had been abandoned. There was no historic occupation here.

"Either warfare or famine caused the people to leave," said Vern. "The people in the pueblos always came back. But in the Sixteenth Century, they were finally abandoned."

We pored over Pueblo Blanco. An arroyo had since sliced through the site. The long, searching tendrils of squash plants, some bearing small gourds, now dotted the site. Overgrown mounds sequestered the room-blocks. A conical depression meant an underlying kiva. Vern snatched up handfuls of a yellow-headed plant, pueblo tea, to be brewed when he got home.

One of the scholars at first denied that the walls of the pueblo here were constructed of sandstone. There wasn't enough sandstone, she told me. I wondered. Sandstone was readily available, at least for some buildings. It was durable, unlike adobe. And it was easy to fashion into blocks. Why didn't they use it? Then I noticed that some of the mounds overlying the room blocks were littered with chunks of sandstone debris. So why were these stones here? It was obvious — to me, anyway. The stones must have been used to erect the pueblo's walls, which had since tumbled down. I shared my observations and thoughts with the scholar. She ruminated on it and nodded, "They probably did use sandstone."

We piled into the vans and retraced our path back to the asphalt highway.

We turned off the paved highway onto a dirt road that was scratched across the vast countryside upon which shrubs and bushes were scattered. Halfway up a hill, we parked near the entrance to a turquoise mine. The owner of the mine, Doug Magness, greeted us. Clad in denim, our lanky, dark-haired host had a receding hairline, and a thick moustache that merged with a bearded chin. I guessed him to be in his forties. When not hanging around the mine, Doug fashioned jewelry, which he marketed. He invited us to take a seat on the double row of stone benches at the edge of the parking area. We fanned out along the benches and started to take our seats, when one of the ladies, Ruth, screamed. All heads turned.

"A snake!" she shrieked.

After this morning's caution about rattlesnakes, I fully expected to come face to face with one of those pit vipers. But no. This yard-long, harmless serpent was beautifully patterned with mahogany and tan bands circling its slender body.

"That's just a red racer," said Doug nonchalantly.

Living up to its name, the snake bolted from the scene.

Doug mentioned that the Indians extracted turquoise here at least a thousand years ago. Volcanic activity 35 million years ago "pushed up minerals that cooled off rapidly." Turquoise was thus brought close to the surface. The mine produced "really fine, blue, beautiful quality material." But "the Spanish didn't have a real high regard for turquoise." The gemstone was heavily mined here during the 1880s and 1890s. The "last real active production was no later than 1929 or 1930." Doug's interest in the mine derived more from a passion for history than a desire to make a buck. There were no new excavations underway. Doug "reclaimed some scraps" of turquoise from the piles of stony debris around the mine. Although he did utilize these turquoise scraps in his jewelry, he could buy the mineral cheaper on the open market than he could reclaim it here. The Chinese produced bushels of it. But the turquoise from Doug's mine had sentimental value. Hard to put a price tag on that.

With that proem, Doug led us to the mine, known in modern times as the Tiffany Mine (yes, *that* Tiffany). A short gravel path led from the benches to the mine entrance, which was shored up with aging timbers. We carefully stepped, single file, down the dark, narrow passageway that had been hacked through the rock. A smidgen of light leaked in from the other end of the tunnel. In a minute we had passed through the shaft and were standing in an underground clearing with a volume of a large living room capped by a cathedral ceiling. From an aperture in the hill's grassy surface, some twenty feet above me, sunlight filtered into the mine. This irregular gash in the earth was manmade. The prehistoric Indians started the process. They chopped away at the surface, with hand-held stone tools known as malls, to extract the turquoise. Over centuries their mining efforts produced an elongated pit about ten feet across. From the chop marks I saw on the overhead walls of the gap, it seemed the Indians dug the hole down to a depth of maybe ten feet. From that depth, the pit was extended to its present level, where I stood, by the modern technique of blasting. Doug indicated how to discern, along the rocky walls of the opening, where the Indians' digging ended and the blasting began. The dynamited sections came away in larger chunks, leaving the walls with sharper features than the softer topology caused by the Indians. The tunnel we had just traversed was constructed in the 1890s to gain access to the lower part of the pit where I now stood.

I suffered from misconceptions when I walked into the mine. I envisioned something on the order of a gold mine, with long shafts that bored deep into the earth, coal cars that shuttled ore along miles of railroad tracks, sweaty and sooty miners who hacked away in the light of their helmet lamps, deafening jackhammers that ripped into veins of precious minerals. I had watched too many documentaries on South African gold mines. This mine was the antithesis of what I had imagined. There had never been any long shafts, or coal cars, or railroad tracks. I doubt that the miners ever got covered with soot. I didn't see any jackhammer tracks on the walls. The miniature cavern in which I was standing was all there was to the mine. And there had never been any lodes of the gem. Unlike a rich vein of gold, the turquoise here was found in fragments embedded in the rock. It had to be chipped out, bit by bit.

I examined the gray walls closely. Some were still sprinkled with the vivid gem, which sparkled against the drab background. I

examined a pile of fist-sized malls that Doug had collected and assembled on a rocky ledge. I grasped one of those stones and tried to
imagine being a prehistoric Indian miner. It must have been arduous labor indeed.

*   *   *

Our vans trekked south from Albuquerque along a two-lane
highway through mile after mile of flat grassland. Scarcely any vehicles shared the road with us. There were no buildings in sight. To
the west, the Rio Grande streamed southward. To the east, the
Manzano Mountains paralleled our route. Scattered head of cattle
grazed in fenced-in, roadside pastures. The rising sun in a blank,
pastel-blue backdrop foretold of another hot day. As we turned left
and headed into the Manzano range, the fields became mottled with
juniper and piñon trees. We would be visiting the abandoned sites
of the Salinas region, in central New Mexico, which contained the
farthest southeastern extension of the prehistoric pueblos. Three
sites in particular would occupy our day: Abó, Gran Quivira and
Quarai.

The area derived its name (Salinas) from the salt lakes to the
east of the mountains, in the Estancia Basin. Before the last ice age,
a vast lake existed there. The glaciers never got that far south, yet
the heavy precipitation did. But over ensuing millennia, the rains
dissipated. The lake dried up. Residues of concentrated salts remained. Salt flats and shallow ephemeral "lakes," only inches deep,
replaced the original lake.

Pithouses appeared in the Basin about 600 A.D. By 950, Abó
Pass was inhabited by Mogollon pithouse builders from the south.
Pottery came into vogue as the people settled into semi-permanent
dwellings. Nomadic groups tended not to develop these clay vessels, as they were too heavy and fragile for travel. The style of pottery initially utilized by the pithouse occupants depicted the
Mogollon origin. Two centuries later, Anasazi-style pottery predomi-
nated in the region. Pithouse construction evolved into above-ground
jacal structures, where wicker walls of woven sticks were filled and
coated with mud. Anasazi builders later improved this architecture
by erecting the jacal walls on stone foundations and facing the walls

with stone slabs. Prehistoric Indians in the basin employed this method at Abó, for instance. But Anasazi influence in the Basin lagged behind Anasazi development elsewhere in the Southwest. By 900 A.D., Anasazi stone structures began to appear in other areas. Originally employed as storage facilities, these permanent buildings eventually became living quarters as well. While the pueblos at Chaco Canyon, 200 miles to the northwest, reached their cultural zenith during the Tenth and Eleventh Centuries, the peoples of Estancia Basin were then still residing exclusively in the rudimentary pithouses. The Mesa Verde area, in southwestern Colorado, started fluorescing about the middle of the Twelfth Century. There was an explosion of new pottery styles, massive building projects, and expanding ceremonialism. Yet, it wasn't until after 1300 A.D., when Mesa Verde was abandoned, that stone villages graced the landscape in Estancia Basin.

Our first stop of the day was at Abó, situated in a pass through the Manzano Mountains. The pueblo here shared architectural features with other pueblos in the Basin. The stone walls of the multistory buildings were usually sealed with mud plaster. Timber, for roofing beams and door lintels, was collected from the nearby mountains. There was a paucity of petite doorways and windows in the exterior walls. Wooden ladders connected one floor to the next. Many rooms had rooftop entrances. Unfortunately, none of this was evident to us. The ruins were still buried. The site, as we viewed it, was dominated by the hulking remains of the Franciscan mission that later adjoined the pueblo.

Trail map in hand, I took to the path that circumscribed the site. I wandered through the roofless skeleton of what had once been a capacious sandstone church with its appurtenant residential structures. The upper walls of the church were missing. From 1622 to 1673, Spanish priests lived here. Actually, two churches were erected on this spot during this period, with the later, larger edifice being superimposed upon the smaller, earlier version. From within the remnants of the badly eroded walls of the *convento*, I gazed out at surrounding countryside, much of which was punctuated by bulges topped with cholla bushes. These earthy mounds cloaked unexcavated room-blocks. Inexplicably, the cholla bushes prospered on these bumps in the terrain, and were an indicator of underlying ruins. There was evidence of the mission's gardens, which produced such dietary delights as melons, plums, grapes, chili peppers and coriander. In the field beyond the gardens, the priests cultivated wheat and raised cattle.

I passed through the dining hall into the *ambulatorio*, a large, central patio. A round kiva, formed from sandstone blocks and with the roof long gone, took up the middle of the patio. I couldn't get an explanation for the presence of this incongruous structure, which was constructed about the same time as the earlier church.

I entered a now-unroofed passageway that led to the corral, where the priests had immured their cows, sheep, goats and pigs. The kitchen was next door. It was now an empty room. The guide-book informed me that cooking was done here on a large Indian-style open hearth. Along a hallway connecting these two rooms, the priests stored spices, almonds, raisins, chocolate and cigars. Tough life these Franciscans had.

A bank of rooms along one side of the *convento* was the dormitory for the friars. The *portería* was located at one end of this set of rooms. Its floor was paved with flagstones rather than the customary adobe of other mission rooms. The *portería* contained benches and a fireplace when the *convento* was occupied.

Every three years during the Franciscans' tenure here, wagon loads of mission supplies rolled in from Mexico City. In turn, the priests exported salt excavated from the salt lakes to the east. This important commodity was prized in Santa Barbara, Mexico, where it was employed in silver smelting.

I cut short my self-guided tour of the mission, using the limited time we had remaining to explore the pueblo grounds. Abó, built on an outcrop of red sandstone, was first occupied by Tompiro-speaking Indians about 1150 A.D. After 1400, they traded pottery, salt, produce and nuts to nearby pueblos and Plains Indians.

By the 1670s, the combined pressure of famine, drought, disease and Apache raids made life here unbearable. The priests and pueblo dwellers left. Many of the Tompiro refugees migrated to the Piro pueblos on the Rio Grande. They never returned to Abó.

An unexcavated depression in the cholla-strewn landscape along the trail signaled a kiva. Unlike its counterpart I had just viewed within the *convento*, this one was still buried. As with other pueblo peoples, the kiva was a major factor in Tompiro religion. Throughout the quarter-mile trail that looped through the pueblo site, all the pueblo ruins were underground. Nodes and dips in the terrain revealed underlying room-blocks and plazas. It was up to the imagination to reconstruct the long-deserted pueblo.

Back to the vans.

A short ride took us to the Gran Quivira ruins. As at Abó, the site's commanding feature was the crumpled stone remains of the obligatory mission with its attached *convento*. Only the lower walls still stood. The pueblo and mission were abandoned about the time of the exodus from Abó.

The Tompiro inhabitants who had once lived here raised corn, beans, squash, cotton and probably amaranth. Water was scarcer at Gran Quivira than at neighboring Abó and Quarai, which were located near streams. To compensate, the people of Gran Quivira constructed a network of surface-water catchments, cisterns and wells. They gathered seeds and nuts and plants. Turkeys were raised for feathers and nutrition. Hunting brought rabbit, deer, antelope and even bison to the cooking fire.

Ceremonialism was an integral part of the Indian's daily life even after the appearance of the Spaniards. Unlike the tenets of our modern society, there was no demarcation between the sacred and the secular in the pueblos. Religion influenced all aspects of one's existence. There were, of course, festivals associated with crop production — prayers and dances for continuous rain and a generous harvest. But rituals also accompanied hunting, marriage and death, for instance.

Anasazi town planning was evident in the layout of the masonry pueblo here. Plazas were centrally located within the configuration of the room-blocks. Rather than simply separating the blocks of rooms, the plazas served a vital function for the community. Much of daily activity took place in the pueblo plazas: women cooked and fashioned pottery, kids played, dogs barked, turkeys scratched in the dirt, men chipped out new projectile points. The plazas were pitted with subterranean kivas. Fires cooked the food, fired the pottery, heated the rooms.

The natives here were ardent traders. They offered corn, salt and cotton *mantas* as their currency. From the Plains Indians to the east, Gran Quivira imported hides and jerky. Flint, from quarries in west Texas, found its way to the pueblo. Mussels, from Texas rivers, were a delicacy here. From Mexico came macaws, highly sought as pets and prized for their handsome feathers. Seashells were acquired for ornamentation.

We followed the paved path from the parking lot up a hillock to the ruins. The church and *convento* were the first stop on the tour. I skipped that, opting to devote my entire time to the pueblo ruins. Mound 7 had been excavated decades ago and, fortunately, *not* backfilled. I eagerly set forth to explore the site. A rectangular grid of small, square, stone rooms, now devoid of roofs and upper walls, was draped across the mound. Near the center of this cluster, the floor of one room was missing. I peeked down into the room. Below where the floor should have been was another room, part of an earlier pueblo structure. That prior pueblo complex was arranged in a circular pattern over the mound. Other than what I was able to glimpse through this floorless room, that prior construction was invisible. It lay abandoned for years before being covered by the erection of the later pueblo complex, which I was now poring over. I encountered this philosophy, of one building phase superimposed upon another, in Mesoamerica, where it had been prevalent.

This second phase of development occurred about 1545 A.D., and resulted in the creation of over 200 new rooms. Concurrent with this construction was the introduction of two foreign cultural traits. The Mogollon-inspired pottery was superseded by Tabirá ware, with its plain, black-on-white, and polychrome versions. The same local clay was used, but with a different tempering grog and concept of decoration. Burial practices changed dramatically. At least as far back as 1300 A.D., the dead at Gran Quivira were wrapped and bound with the knees tucked under the chin, then interred in trash heaps in front of the houses. But after 1545, half the bodies buried in Mound 7 had been cremated. These ceramic traits and mortuary practices suggested a Zuni influence.

I leaned over the low walls of one room that still contained evidence of having served as a grinding station. Three metates, manos resting on top, were in place. Thin stone slabs, mounted vertically between the metates, were in situ. They defined and separated the workspaces. Three women would have labored here, side by side, gossiping and grinding.

The walls I inspected seemed composed of blocks of sandstone, shale and limestone. I looked closely into the subterranean kivas, their roofs long gone, for signs of the murals Carol said were once there. They, too, had disappeared over time. In the pueblo's heyday, kiva walls were plastered with multiple layers upon which the murals were painted. We would glimpse such works of art at another site.

The peoples of the Estancia Basin were spared Coronado's foreboding intrusion in the 1540s. But in 1598, the Spaniards blew into town. Pueblo life was never the same. The conquistadors implemented the *encomienda* system. An individual favored by the Spanish crown was appointed an *encomendero*, which entitled him to collect annual tribute from an Indian village. The tribute was often paid in the form of locally produced goods such as corn or *mantas*. Under an alternate method, *repartimiento*, the pueblo dwellers were burdened with a labor tax. The law prohibited both systems from being utilized simultaneously, but this was one decree that wasn't rigorously followed.

The civil authorities, who enforced the requisition of goods and labor from the Indians, were often at odds with the Franciscan missionaries over these tax practices. Church and state usually had divergent goals. The priests' animus was conversion of the natives to Christianity, rather than the accumulation of personal wealth. At times there was a tug of war, between church and state, over the allegiance of the Indians, who were whipsawed in the process. These disputes, between these two branches of Spanish authority, were not always amicably resolved.

For example, in 1613 Governor Peralta sent armed troops to collect tribute from Taos Pueblo during a holy day, in blatant defiance to the resident priest, who demanded the soldiers stay away. When the soldiers arrogantly marched and rode into the pueblo anyway, the priest became enraged at what he considered blasphemous conceit. He thereupon declared himself an agent of the dreaded Inquisition, which still struck terror in the hearts of even the staunchest soldiers. The audacious man of the cloth arrested the governor in front of his own men, and imprisoned the stunned administrator in his own colony. Talk about nerve!

Quarai was set in a sparse woodland that showcased juniper trees and cholla bushes. Cottonwood trees lined the banks of the nearby spring-fed stream at the base of the Manzano Mountains. Sandstone was abundantly available as a building material. Pueblo ruins dated back to at least 1300 A.D. Unlike their neighbors in Abó and Gran Quivira, the inhabitants of Quarai spoke Tiwa.

As at our two prior stops this day, the remnants of a Spanish mission from the Seventeenth Century presided over the site. I made only a cursory examination of the deteriorated framework of the church and *convento*, which was discernible from the layout of the crumbled walls. The traditional, mission architectural features were evident. But an unusual structure caught my eye. As at Abó, a kiva dominated a plaza within the *convento*. But this kiva at Quarai was square. The roof had long since disappeared. The tops of the stone walls now came up to the level of the ground upon which I stood. I peered down into the spacious kiva. A square fire pit was delineated by stone slabs shoved vertically into the dirt floor. The compulsory ventilator shaft, at the base of one of the walls, was framed with the building stones. The shaft, lined with stones, led backward and upward to the surface.

The cruciform church must have been impressive when it stood intact. With towering sandstone walls forty feet high, the lofty and spacious building enclosed a vast quantity of space, unlike anything the Indians had ever seen. Walls once were plastered white, with dados tinted in patterns of red, black, yellow and blue. Above them, paintings had hung along the wall. Giant ceiling beams would have connected to the upper walls. It must have been an awesome scene for the natives to behold.

The priests here had customarily worn a habit of coarse gray sackcloth under a habit of white sackcloth, with a scapular and rosary. The cord of patron St. Francis of Assisi was draped around the waist. Sandals, woolen stockings or leggings, a heavy blue cloak and a flat friar's hat completed the cumbersome outfit. I couldn't imagine anyone walking around in all that in central New Mexico during the Seventeenth Century, except perhaps during the winter nights.

As their Salinas counterparts had done in Abó and Gran Quivira, the priests and natives here drifted away during the 1670s, for similar reasons.

I exited the mission and wandered over the surrounding fields. Although nine mounds of pueblo rooms occupied the area, there were no Indian ruins to be viewed. This was another unexcavated site. Yawn. I would liked to have explored the ruins of the pueblo, which reached three stories and contained hundreds of rooms, but was now buried out of sight.

* * *

The daily vehicle rotation put Joan and me in the third row of the van that Vern drove. His wife and kids, along for the visit to the Keresan-speaking village of Acoma, took up the row ahead of us. As we headed west from Albuquerque along I-40, I was amazed at how well the kids behaved. They sat quietly, observing the passing scenery. Joan was particularly excited about touring Acoma, one of the locations on her travel wish-list. The pueblo, still inhabited after centuries of occupation, was erected atop a virtually inaccessible mesa. Our rear window framed the rising sun as we traversed the flat landscape. Mesas and hills punctuated the countryside to the south. Carol, driving one of the other vehicles, used the intercom system that connected the vans to brief us on our forthcoming destination.

There has been occupation in the area since about 600 A.D. Acoma liked to use that date as its point of origin, but "that's not supported by the evidence," said Carol. "Around 1300, they started living on top."

Someone naturally asked which of the pueblos was the oldest continuously inhabited city in the country.

"Acoma claims it," responded Carol.

But there was a dispute.

"Taos could claim the honor," Vern chimed in over the intercom. "We've been here since time began."

Carol continued. "About 1599, Spanish soldiers transited the area. The Acomas slaughtered a bunch of them." The Spaniards thereupon exacted a terrible vengeance. They rounded up all the villagers they could nab, killing and enslaving many of them. "All the men had their right foot cut off, then they were put into bondage."

A side road led from the interstate southward through barren terrain. Within twenty minutes we pulled into the pueblo's visitors' center. Two sides of the parking lot were jammed with display tables, end to end, of the Indian vendors who operated out of their vehicles. Relaxing beneath umbrellas, the natives marketed their wares to curious sightseers. It was the Indians' version of a flea market. Bowls, pots, dishes and other clay vessels and figures, and jewelry of silver and turquoise, awaited our perusal. Other tourists were already picking through the goods. But our group had little time to scout the merchandise, as the tour bus was loading for the trip up to the mesa top. Off-reservation vehicles weren't allowed to drive up to the mesa. A mile away, the mesa burst onto the featureless, horizontal landscape. At the top of its sheer walls, I could make out the shape of the pueblo. Now I got excited.

Carol introduced us to Robert, an Acoma Indian who would be our guide this morning. Tall, dark-complected, with long jet-black hair worn loose, Robert was clad in a black T-shirt and black jeans. I guessed him to be in his early twenties. His face was making a valiant attempt to sprout a moustache, which barely contrasted with his sable skin. The black outline of a tattoo, which I couldn't decipher, adorned his entire right deltoid. He was an art student who vended his jewelry creations. Despite being soft-spoken, he wasn't bashful about marketing his works.

Before our gang loaded onto the bus, we unloaded our kidneys. Once up on the mesa, we'd have to hold our water. The pueblo there had neither electricity, running water, nor plumbing. I made another obligatory stop, at the visitors' center. To take along a camera, a visitor had to cough up a surcharge. I forked over ten dollars (for Joan and me) to the young Indian cashier, who curtly took my money as though she were doing me a favor. She shoved two sticky labels at me, which were to be visibly displayed on the cameras.

We piled into the undersized bus. There were more derriéres than bus seats. We crowded together, becoming very intimate with the fellow passengers on either side. Another Acoma resident, Reva,

PUEBLO HOMES AT ACOMA

climbed aboard. Small and middle-aged, she would escort us around the pueblo when we got to the top of the mesa. She educated us about the two forms of crafts that would be available. One was "traditional," signifying that the item was entirely handmade. The other, "ceramic," denoted a piece that was cast in a mold, then sold to the artist who thereupon decorated it by hand. The ceramic wares would "look better," Reva said. But the objects produced from scratch by the craftsman were more desirable despite not being perfectly formed. The bus groaned its way up the steep road leading to the summit. The driver had to stop and downshift as we crept uphill. I was concerned that our overloaded vehicle might backslide. But we — finally — reached the village.

A network of mud-coated pueblo buildings, some stacked two or three stories high and separated by vacant dirt streets, spread over the entire mesa top. There was little visible activity until we pulled in. As soon as we alighted from the bus, Reva demanded to see our "camera tags." Heaven forbid someone should sneak an untaxed camera into town. As we displayed our cameras in unison, Reva walked down our line and visually inspected each and every one of them!

"Don't take anyone's picture unless you get permission," she said sternly. "Ask first!"

Like sheep following a shepherd, we trailed Reva along the short, dusty roads. Doors opened from houses that lined our route. Out came the vendors, usually women, some with kids in tow. They set up curbside stands that showcased their merchandise, mostly pottery vessels. Reva led us by every display, pausing long enough for us to survey the goods. Our course through this ancient pueblo took us from one merchant, straight to the next, and so on, like connecting the dots. We never got a chance to peek into any of the houses or have any meaningful dialogue with the inhabitants (other than to make a purchase). I browsed through the pottery, but I was more intent on looking around this interesting town. Unfortunately, Reva didn't allow us to wander off. We were more regimented than raw recruits at Parris Island. Everyone I encountered was in the business of selling wares to the tourists. Two other groups of sightseers, also led by Acoma guides, roamed the village. Straggly dogs of undeterminable pedigree loitering in the shadows, looked on with disinterest. Other than the busses that occasionally shuttled tourists to and from the mesa, there was no vehicular traffic. A few native-owned cars and pickups were parked beside the buildings. Except for a couple of cottonwood trees, I didn't see any plants. From the edge of the precipice, I gazed down hundreds of feet to the sparsely vegetated countryside. Other mesas, with steep, bare sides, interrupted the monotonous landscape, which extended to the horizon. Along the slope immediately below me was a hodgepodge of outhouses. The solar orb was rapidly scaling the clear, cerulean sky. Another hot day.

We followed Reva to the Spanish-style church with its adjacent cemetery. No photos allowed, of course. The spacious edifice was originally built in 1629 as a fortress. Its high windows attested to its defensive nature. During the Pueblo Revolt in 1680, it was partially destroyed. The tall exterior walls were now plastered with mud and straw. We strolled in through the wide double doors, onto a floor of packed dirt. The ceiling had to be three stories high. Murals of corn and rainbows, connoting a plentiful harvest, decorated the whitewashed walls. Above them, Christian pictures hung in wooden frames. A balcony extended from the rear, above the entrance. On the wall behind the balcony, other murals depicted a "moon-face" and five-pointed star above a rainbow that arced over a stylized pueblo. As with so many other indigenous peoples in the New World who were conquered by the Spaniards, the Acoma residents blended native religious beliefs with Christian doctrines. The altar, some 100 feet from the entrance, seemed remote. Only a few rows of crudely hewn pews were lined up in front of the altar. The intervening space, between the entrance and the pews, was empty. We traversed that gap. The altar was emblazoned with Christian icons, carved and painted in a bygone century by the Spaniards. Joan later chanced upon a magnificent black-and-white blowup of the exterior of the church when we returned to Florida. Ansel Adams had captured the structure during his acclaimed excursion, The Mural Project, in the early Forties.

Reva escorted us out of the church and back to the pottery tour. I took a surfeit of photos. Whenever an Indian was in the picture, or at least in the foreground, I did seek permission. Most of my photo subjects granted it. But as I lined up a shot of one merchant and his crafts, he waved me off. I could only take a picture if I bought a pot, he said. That really rubbed my fur the wrong way. So I told him I didn't want his ugly face on my film anyway. As I walked away, he mumbled something in a language I didn't understand. It's just as well I didn't.

Many of the houses had wooden ladders reaching from the ground to the roof, or from one floor to the next. Reva pointed out an above-ground active kiva. A ladder on the roof disappeared into its depths. The interior of the kiva was totally obscured, by the walls and roof, from the view of passers-by. Women were not allowed entry, she said, except for "social dances." At other times the men there were inaccessible to the women. A hole was cut into the exterior wall of the kiva in case a lady absolutely had to contact her man. She could then call to him through the opening. Otherwise, stay away. Wait until the feminists find out about this!

Bent stove pipes poked out from the walls of some houses and reached skyward. Many of the pueblo dwellers cooked and heated with wood-burning stoves. Others used propane. *Hornos*, some with charcoal stains around the door, hunched beside a few of the buildings. One enterprising woman operated a lunch wagon. She made a couple of sales. Joan anted up and walked away with a handful of

POTTERY FOR SALE AT ACOMA

tamale. Even Reva got one. I tasted a piece of Joan's. It was spicy, juicy and surprisingly delicious.

Reva made reference to a three-story row of houses. The bottom floor, she said, was for storage. Above that was the living area. The top story contained the kitchen. The adobe blocks weren't made at the pueblo. They were purchased from a manufacturer in Albuquerque. On a nearby house under construction, I noticed a wall being erected from what seemed an unusual material: concrete blocks. Most of the adobe homes had screens over the doors and windows. Wooden roof posts protruded beyond the walls of some buildings.

Despite being turned off by the excessive commercialism during our tour, I was determined to leave with a sample of native craftsmanship. I journeyed from stand to stand, snapping photos and browsing through merchandise. An unusual piece caught my eye, something other than the myriad of pots and bowls I had thus far encountered — a large turtle effigy of fired clay. Upon its back and head rode a large dog and about a dozen human adults, some clutching children to their breasts. The handmade object was painted in white, black and russet. I knew it had symbolic significance.

"What is this?" I asked the vendor, as I grasped and examined it.

She told me the tale of the turtle. A flood had swept over the land, engulfing the town and dooming the people. Along came the turtle to the rescue. The drowning people pulled themselves onto the back of the turtle and rode to safety.

That did it. I had to have this piece. "How much do you want for it?"

"One hundred fifty dollars."

A lot of money — but worth it, to me anyway. "How about a hundred dollars?"

"Sure."

That was too quick. Damn, I probably could have bought it for less. But it was still a bargain. I had her wrap the fragile work of art in a thick cushion of crumpled newspaper.

Reva urged us to move along, as the "hour was almost over." Oh, were we under a time constraint? That was news to me. I guess the bus had to get back to the visitors' center to ferry another load of fare-paying sightseers to the village. Our brief visit was more like a whirlwind shopping spree than an archeology tour.

Joan noticed one ancient character seated in the shadows. She just had to capture him on film. But to gain his permission, she was required to purchase a bundle of his Navajo tea for a dollar. On top of that, he finagled another buck out of her. Sort of a model fee, I guess.

Joan's camera automatically rewound the roll of film when the last picture was taken. The sudden loud whir of the rewinding camera startled Ruth, who was probably still shaken up from her encounter with the snake back at the turquoise mine. She clutched at Joan and gasped.

Reva gave us the choice of riding the bus back to the visitors' center or climbing down a precarious stairway cut into the side of the precipice. Several of us opted for the hike down. It was indeed a steep climb — but fun. Handholds, hacked into the rock, came in handy.

From the visitors' center, we loaded into the vans for the short jaunt to nearby Enchanted Mesa, where we would have lunch. Beneath spreading juniper trees, with the Mesa as a backdrop, Jim set up the buffet table. We had the entire bucolic setting to ourselves. We lounged in the shade and chowed down the salad, corn and fruit, as Robert described how he and his family tended their cattle. They herded the animals into the mountains for the summer, then drove them back to the valley for the winter. Robert had a close relationship with his environment.

"Respect the land and your animals, and they'll respect you," he said.

Bellies full, we rolled into the Coronado State Monument. Carol informed us that this was "the only place in the U.S. to see real kiva murals." The abandoned Pueblo IV site, Kuaua, had been excavated during the 1930s. Its kiva, restored in modern times, had been built over an abandoned or destroyed kiva. Tiwa-speaking people resided here in the two or three centuries prior to the arrival of the Spaniards. Kuaua was one of twelve pueblos, strung along the Rio Grande, comprising the Tiguex Province. Coronado's incursion into the Southwest in 1540 took him through the area. With some 300 Spanish soldiers, 1000 Indian allies and slaves, 1000 horses and 500 mules, he sought the legendary Seven Cities of Cíbola and its purported riches. The expedition camped at Kuaua.

One of the Spaniards, Pedro de Castaneda, wrote in 1540 of his detailed observations of pueblo life here. He was impressed with the architecture, work ethic and the "harmonious way of life" of the people:

> "There is no drunkenness among them nor sodomy nor sacrifices, neither do they eat flesh, but they are usually at work."

Years later, another Spaniard, Gaspar Pedro de Villagra, chronicled his observations:

> "The towns have no definite streets. Houses are well built, with square walls, three, four, five, six and even seven stories high with windows and terraces. Men spin and weave, while women cook and build houses. They

wear cotton garments. These are peaceful people. They are excellent swimmers, good fishermen and expert planters. There is complete equality, with no authoritative figures."

The Indians at first accommodated the treasure seekers, providing them with food, shelter and supplies. But the initial harmony between Indians and Spaniards turned to discord. The guests became oppressors. Friction developed. Then confrontation. Finally, rebellion. As with most encounters with the heavily armed Spaniards, the Tigeux natives lost. Disheartened, they eventually abandoned their villages.

The renowned Kuaua murals were now housed here at the modest museum, which sat within the pueblo site. The murals, faded, tattered and incomplete, lined the walls in a dozen glass cases. They were difficult to make out. Originally they had been painted in yellow, black, white and red. I could distinguish many half-sized human figures, some with a kilt, waistband and feathered headdress. Rattlesnakes and lightning bolts were somehow interrelated and symbolized messengers to the gods. One human figure was associated with jimson weed, which a placard noted was "known for its hallucinogenic properties." A macaw mask and form represented "Sky Father," whose "all-seeing eye beholds everything that transpires." A frontal view of another human figure, tears streaming down his face, was adorned with conch rattles. There were deer tracks, a handprint and a dragonfly. A white rabbit supposedly portrayed a rabbit hunt. Many other figures and symbols were indiscernible to me. But I was elated at glimpsing these magnificent works of art. Until this trip I hadn't been aware that kivas even had murals. I queried Carol for an interpretation of the murals.

"No one knows what it all means," she said. "Modern pueblo people can recognize some masks. But these were secret societies. We would have to have lived in this village to understand these murals."

We followed Carol and Vern out of the museum to the dirt path that meandered through the surrounding ruins. The reconstructed kiva monopolized the immediate scene. Although a subterranean structure, its upper walls and roof extended four feet into the air.

ON TOP OF RECONSTRUCTED KIVA AT KUAUA

Six huge roofing timbers protruded from the upper walls above ground level. The entire pueblo site was carpeted with weeds and grasses in various shades of brown and green. Strings of mountains, tinted gray and purple, lined the background, their peaks poking into a cloud-strewn sky. The parching sun, on its downward arc, was finally relenting. We scrambled onto the kiva's roof and stepped down the ladder that connected the roof opening to the kiva's interior, about ten feet below. The squarish single-room kiva was spacious enough to hold all of us at once, although we were crowded. In most respects this kiva was typical of others, but its distinguishing feature was, of course, the murals, vividly recreated here. The figures were more recognizable than the originals at the museum, but their significance was still a mystery.

One figure, clad in kilt and headdress, held a stylized corn stalk. Tears seemed to drip from his eyes. The lower half of his face was tinted black. From the beak of a nearby bird in flight, a copious stream of something, possibly rain, flowed down. A rattlesnake was drawn above the bird.

In another scene, a totally black human figure, outlined in white, with white circles for eyes and mouth, faced forward. One hand held a white jug. The other hand grasped a black cylindrical object which no one could identify. A cloud terrace with "rain" pouring down was sketched above his head. To his side, a standing "duck" spewed "rain" from its bill.

Another wall displayed a frontal view of two man-figures adjacent to one another, each clad in a black kilt and white waist sash with "tassels." One wore a single feather in his hair and had a yellow band painted across the top half of his face. A mask? The head of the other man was not drawn, as this portion of the figure was missing from the original mural. The legs of both men were stark white, possibly from stockings or body paint. The torsos were painted yellow, the hands red. A black pot dangled from the left hand of each man. From it flowed two streams of "rain." The "rain" spilled onto larger pots at foot level, which overflowed with more "rain." Inexplicable yellow circles, black triangles and white lines occupied the space between the two men.

Other birds, one of which may have been a bald eagle, spewed "rain" from their mouths. A black fish squirted a solid arc of something into the air. A black pot bubbled "rain" out. A zigzag of black lines with a white point shot straight up from the top of the pot. Lightning?

We climbed out of the kiva and set off on our own to explore the residual of the site. The adobe walls of the pueblo buildings were badly decayed. Little remained but the lower portions of a few walls on the ground floor. The upper floors were totally gone. The architecture and layout of the village were only imaginable. But the kiva art, even as recreated, made the visit to this site memorable.

Our group rendezvoused one last time for the farewell dinner in Albuquerque. In a sense it was a joyous occasion, as we relived our recent interesting experiences over food and drink. But sad, too, since our fellow travelers, whom we'd come to know and like, would be scattering throughout the country in the morning. Jim and the scholars, Vern and Carol, had some closing words. Jim sincerely thanked us for our participation in the trip. It was we who should have thanked him for his superb efforts at organizing the venture and keeping it flowing smoothly. Carol ebulliently expressed gratitude at having been invited aboard as a guide. She thoroughly enjoyed the trip and was looking forward to trying it again. Vern, in his humble manner, said he was pleased at having been part of the team.

During the excursion, one of us, Robbie, came up with the idea of getting an inexpensive gift for each of the trip leaders — a token of our appreciation. We all chipped in. Until she made the presentations at the dinner, I didn't know what she had picked out. Jim, then Carol, opened their tiny packages. Each was delighted as they proudly held aloft a Zuni fetish. Vern was next. I watched his face closely as he unwrapped his small box. Another Zuni fetish. His face didn't burst into a smile. He stared at the object for a couple of pregnant seconds, then forced a hint of a grin as he held it up for all to see. A Zuni fetish for a Taos Indian? Was that analogous to presenting a Bible to a Hindu? Was this a monumental faux pas? I could only guess what was going through Vern's mind. Was he thinking that us whites couldn't differentiate between Indian tribes? Seen one, seen 'em all? I hoped he realized that our intentions, if not our deeds, were noble.

Then we said our good-byes.

✳   ✳   ✳

Joan and I hung around town another day, to view magnificent rock art just beyond the city's western limits. After breakfast, we rented a car and drove into Petroglyph National Monument at Boca Negra Canyon. Only a few other curious souls were clambering over the craggy hillside of the park's three sightseeing trails, as the stark sun vaulted unimpeded into the heavens. Parking near the farthest trail, we stood at the base of the West Mesa escarpment, a seventeen-mile ridge of basalt boulders created by volcanic eruptions about 150,000 years ago. Over the ensuing millennia, the Rio Grande eroded away the basalt caprock of the ridge. Huge pieces of caprock were undermined by the river and dislodged. These boulders tumbled along the sides of the escarpment. Exposure to the elements and the microbes left a veneer of desert vanish over the rocks. The petroglyphs were etched into this coating, yielding images of high contrast. Many of the older figures were repatinated. Around 1000 B.C., the Indians began carving on the rocks here. The majority of these drawings were done in the Rio Grande style, which developed suddenly about 1300 A.D. and continued until 1680. These dates coincide with the dramatic increase in local populations and the construction of dozens of pueblos along the Rio Grande. Common images for this style included: animals, four-pointed stars, spirals and animal tracks.

We set off along the Mesa Point Trail, picking our way through the massive rocks to the top of the ridge. An isolated boulder, totally encrusted with desert vanish except where petroglyphs were incised, bore a square outline partially filled with images. I could easily make out a four-pointed star and a cloud terrace within the square. Other designs were unrecognizable to me. Another isolated boulder contained two birds, face to face, connected at the breast. To their right was what I guessed to be a headdress. To the right of that was another four-pointed star.

One enterprising prehistoric artist used a natural hole in a rock for the eye of his bird figure. Footprints and handprints adorned other rocks. Another bore a dragonfly, a water symbol. The face of one rock held two cat-like animals, their tails raised.

I noticed a shallow, rectangular depression in one of the boulders. A brochure indicated that "grinding spots" had been found throughout the escarpment. Speculation held that these were used for grinding corn and seed, sharpening tools, preparing medicinal or ritual potions, or crushing ingredients for pigments.

The sinuous shape of an extensive serpent covered the side of one large rock. Its head was bedecked with what were probably feathers or horns. A "horned mask" was etched above it.

Even Kokopelli was represented here. This mythical flute player was ubiquitous in the rock art of the Southwest, all the way from the San Juan Basin and Monument Valley south to Casas Grandes in Mexico. An important figure to the dwellers of the Rio Grande pueblos, this hunchback icon was also significant to the Navajo and Hopi. In some instances, it was depicted as a phallic symbol.

Not all the designs were prehistoric. A Christian cross was scratched into a rock, apparently by a shepherd during the 1700s or 1800s.

The next self-guided tour, along the Macaw Trail, was brief. Two macaw petroglyphs attested to the prehistoric presence of this non-native bird, which was imported from Mexico as a trade item. One of the macaws was encased in what seemed to be a cage, perhaps a device to transport or house the bird. An enigmatic shape appearing on other rocks was proclaimed by the brochure to represent a yucca seedpod.

We paused at the pavilion at the base of this trail to quench our thirst and daub on more sunscreen before exploring the nearby Cliff Base Trail. Two boulders along this third and final trail each possessed a four-pointed "star-face," the top point of which was transformed into a "headdress." One had bird talons beneath the face. The other face bore a demoniac expression. There were outlines of stylized human figures in frontal view. One had upraised arms and some sort of head ornamentation.

Joan and I stepped off the trail and onto the adjacent boulders to get a better shot of some images. A ranger promptly warned us to get back on the trail. Yes, we did get the photos.

A poorly preserved "shield figure" with upraised arms was discernible. Drawn with stick-like arms and legs, its shield totally covered its torso. A horizontal row of three triangles lined the top third of the shield. Two streams of "rain" poured down from the triangles. Other rocks depicted: birds, spirals, a "lizard," serpents and masked faces. A boulder just off the trail bore the shallow scoop of another grinding spot.

RESOURCES

The Archaeological Conservancy
5301 Central Avenue, NE
Suite 1218
Albuquerque, NM 87108
(505) 266-1540
e-mail: archcons@nm.net
web site: www.gorp.com/archcons/
The Conservancy offers various archeological trips to the Southwest, Mississippi Valley and Mesoamerica. Destinations tend to vary from year to year.

Crow Canyon Archaeological Center
23390 Road K
Cortez, CO 81321
(800) 422-8975, (970) 565-8975
e-mail: Webmaster@crowcanyon.org
web site: www.crowcanyon.org/
The Center offers several archeological trips throughout the Southwest, to sites such as Chaco Canyon, Mesa Verde, Aztec Ruins and Canyon de Chelly.

Earthwatch Institute
680 Mt. Auburn St.
Watertown, MA 02471
(800) 776-0188
e-mail: info@earthwatch.org
web site: www.earthwatch.org/
Earthwatch offers archeological expeditions with hands-on digging into ancient sites.

For information about some national parks and monuments with archeological sites or features in the Southwest:

Mesa Verde National Park
PO Box 8
Mesa Verde, CO 81330
web site: www.mesaverde.org/mvnp.html

Chaco Culture National Historical Park
PO Box 220
Nageezi, NM 87037
(505) 786-7014
web site: www.nps.gov/chcu/

Casa Grande Ruins National Monument
1100 Ruins Road
Coolidge, AZ 85228
(520) 723-3172
web site: www.nps.gov/cagr/

Canyon de Chelly National Monument
PO Box 588
Chinle, AZ 86503
(520) 670-5500
web site: www.nps.gov/cach/

Petroglyph National Monument
6001 Unser Blvd., NW
Albuquerque, NM 87120
(505) 899-0205
web site: www.nps.gov/petr/

Aztec Ruins National Monument
PO Box 640
84 County Road 2900
Aztec, NM 87410
(505) 334-6174
e-mail: azru-interpretation@nps.gov
web site: www.nps.gov/azru/

Arkansas Post National Monument
1741 Old Post Road
Gillett, AR 72055
(870) 548-2207
web site: www.nps.gov/arpo/

Poverty Point National Monument
c/o Poverty Point State Commemorative Area
PO Box 248
Epps, LA 71237
web site: www.nps.gov/popo/

Salinas Pueblo Missions National Monument
(for the Abó, Quarai and Gran Quivira sites)
PO Box 517
Mountainair, NM 87036
(505) 847-2585
web site: www.nmculture.org/HTML/direct.htm

For information about Parkin, a state archeological site in Arkansas:

Dr. Jeff Mitchem
Arkansas Archeological Survey
PO Box 241
Parkin, AR 72373
(870) 755-2119
e-mail: jeffmitchem@juno.com
web site:
www.uark.edu/campus-resources/archinfo/parkin.html

For information about the existing Indian pueblos in New Mexico, including Acoma, Taos and Picuris:

Indian Pueblo Cultural Center
2401 12th Street NW
Albuquerque, NM 87192
(505) 843-7270, (800) 766-4405
web site: www.indianpueblo.org/index.shtml#toc

BIBLIOGRAPHY

Adams, Daniel. "Last Ditch Archeology." *Science 83*, (December, 1983), pp. 28-37.

Adams, E. Charles. *Walpi Archaeological Project*. Flagstaff, AZ: Museum of Northern Arizona.

Adams, Richard. *Prehistoric America*. Boston: Little, Brown and Co., 1977.

Ambler, J. Richard. *The Anasazi*. Flagstaff, AZ: Museum of Northern Arizona, 1989.

Anasazi. A National Park film. Distributed by INTERpark, Cortez, CO. VCR video, 24 min.

Anonymous. "U.S. Offers Land In Effort To End Tribal Dispute." *The Miami Herald*, (November 26, 1992), p. 22B.

Arnold, David. "Pueblo Pottery — 2,000 Years Of Artistry." *National Geographic*, (November, 1982), pp. 593-605.

Aveni, A.F. *Skywatchers Of Ancient Mexico*. Austin, TX: University of Texas Press, 1980.

Barnes, F.A. *Canyon Country Prehistoric Rock Art*. Salt Lake City, UT: Wasatch Publishers Inc., 1982.

Barry, John. *American Indian Pottery*. Florence, AL: Books Americana, 1981.

Bartlett, Michael, Thomas Kolaz and David Gregory. *Archaeology In The City*. Tucson, AZ: University of Arizona Press, 1986.

Bawden, Garth. "A Long Line Of Brilliant Societies." *Archaeology*, Vol. 42 (May, 1898), pp. 54-59.

Bezy, John. "The Geology Of Pecos." *Exploration*, (1981), pp. 23-25.

Canyon de Chelly & Hubbell Trading Post. Finley-Holiday Film Corp., Whittier, CA. VCR video, 30 min. 1989.

Carlson, John. "Rise And Fall Of The City Of The Gods." *Archaeology*, (November/December, 1993), pp. 58-69.

Cunkle, James. *Talking Pots*. Phoenix, AZ: Golden West Publishers, 1993.

Cussler, Clive. *Inca Gold*. New York: Simon & Schuster, 1994.

Dedera, Don. *Navajo Rugs*. Flagstaff, AZ: The Northland Press, 1975.

Dixon, E. James. "The Origins Of The First Americans." *Archaeology*, March/April, 1985), pp. 22-27.

Doyel, David. "The Prehistoric Hohokam Of The Arizona Desert." *American Scientist*, Vol. 67 (September-October, 1979), pp. 544-554.

Dozier, Edward. *The Sonoran Desert*. Tucson, AZ: University of Arizona Press, 1968.

Dutton, Bertha. *American Indians Of The Southwest*. Albuquerque, NM: University of New Mexico Press, 1983.

Ellis, G. Lain. "Cultural And Landscape Influences On Tucson Basin Hohokam Settlement." *American Anthropologist*, Vol 93 (March, 1991), pp. 125-137.

Ferguson, William and Arthur Rohn. *Anasazi Ruins Of The Southwest In Color*. Albuquerque, NM: University of New Mexico Press, 1987.

Fontana, Bernard. *Of Earth And Little Rain*. Tucson, AZ: University of Arizona Press, 1989.

Grant, Campbell. *Canyon De Chelly, Its People And Rock Art*. Tucson, AZ: University of Arizona Press, 1978.

Grant, Campbell. *Rock Art Of The American Indian*. Golden, CO: Outbooks, 1981.

Haury, Emil. *The Hohokam: Desert farmers And Craftsmen, Snaketown, 1964-1965*. Tucson, AZ: University of Arizona Press, 1976.

Haury, Emil. *The Stratigraphy And Archaeology Of Ventana Cave*. 2nd ed. Tucson, AZ: University of Arizona Press, 1975.

Hayes, Alden. "The Jumanos Pueblos." *Exploration*, (1982), pp. 11-15.

Hillerman, Tony. *A Thief Of Time.* New York: Harper & Row, 1988.

James, George. *Indian Blankets And Their Makers.* Glorieta, NM: The Rio Grande Press Inc., 1974.

Kessell, John. "The Presence Of The Past: Pecos Pueblo." *Exploration,* (1981). pp. 12-14.

Kubler, George. *The Religious Architecture Of New Mexico.* Albuquerque, NM: University of New Mexico Press, 1972.

Lang, Richard. "Early Prehistory In The Estancia Basin." *Exploration,* (1982), pp. 2-5.

Lekson, Stephen, Thomas Windes, John Stein and W. James Judge. "The Chaco Canyon Community." *Scientific American,* Vol. 259 (July, 1988), pp. 100-109.

Lekson, Stephen. "Rewriting Southwestern Prehistory." *Archaeology,* (January/February, 1997), pp. 52-55.

Lister, Robert. *Those Who Came Before.* Tucson, AZ: University of Arizona Press, 1983.

MacMahon, James. *Deserts.* New York: Alfred A. Knopf, 1985.

Marana Community In The Hohokam World, The, ed. Suzanne Fish, Paul Fish and John Madsen. Tucson, AZ: University of Arizona Press, 1992.

Martineau, LaVan. *The Rocks Begin To Speak.* Las Vegas, NV: KC Publications, 1987.

Masse, Bruce. "Prehistoric Irrigation Systems In The Salt River Valley, Arizona." *Science,* Vol. 214 (1981), pp. 267-270.

McGuire, Randall and Michael Schiffer. Hohokam And Patayan: *Prehistory Of Southwestern Arizona.* New York: Academic Press, 1982.

Mesa Verde National Park. Finley-Holiday Film Corp., Whittier, CA. Distributed by INTERpark, Cortez, CO., VCR video, 60 min.

Murphy, Dan. "Salinas: A View Through Time." *Exploration,* (1982), pp. 6-10.

Noble, Grant. *Ancient Ruins Of The Southwest.* Flagstaff, AZ: Northland Press, 1981.

Nordby, Larry. "The Prehistory Of The Pecos Indians." *Exploration,* (1981), pp. 5-11.

Ortiz, Alfonso. *The Pueblo.* New York: Chelsea House Publishers, 1994.

Patterson, Alex. *A Field Guide To Rock Art Symbols Of The Greater Southwest.* Boulder, CO: Johnson Books, 1992

Pike, Donald. Anasazi, *Ancient People Of The Rock.* New York: Crown Publishers, 1974.

Plog, Stephen. *Stylistic Variation In Prehistoric Ceramics. Design Analysis In The American Southwest.* Cambridge, MA: Cambridge University Press, 1980.

Plotkin, Mark. *Tales Of A Shaman's Apprentice.* New York: Penguin Books, 1993.

Russell, Sharman. "Playing Ball With The Gods." *American Archaeology,* (Winter, 1997 98), pp. 18-23.

Schaafsma, Polly. "Tompico Rock Art." *Exploration,* (1982), pp. 17-19.

Schaafsma, Polly. *Indian Rock Art Of The Southwest.* Albuquerque, NM: University of New Mexico Press, 1974.

Schaafsma, Polly. *Indian Rock Art Of The Southwest.* Albuquerque, NM: University of New Mexico Press, 1980.

Sheridan, Thomas and Gary Nabhan. "Living With A River." *The Journal Of Arizona History,* Vol. 265 (July, 1991), pp. 80-86.

Simmons, Marc. "Pecos Pueblos On The Sante Fe Trail." *Exploration,* (1981), pp. 2-4.

Thomas, David Hurst, Jay Miller, Richard White, Peter Nabokov and Philip J. Deloria. *The Native Americans: An Illustrated History.* Atlanta, GA: Turner Publishing, Inc., 1993.

Towns And Temples Along The Mississippi, ed. David Dye and Cheryl Cox. Tuscaloosa, AL: The University of Alabama Press, 1990.

Weaver, Kenneth. "Magnetic Clues Help Date The Past." *National Geographic*, (May, 1967), pp. 696-701.

Wilcox, David and Charles Sternberg. *Hohokam Ballcourts And Their Interpretation*. Tucson, AZ: University of Arizona Press, 1983.

Wilford, John. "Study Of Ancient Indian Site Puts Early American Life In New Light." *New York Times*, (September 19, 1997), pp. A1, A9.

Wilson, John. "Quarai: A Turbulent History." *Exploration*, (1982), pp. 20-25.

Wisner, George. "On The Trail Of The First Americans." *American Archaeology*, (Summer, 1997), pp. 13-17.

Young, John. *Kokopelli*. Palmer Lake, CO: Filter Press, 1990.

INDEX

Woodlands Period, 182, 187, 188, 192
woodpecker, 128

Y

Yucatan Peninsula, 111
yucca, 27, 29, 126, 146, 168, 213, 231, 268

Z

zaguán, 208
ziggurat, 94
Zuni, 34, 73, 252
Zuni fetish, 266

About the Author

Thom Tansey

Thom Tansey, a native of Massachusetts, holds a degree in biochemistry and a law degree. He currently practices law in Ft. Lauderdale, Florida.

Thom began his travel adventures some 20 years ago with a four-day jaunt to Costa Rica to climb an active volcano, wade in shark-infested waters, and mingle with the locals. It was a brief trip, but it set the stage for a lifetime of travel and learning.

Since then, he has excavated dinosaur bones, explored ancient ruins, learned to fly helicopters and airships, become certified in nitrox diving, rafted whitewater rivers, and taken lessons in hot air balloons, hang gliders, and aerobatic planes. He has swum with manatees, frolicked with dolphins, cruised the Everglades in an airboat, learned to Eskimo-roll a kayak, and taken professional auto-racing courses.

He has been helicoptered to ice floes in the St. Lawrence River in the dead of winter to witness the birth of thousands of snow-white harp seals, patrolled the arctic tundra in a rugged buggy to photograph the annual migration of the polar bears onto the ice of Hudson Bay, snowmobiled through Yellowstone National Park for close-up views of the bison and elk foraging through the snow, among many other exciting experiences.

Thom's future adventure travel plans include continued exploration of Mayan ruins, diving with sharks, and digging up Ice Age mammals. He is currently working on the next volume in The Bonehunter Series, which will cover his experiences finding and excavating dinosaur bones, some as old as 150 million years.